MW00845133

Learning Scrapy

Learn the art of efficient web scraping and crawling with Python

Dimitrios Kouzis-Loukas

[PACKT] open source*
PUBLISHING   community experience distilled

BIRMINGHAM - MUMBAI

Learning Scrapy

Copyright © 2016 Packt Publishing

All rights reserved. No part of this book may be reproduced, stored in a retrieval system, or transmitted in any form or by any means, without the prior written permission of the publisher, except in the case of brief quotations embedded in critical articles or reviews.

Every effort has been made in the preparation of this book to ensure the accuracy of the information presented. However, the information contained in this book is sold without warranty, either express or implied. Neither the author, nor Packt Publishing, and its dealers and distributors will be held liable for any damages caused or alleged to be caused directly or indirectly by this book.

Packt Publishing has endeavored to provide trademark information about all of the companies and products mentioned in this book by the appropriate use of capitals. However, Packt Publishing cannot guarantee the accuracy of this information.

First published: January 2016

Production reference: 1220116

Published by Packt Publishing Ltd.
Livery Place
35 Livery Street
Birmingham B3 2PB, UK.

ISBN 978-1-78439-978-8

www.packtpub.com

Credits

Author
Dimitrios Kouzis-Loukas

Reviewer
Lazar Telebak

Commissioning Editor
Akram Hussain

Acquisition Editor
Subho Gupta

Content Development Editor
Kirti Patil

Technical Editor
Siddhesh Ghadi

Copy Editor
Priyanka Ravi

Project Coordinator
Nidhi Joshi

Proofreader
Safis Editing

Indexer
Monica Ajmera Mehta

Graphics
Disha Haria

Production Coordinator
Nilesh R. Mohite

Cover Work
Nilesh R. Mohite

About the Author

Dimitrios Kouzis-Loukas has over fifteen years experience as a topnotch software developer. He uses his acquired knowledge and expertise to teach a wide range of audiences how to write great software, as well.

He studied and mastered several disciplines, including mathematics, physics, and microelectronics. His thorough understanding of these subjects helped him raise his standards beyond the scope of "pragmatic solutions." He knows that true solutions should be as certain as the laws of physics, as robust as ECC memories, and as universal as mathematics.

Dimitrios now develops distributed, low-latency, highly-availability systems using the latest datacenter technologies. He is language agnostic, yet has a slight preference for Python, C++, and Java. A firm believer in open source software and hardware, he hopes that his contributions will benefit individual communities as well as all of humanity.

About the Reviewer

Lazar Telebak is a freelance web developer specializing in web scraping, crawling, and indexing web pages using Python libraries/frameworks.

He has worked mostly on projects that deal with automation and website scraping, crawling, and exporting data to various formats, including CSV, JSON, XML, and TXT, and databases such as MongoDB, SQLAlchemy, and Postgres.

He also has experience in frontend technologies and the languages: HTML, CSS, JS, and jQuery.

www.PacktPub.com

Support files, eBooks, discount offers, and more

For support files and downloads related to your book, please visit www.PacktPub.com.

Did you know that Packt offers eBook versions of every book published, with PDF and ePub files available? You can upgrade to the eBook version at www.PacktPub.com and as a print book customer, you are entitled to a discount on the eBook copy. Get in touch with us at service@packtpub.com for more details.

At www.PacktPub.com, you can also read a collection of free technical articles, sign up for a range of free newsletters and receive exclusive discounts and offers on Packt books and eBooks.

https://www2.packtpub.com/books/subscription/packtlib

Do you need instant solutions to your IT questions? PacktLib is Packt's online digital book library. Here, you can search, access, and read Packt's entire library of books.

Why subscribe?

- Fully searchable across every book published by Packt
- Copy and paste, print, and bookmark content
- On demand and accessible via a web browser

Free access for Packt account holders

If you have an account with Packt at www.PacktPub.com, you can use this to access PacktLib today and view 9 entirely free books. Simply use your login credentials for immediate access.

Table of Contents

Preface

Let me take a wild guess. One of these two stories is curiously similar to yours:

Your first encounter with Scrapy was while searching the net for something along the lines of "web scraping Python". You had a quick look at it and thought, "This is too complex...I just need something simple." You went on and developed a Python script using requests, struggled a bit with beautiful soup, but finally made something cool. It was kind of slow, so you let it run overnight. You restarted it a few times, ignored some semi-broken links and non-English characters, and in the morning, most of the website was proudly on your hard disk. Sadly, for some unknown reason, you didn't want to see your code again. The next time you had to scrape something, you went directly to scrapy.org and this time the documentation made perfect sense. Scrapy now felt like it was elegantly and effortlessly solving all of the problems that you faced, and it even took care of problems you hadn't thought of yet. You never looked back.

Alternatively, your first encounter with Scrapy was while doing research for a web-scraping project. You needed something robust, fast, and enterprise-grade, so most of the fancy one-click web-scraping tools were out of question. You needed it to be simple but at the same time flexible enough to allow you to customize its behavior for different sources, provide different types of output feeds, and reliably run 24/7 in an automated manner. Companies that provided scraping as a service seemed too expensive and you were more comfortable using open source solutions than feeling locked on vendors. From the very beginning, Scrapy looked like a clear winner.

No matter how you got here, I'm glad to meet you on a book that is entirely devoted to Scrapy. Scrapy is the secret of web-scraping experts throughout the world. They know how to maneuver it to save them hours of work, deliver stellar performance, and keep their hosting bills to an absolute minimum. If you are less experienced and you want to achieve their results, unfortunately, Google will do you a disservice. The majority of Scrapy information on the Web is either simplistic and inefficient or complex. This book is an absolute necessity for everyone who wants accurate, accessible, and well-organized information on how to make the most out of Scrapy. It is my hope that it will help the Scrapy community grow even further and give it the wide adoption that it rightfully deserves.

What this book covers

Chapter 1, *Introducing Scrapy*, will introduce you to this book and Scrapy, and will allow you to set clear expectations for the framework and the rest of the book.

Chapter 2, *Understanding HTML and XPath*, aims to bring web-crawling beginners up to speed with the essential web-related technologies and techniques that we will use thereafter.

Chapter 3, *Basic Crawling*, is where we learn how to install Scrapy and crawl a website. We develop this example step by step by showing you the methodology and the way of thinking behind every action. After this chapter, you will be able to crawl the majority of simple websites.

Chapter 4, *From Scrapy to a Mobile App*, shows us how we can use our scraper to populate a database and feed a mobile application. After this chapter, you will have a clear appreciation of the benefits that web crawling brings in time to market terms.

Chapter 5, *Quick Spider Recipes*, demonstrates more powerful spider features, allowing us to log in, scrape faster, consume APIs, and crawl lists of URLs.

Chapter 6, *Deploying to Scrapinghub*, shows us how to deploy spiders to Scrapinghub's cloud servers and enjoy availability, easy deployment, and control.

Chapter 7, *Configuration and Management*, is a well-organized presentation of the impressive number of features that one can enable and fine-tune using Scrapy's configuration.

Chapter 8, Programming Scrapy, takes our knowledge to a whole new level by showing us how to use the underlying Twisted engine and Scrapy's architecture to extend every aspect of its functionality.

Chapter 9, Pipeline Recipes, presents numerous examples where we alter Scrapy's functionality to insert into databases such as MySQL, Elasticsearch, and Redis, interface APIs, and legacy applications with virtually no degradation of performance.

Chapter 10, Understanding Scrapy's Performance, will help us understand how Scrapy spends its time, and what exactly we need to do to increase its performance.

Chapter 11, Distributed Crawling with Scrapyd and Real-Time Analytics, is our final chapter showing how to use scrapyd in multiple servers to achieve horizontal scalability, and how to feed crawled data to an Apache Spark server that performs stream analytics on it.

What you need for this book

Lots of effort was put into making this book's code and content available for as wide an audience as possible. We want to provide interesting examples that involve multiple servers and databases, but we don't want you to have to know how to set all these up. We use a great technology called Vagrant to automatically download and set up a disposable multiserver environment inside your computer. Our Vagrant configuration uses a virtual machine on Mac OS X and Windows, and it can run natively on Linux.

For Windows and OS X, you will need a 64-bit computer that supports either Intel or AMD virtualization technologies: VT-x or AMD-v. Most modern computers will do fine. You will also need 1 GB of memory that is dedicated to the Virtual Machine for most chapters with the exception of *Chapter 9, Pipeline Recipes*, and *Chapter 11, Distributed Crawling with Scrapyd and Real-Time Analytics*, which require 2 GB. *Appendix A, Installing Prerequisites*, has all the details of how to install the necessary software.

Scrapy itself has way more limited hardware and software requirements. If you are an experienced user and you don't want to use Vagrant, you will be able to set Scrapy up on any operating system even if it has limited memory using the instructions that we provide in *Chapter 3, Basic Crawling*.

After you successfully set up your Vagrant environment, you will be able to run examples from the entire book (with the obvious exceptions of *Chapter 4, From Scrapy to a Mobile App*, and *Chapter 6, Deploying to Scrapinghub*) without the need for an Internet connection. Yes, you can enjoy this book on a flight.

Who this book is for

This book tries to accommodate quite a wide audience. It should be useful to:

- Web entrepreneurs who need source data to power their applications
- Data scientists and Machine Learning practitioners who need to extract data for analysis or to train their models
- Software engineers who need to develop large-scale web-scraping infrastructure
- Hobbyists who want to run Scrapy on a Raspberry Pi for their next cool project

In terms of prerequisite knowledge, we tried to require a very small amount of it. This book presents the basics of web technologies and scraping in the earliest chapters for those who have very little web-scraping experience. Python is easily readable and most of what we present in the spider chapters should be fine for anyone with basic experience of any programming language.

Frankly, I strongly believe that if someone has a project in mind and wants to use Scrapy, they will be able to hack the examples of this book and have something up and running within hours even with no previous scraping, Scrapy, or Python experience.

After the first half of the book, we become more Python-heavy, and at this point, beginners may want to allow themselves a few weeks of basic Scrapy experience before they delve deeper. At this point, more experienced Python/Scrapy developers will enjoy learning event-driven Python development using Twisted and the very interesting Scrapy internals. For the performance chapter, some mathematics intuition may be beneficial, but even without it, most diagrams should make a clear impression.

Conventions

In this book, you will find a number of text styles that distinguish between different kinds of information. Here are some examples of these styles and an explanation of their meaning.

Code words in text, database table names, folder names, filenames, file extensions, pathnames, dummy URLs, user input, and Twitter handles are shown as follows: "The `<head>` part is important to indicate meta-information such as character encoding."

A block of command line is set as follows:

```
$ python
>>> from twisted.internet import defer
>>> # Experiment 1
>>> d = defer.Deferred()
>>> d.called
False
>>> d.callback(3)
>>> d.called
True
>>> d.result
3
```

New terms and **important words** are shown in bold. Words that you see on the screen, for example, in menus or dialog boxes, appear in the text like this: "Clicking the **Next** button moves you to the next screen."

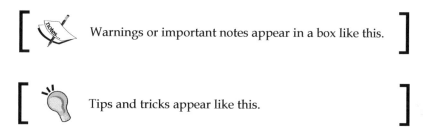

Warnings or important notes appear in a box like this.

Tips and tricks appear like this.

Reader feedback

Feedback from our readers is always welcome. Let us know what you think about this book—what you liked or disliked. Reader feedback is important for us as it helps us develop titles that you will really get the most out of.

To send us general feedback, simply e-mail feedback@packtpub.com, and mention the book's title in the subject of your message.

If there is a topic that you have expertise in and you are interested in either writing or contributing to a book, see our author guide at www.packtpub.com/authors.

Customer support

Now that you are the proud owner of a Packt book, we have a number of things to help you to get the most from your purchase.

Downloading the example code

You can download the example code files from your account at http://www.packtpub.com for all the Packt Publishing books you have purchased. If you purchased this book elsewhere, you can visit http://www.packtpub.com/support and register to have the files e-mailed directly to you.

Errata

Although we have taken every care to ensure the accuracy of our content, mistakes do happen. If you find a mistake in one of our books—maybe a mistake in the text or the code—we would be grateful if you could report this to us. By doing so, you can save other readers from frustration and help us improve subsequent versions of this book. If you find any errata, please report them by visiting http://www.packtpub.com/submit-errata, selecting your book, clicking on the **Errata Submission Form** link, and entering the details of your errata. Once your errata are verified, your submission will be accepted and the errata will be uploaded to our website or added to any list of existing errata under the Errata section of that title.

To view the previously submitted errata, go to https://www.packtpub.com/books/content/support and enter the name of the book in the search field. The required information will appear under the **Errata** section.

Piracy

Piracy of copyrighted material on the Internet is an ongoing problem across all media. At Packt, we take the protection of our copyright and licenses very seriously. If you come across any illegal copies of our works in any form on the Internet, please provide us with the location address or website name immediately so that we can pursue a remedy.

Please contact us at `copyright@packtpub.com` with a link to the suspected pirated material.

We appreciate your help in protecting our authors and our ability to bring you valuable content.

Questions

If you have a problem with any aspect of this book, you can contact us at `questions@packtpub.com`, and we will do our best to address the problem.

1
Introducing Scrapy

Welcome to your Scrapy journey. With this book, we aim to take you from a Scrapy beginner—someone who has little or no experience with Scrapy—to a level where you will be able to confidently use this powerful framework to scrape large datasets from the web or other sources. In this chapter, we will introduce you to Scrapy and talk to you about some of the great things you can achieve with it.

Hello Scrapy

Scrapy is a robust web framework for scraping data from various sources. As a casual web user, you will often find yourself wishing to be able to get data from a website that you're browsing on a spreadsheet program like Excel (see *Chapter 3, Basic Crawling*) in order to access it while you're offline or to perform calculations. As a developer, you'll often wish to be able to combine data from various data sources, but you are well aware of the complexities of retrieving or extracting them. Scrapy can help you complete both easy and complex data extraction initiatives.

Scrapy is built upon years of experience in extracting massive amounts of data in a robust and efficient manner. With Scrapy, you are able to do with a single setting what would take various classes, plug-ins, and configuration in most other scraping frameworks. A quick look at *Chapter 7, Configuration and Management* will make you appreciate how much you can achieve in Scrapy with a few lines of configuration.

From a developer's perspective, you will also appreciate Scrapy's event-based architecture (we will explore it in depth in *Chapter 8, Programming Scrapy* and *Chapter 9, Pipeline Recipes*). It allows us to cascade operations that clean, form, and enrich data, store them in databases, and so on, while enjoying very low degradation in performance—if we do it in the right way, of course. In this book, you will learn exactly how to do so. Technically speaking, being event-based, Scrapy allows us to disconnect latency from throughput by operating smoothly while having thousands of connections open. As an extreme example, imagine that you aim to extract listings from a website that has summary pages with a hundred listings per page. Scrapy will effortlessly perform 16 requests on that site in parallel, and assuming that, on an average, a request takes a second to complete, you will be crawling at 16 pages per second. If you multiply that with the number of listings per page, you will be generating 1600 listings per second. Imagine now that for each of those listings you have to do a write to a massively concurrent cloud storage, which takes 3 seconds (very bad idea) on an average. In order to support the throughput of 16 requests per second, it turns out that we need to be running $1600 \cdot 3 = 4800$ write requests in parallel (you will see many such interesting calculations in *Chapter 9, Pipeline Recipes*). For a traditional multithreaded application, this would translate to 4800 threads, which would be a very unpleasant experience for both you and the operating system. In Scrapy's world, 4800 concurrent requests is business as usual as long as the operating system is okay with it. Furthermore, memory requirements of Scrapy closely follow the amount of data that you need for your listings in contrast to a multithreaded application, where each thread adds a significant overhead as compared to a listing's size.

In a nutshell, slow or unpredictable websites, databases, or remote APIs won't have devastating consequences on your scraper's performance, since you can run many requests concurrently, and manage everything from a single thread. This translates to lower hosting bills, opportunity for co-hosting scrapers with other applications, and simpler code (no synchronization necessary) as compared to typical multithreaded applications.

More reasons to love Scrapy

Scrapy has been around for more than half a decade, and is mature and stable. Beyond the performance benefits that we mentioned in the previous section, there are several other reasons to love Scrapy:

- Scrapy understands broken HTML

  You can use Beautiful Soup or lxml directly from Scrapy, but Scrapy provides **selectors**—a higher level XPath (mainly) interface on top of lxml. It is able to efficiently handle broken HTML code and confusing encodings.

- Community

  Scrapy has a vibrant community. Just have a look at the mailing list at `https://groups.google.com/forum/#!forum/scrapy-users` and the thousands of questions in Stack Overflow at `http://stackoverflow.com/questions/tagged/scrapy`. Most questions get answered within minutes. More community resources are available at `http://scrapy.org/community/`.

- Well-organized code that is maintained by the community

  Scrapy requires a standard way of organizing your code. You write little Python modules called spiders and pipelines, and you automatically gain from any future improvements to the engine itself. If you search online, you will find quite a few professionals who have Scrapy experience. This means that it's quite easy to find a contractor who will help you maintain or extend your code. Whoever joins your team won't have to go through the learning curve of understanding the peculiarities of your own custom crawler.

- Growing feature set but also quality focused

  If you have a quick look at the Release Notes (`http://doc.scrapy.org/en/latest/news.html`), you will notice that there is a growth, both in features and in stability/bug fixes.

About this book: aim and usage

With this book, we aim to teach you Scrapy by using focused examples and realistic datasets. Most chapters focus on crawling an example property rental website. We chose this, because it's representative of most of the web crawling projects, allows us to present interesting variations, and is at the same time simple. Having this example as the main theme helps us focus on Scrapy without distraction.

We start by running small crawls of a few hundred pages, and we scale it out to performing distributed crawling of fifty thousand pages within minutes in *Chapter 11, Distributed Crawling with Scrapyd and Real-Time Analytics*. In the process, we will show you how to connect Scrapy with services like MySQL, Redis, and Elasticsearch, use the Google geocoding API to find coordinates for the location of our example properties, and feed Apache Spark to predict the keywords which affect property prices the most.

Be prepared to read this book several times. Maybe you can start by skimming through it to understand its structure. Then read a chapter or two, learn, experiment for a while, and then move further. Don't be afraid to skip a chapter if you feel familiar with it. In particular, if you know HTML and XPath, there's no point spending much time on *Chapter 2, Understanding HTML and XPath*. Don't worry; this book still has plenty for you. Some chapters like *Chapter 8, Programming Scrapy* combine the elements of a reference and a tutorial, and go in depth into programming concepts. That's an example of a chapter one might like to read a few times, while allowing a couple of weeks of Scrapy practice in between. You don't need to perfectly master *Chapter 8, Programming Scrapy* before moving, for example, to *Chapter 9, Pipeline Recipes*, which is full of applications. Reading the latter will help you understand how to use the programming concepts, and if you wish, you can reiterate as many times as you like.

We have tried to balance the pace to keep the book both interesting and beginner-friendly. One thing we can't do though, is teach Python in this book. There are several excellent books on the subject, but what I would recommend is trying a bit more relaxed attitude while learning. One of the reasons Python is so popular is that it's relatively simple, clean, and it reads well as English. Scrapy is a high-level framework that requires learning from Python beginners and experts alike. You could call it "the Scrapy language". As a result, I would recommend going through the material, and if you feel that you find the Python syntax confusing, supplement your learning with some of the excellent online Python tutorials or free Python online courses for beginners at Coursera or elsewhere. Rest assured, you can be quite a good Scrapy developer without being a Python expert.

The importance of mastering automated data scraping

For many of us, the curiosity and the mental satisfaction in mastering a cool technology like Scrapy is sufficient to motivate us. As a pleasant surprise, while learning this great framework, we enjoy a few benefits that derive from starting the development process from data and the community instead of the code.

Developing robust, quality applications, and providing realistic schedules

In order to develop modern high-quality applications, we need realistic, large datasets, if possible, before even writing a single line of code. Modern software development is all about processing large amounts of less-than-perfect data in real time to extract knowledge and actionable insights. When we develop software and apply it to large datasets, small errors and oversights are difficult to detect and might lead us to costly erroneous decisions. It's easy, for example, to overlook entire states while trying to study demographics, just because of a bug that silently drops data when the state name is too long. By carefully scraping, and having production-quality, large, real-world datasets during development (or even earlier) during design exploration, one can find and fix bugs, and make informed engineering decisions.

As another example, imagine that you want to design an Amazon-style "if you like this, you might also like that"-style recommendation system. If you are able to crawl and collect a real-world dataset before you even start, you will quickly become aware of the issues related to invalid entries, discontinued products, duplicates, invalid characters, and performance issues due to skewed distributions. Data will force you to design algorithms robust enough to handle the products bought by thousands of people as well as new entries with zero sales. Compare that to software developed in isolation that will later, potentially after weeks of development, face the ugliness of real-world data. The two approaches might eventually converge, but the ability to provide schedule estimates you can commit to, and the quality of software as the project's time progresses will be significantly different. Starting from data, leads to a much more pleasant and predictable software development experience.

Developing quality minimum viable products quickly

Large realistic datasets are even more essential for start-ups. You might have heard of the "Lean Startup", a term coined by *Eric Ries* to describe the business development process under conditions of extreme uncertainty like tech-start-ups. One of the key concepts of that framework is that of the **minimum viable product (MVP)**—a product with limited functionality that one can quickly develop and release to a limited audience in order to measure reactions and validate business hypotheses. Based on the reactions, a start-up might choose to continue with further investments, or "pivot" to something more promising.

Some aspects of this process that are easy to overlook are very closely connected with the data problems that Scrapy solves for us. When we ask potential customers to try our mobile app, for example, we as developers or entrepreneurs ask them to judge the functionality imagining how this app will look when completed. This might be a bit too much imagining for a non-expert. The distance between an app which shows "product 1", "product 2", and "user 433", and an application that provides information on "Samsung UN55J6200 55-Inch TV", which has a five star rating from user "Richard S." and working links that take you directly to a product detail page (despite the fact we didn't write it), is significant. It's very difficult for people to judge the functionality of an MVP objectively, unless the data that we use is realistic and somewhat exciting.

One of the reasons that some start-ups have data as an afterthought is the perception that collecting them is expensive. Indeed, we would typically need to develop forms, administration screens, and spend time entering data — or we could just use Scrapy and crawl a few websites before writing even a single line of code. You will see in *Chapter 4*, *From Scrapy to a Mobile App*, how easy it is to develop a simple mobile app as soon as you have data.

Scraping gives you scale; Google couldn't use forms

While on the subject of forms, let's consider how they affect the growth of a product. Imagine for a second Google founders creating the first version of their engine incorporating a form that every webmaster has to fill, and copy-paste the text for every page on their website. They should then accept the license agreement to allow Google to process, store, and present their content while pocketing most of the advertising profits. Can you imagine the incredible amount of time and effort required to explain the vision and convince people to get involved in this process? Even if the market was starving for an excellent search engine (as it proved to be the case), this engine wouldn't be Google because its growth would be extremely slow. Even the most sophisticated algorithms wouldn't be able to offset the lack of data. Google uses web crawlers that move through links from page to page, filling their massive databases. Webmasters don't have to do anything at all. Actually, it requires a bit of effort to prevent Google from indexing your pages.

The idea of Google using forms might sound a bit ridiculous, but how many forms does a typical website require a user to fill? A login form, a new listing form, a checkout form, and so on. How much do those forms really cost by hindering application's growth? If you know your audience/customers enough, it is highly likely that you have a clue on the other websites they are typically using, and might already have an account with. For example, a developer will likely have a Stack Overflow and a GitHub account. Could you—with their permission—scrape those sites as soon as they give you their username, and auto-fill their photos, their bio, and a few recent posts? Can you perform some quick text analytics on the posts they are mostly interested in, and use it to adapt your site's navigation structure and suggested products or services? I hope you can see how replacing forms with automated data scraping can allow you to better serve your audience, and grow at web-scale.

Discovering and integrating into your ecosystem

Scraping data naturally leads you to discover and consider your relationship with the communities related to your endeavors. When you scrape a data source, naturally some questions arise: Do I trust their data? Do I trust the companies who I get data from? Should I talk to them to have a more formal cooperation? Am I competing or cooperating with them? How much would it cost me to get these data from another source? Those business risks are there anyway, but the scraping process helps us become aware of them earlier, and develop mitigation strategies.

You will also find yourself wondering what do you give back to those websites or communities? If you give them free traffic, they will likely be happy. On the other hand, if your application doesn't provide some value to your source, maybe your relationship is a bit ephemeral unless you talk to them and find a way to cooperate. By getting data from various sources, you are primed to develop products friendlier to the existing ecosystem that respect established market players, disrupting only when it's worth the effort. Established players might also help you grow faster—for example, if you have an application that uses data feeds from two or three distinct ecosystems of a hundred thousand users each, your service might end up connecting three hundred thousand users in a creative way which benefits everybody. For example, if you create a start-up that combines a rock music and a t-shirt printing community, you end up with a mixture of two ecosystems, and both you and the communities will likely benefit and grow.

Being a good citizen in a world full of spiders

There are a few things one needs to be aware of while developing scrapers. Irresponsible web scraping can be annoying and even illegal in some cases. The two most important things to avoid are **denial-of-service (DoS)** attack like behavior and violating copyrights.

In the first one, a typical visitor might be visiting a new page every few seconds. A typical web crawler might be downloading tens of pages per second. That is more than ten times the traffic that a typical user generates. This might reasonably make the website owners upset. Use throttling to reduce the traffic you generate to an acceptable user-like level. Monitor the response times, and if you see them increasing, reduce the intensity of your crawl. The good news is that Scrapy provides out-of-the-box implementation of both these functionalities (see *Chapter 7, Configuration and Management*).

On copyrights, obviously, take a look at the copyright notice of every website you scrape, and make sure you understand what is allowed and what is not. Most sites allow you to process information from their site as long as you don't reproduce them claiming that it's yours. What is nice to have is a User-Agent field on your requests that allows webmasters to know who you are and what you do with their data. Scrapy does this by default by using your BOT_NAME as a User-Agent when making requests. If this is a URL or a name that clearly points to your application, then the webmaster can visit your site, and learn more about how you use their data. Another important aspect is allowing any webmaster to prevent you from accessing certain areas of their website. Scrapy provides functionality (RobotsTxtMiddleware) that respects their preferences as expressed on the web-standard robots.txt file (see an example of that file at http://www.google.com/robots.txt). Finally, it's good to provide the means for webmasters to express their desire to be excluded from your crawls. At the very least, it must be easy for them to find a way to communicate with you and express any concerns.

Laws differ from country to country, and I'm by no means in a position to give legal advice. Please seek professional legal advice if you feel the need before relying too heavily on scraping for your projects. This applies to the entire content of this book.

What Scrapy is not

Finally, it's easy to misunderstand what Scrapy can do for you mainly because the terms *Data Scraping* and all the related terminology is somewhat fuzzy, and many terms are used interchangeably. I will try to clarify some of these areas to prevent confusion and save you some time.

Scrapy is *not* Apache Nutch, that is, it's not a generic web crawler. If Scrapy visits a website it knows nothing about, it won't be able to make anything meaningful out of it. Scrapy is about extracting structured information, and requires manual effort to set up the appropriate XPath or CSS expressions. Apache Nutch will take a generic page and extract information, such as keywords, from it. It might be more suitable for some applications and less for others.

Scrapy is *not* Apache Solr, Elasticsearch, or Lucene; in other words, it has nothing to do with a search engine. Scrapy is not intended to give you references to the documents that contain the word "Einstein" or anything else. You can use the data extracted by Scrapy, and insert them into Solr or Elasticsearch as we do at the beginning of *Chapter 9, Pipeline Recipes*, but that's just a way of using Scrapy, and not something embedded into Scrapy.

Finally, Scrapy is *not* a database like MySQL, MongoDB, or Redis. It neither stores nor indexes data. It only extracts data. That said, you will likely insert the data that Scrapy extracts to a database, and there is support for many of them, which will make your life easier. Scrapy isn't a database though, and its outputs could easily be just files on a disk or even no output at all—although I'm not sure how this could be useful.

Summary

In this chapter, we introduced you to Scrapy, gave you an overview of what it can help you with, and described what we believe is the best way to use this book. We also presented several ways with which automated data scraping can benefit you by helping you quickly develop high-quality applications that integrate nicely with existing ecosystems. In the following chapter, we will introduce you to HTML and XPath, two very important web languages that we will use in every Scrapy project.

2
Understanding HTML and XPath

In order to extract information from web pages, you have to understand a little bit more about their structure. We will have a quick look at HTML, the tree representation of HTML, and XPath as a way of selecting information on web pages.

HTML, the DOM tree representation, and the XPath

Let's spend some time understanding the process that takes place from when a user types a URL on the browser (or more often, when he/she clicks on a link or a bookmark) until a page is displayed on the screen. From the perspective of this book, this process has four steps:

- A URL is typed on the browser. The first part of the URL (the domain name, such as gumtree.com) is used to find the appropriate server on the web, and the URL along with other data like cookies form a request which is sent to that server.

- The server replies by sending an HTML page to the browser. Note that the server might also return other formats, such as XML or JSON, but for now we focus on HTML.

- The HTML gets translated to an internal tree representation inside the browser: the infamous **Document Object Model (DOM)**.

- The internal representation is rendered, based on some layout rules, to the visual representation that you see on the screen.

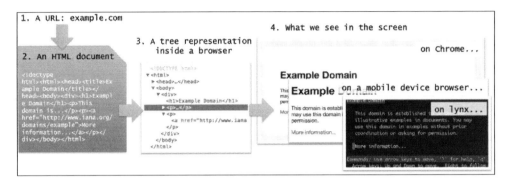

Let's have a look at those steps and the representations of the documents that they require. This will help you in locating the text that you want to scrape and in writing programs that retrieve it.

The URL

For our purposes, the URL has two main parts. The first part helps us locate the appropriate server on the net via the **Domain Name System (DNS)**. For example, when you send `https://mail.google.com/mail/u/0/#inbox` to the browser, it creates a DNS request on `mail.google.com`, which resolves the IP address of a suitable server such as `173.194.71.83`. Essentially, `https://mail.google.com/mail/u/0/#inbox` translates to `https://173.194.71.83/mail/u/0/#inbox`.

The rest of the URL is important for the server to understand what the request is all about. It might be an image, a document, or something that needs to trigger an action like sending an e-mail on that server.

The HTML document

The server reads the URL, understands what we are asking for, and replies with an HTML document. This document is essentially a text file that we can open with TextMate, Notepad, vi, or Emacs. Unlike most text documents, an HTML document has a format specified by the World Wide Web Consortium. The specification is certainly beyond the scope of this book, but let's have a look at a simple HTML page. If you head to `http://example.com`, you can see the associated HTML file in your browser by choosing **View Page Source**. The exact process is different on different browsers; on many systems, it's an option you can get by right clicking, and most browsers show the source if you press *Ctrl + U*, or *Cmd + U* on a Mac.

In some pages, this feature might be disabled. and you will have to click on the Chrome menu and then **Tools | View Source**.

The following is currently the HTML code of `http://example.com/`:

```html
<!doctype html>
<html>
  <head>
      <title>Example Domain</title>
      <meta charset="utf-8" />
      <meta http-equiv="Content-type"
             content="text/html; charset=utf-8" />
      <meta name="viewport" content="width=device-width,
             initial-scale=1" />
      <style type="text/css"> body { background-color: ...
             } }</style>
  <body>
      <div>
             <h1>Example Domain</h1>
             <p>This domain is established to be used for
                illustrative examples examples in documents.
                You may use this domain in examples without
                prior coordination or asking for permission.</p>
             <p><a href="http://www.iana.org/domains/example">
                More information...</a></p>
      </div>
  </body>
</html>
```

I formatted the HTML document to be readable, but you might well get all this text in a single line. In HTML, spaces and line breaks don't matter in most contexts.

The text between the angle brackets (for example, `<html>` or `<head>`) is called a *tag*. `<html>` is an opening tag and `</html>` is a closing tag. The only difference is the / character. As this shows, tags come in pairs. Some web pages are sloppy about closing tags (using a single `<p>` tag to separate paragraphs, for instance), but the browser is very permissive and tries to infer where a closing `</p>` tag should be.

Everything between `<p>` and `</p>` is called an HTML *element*. Note that elements might contain other elements, as is the case for the `<div>` element in the example or the second `<p>`, which includes an `<a>` element.

Some tags are a bit more complex, such as `<a href="http://www.iana.org/ domains/example">`. The `href` part with the URL is called an *attribute*.

Finally, many elements include text, such as the `"Example Domain"`, within the `<h1>` element.

The good news is that not all this markup is important for us. The only things that are visible are the elements of the body element: what's between the `<body>` and `</body>` tags. The `<head>` part is important to indicate meta-information such as character encoding, but Scrapy takes care of most of those issues, so it is highly likely that you will never have to pay attention to that part of the HTML page.

The tree representation

Every browser has its own, complex internal data structures with the aid of which it renders web pages. The DOM representation is cross-platform and language-independent, and is supported by most browsers.

To see the tree representation of a web page in Chrome, right-click on the element you are interested in, and select **Inspect Element**. If this feature is disabled, you can still access it by clicking on the Chrome menu and then **Tools | Developer Tools**.

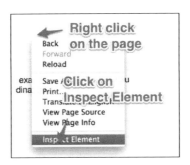

At this point, you see something that looks very similar to the HTML representation, but it's not exactly the same. It's a tree representation of the HTML code. It will look the same regardless of how the original HTML document uses spacing and line breaks. You can click on every element to inspect or manipulate attributes, and such, and see how these changes affect what you see on the screen in real time. For example, if you double-click some text, modify it, and press the *Enter* key, the text on the screen will be updated with the new value. On the right, under the **Properties** tag, you can see the properties of this tree representation, and at the bottom, you can see a breadcrumb-like structure that shows the exact position of your currently selected element in the hierarchy of HTML elements.

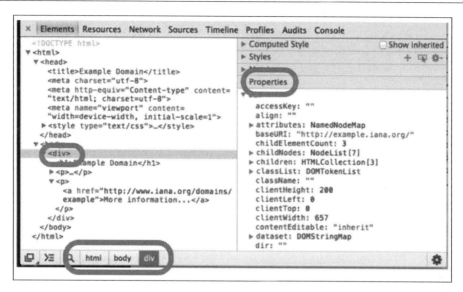

The important thing to keep in mind is that while HTML is just text, the tree representation is an object inside the browser's memory that you can view and manipulate programmatically, and in the case of Chrome, via the **Developer Tools**.

What you see on the screen

The HTML text representation and the tree representation don't have anything that looks like the beautiful view we usually see on our screen. This is actually one of the reasons that HTML has been so successful. It is a document that is meant to be read by humans, and specifies the content of the page, but not the way it's going to render on the screen. This means it's the browser's responsibility to render the HTML document and make it look nice, whether it's a full-featured browser such as Chrome, a mobile device browser, or even a text-only browser such as Lynx.

That said, the evolution of the web spurred great demand for both web developers and users to have more control over how a web page is rendered. CSS was created to give hints on how HTML elements are rendered. For scraping, though, we don't need anything that has to do with CSS.

So, how does the tree representation map to what we see on the screen? The answer lies in what is called the box model. Just as a DOM tree element can contain other elements or text, in the same way, by default, when rendered on the screen, each box representation of an element contains the box representations of the embedded elements. In that sense, what we see on the screen is a two-dimensional representation of the original HTML document—but the tree structure is a part of the representation, in a hidden way. For instance, in the following image, we see how three DOM elements—a `<div>` and two embedded elements, an `<h1>` and a `<p>`— appear in a browser and in the DOM:

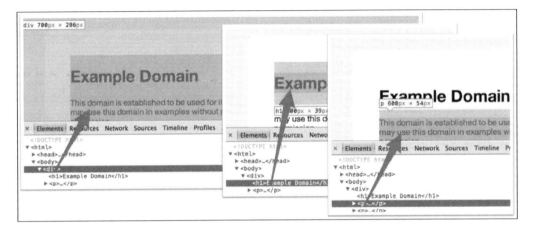

Selecting HTML elements with XPath

If you come from a traditional software engineering background, and have no knowledge of XPath, you will probably worry that, in order to access this information in HTML documents, you will have to do lots of string matching, searching for tags on the document, handling special cases, and so on, or somehow parse the entire tree representation to extract what you want. The good news is that none of those is necessary. You can select and extract elements, attributes, and text with a language called XPath, specially designed for that purpose.

In order to use XPath with Google Chrome, click on the **Console** tab of **Developer Tools** and use the `$x` utility function. For example, you can try `$x('//h1')` on `http://example.com/`. It will move the browser to the `<h1>` element, as shown in the following screenshot:

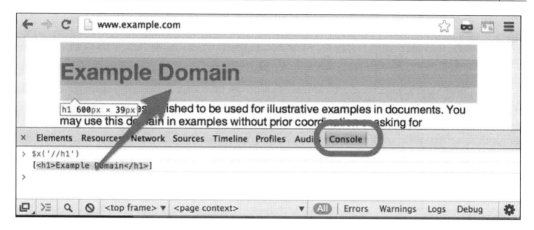

What you will see returned on the Chrome **Console** is a JavaScript array containing the selected elements. If you put your mouse cursor over those variables, the selected elements will be highlighted on the screen. It's very handy.

Useful XPath expressions

The hierarchy of the document starts with the `<html>` element, and you can use element names and slashes to select elements of the document. For example, the following is what various expressions will return from the `http://example.com/` page:

```
$x('/html')
    [ <html>...</html> ]
$x('/html/body')
    [ <body>...</body> ]
$x('/html/body/div')
    [ <div>...</div> ]
$x('/html/body/div/h1')
    [ <h1>Example Domain</h1> ]
$x('/html/body/div/p')
    [ <p>...</p>, <p>...</p> ]
$x('/html/body/div/p[1]')
    [ <p>...</p> ]
$x('/html/body/div/p[2]')
    [ <p>...</p> ]
```

Note that because two `<p>` elements lie under the `<div>` on this particular page, `html/body/div/p` returns two elements. You can use `p[1]` and `p[2]` to access the first and the second element respectively.

Note that Document's title, may be the only interesting element from a scraping perspective, is in the head section, and can be accessed with the following expression:

```
$x('//html/head/title')
   [ <title>Example Domain</title> ]
```

For large documents, you might have to write a very large XPath expressions to reach specific elements. In order to avoid this, the // syntax allows you to get elements of a particular type no matter where they are in the hierarchy. For example, //p will select all the p elements, and //a all the links for us.

```
$x('//p')
   [ <p>...</p>, <p>...</p> ]
$x('//a')
   [ <a href="http://www.iana.org/domains/example">More
information...</a> ]
```

The //a syntax can also be used anywhere in the hierarchy. For example, to find any links under any div, you can use //div//a. Note that //div/a with single slash would give an empty array, because there isn't any `a` directly under `div` in example.com:

```
$x('//div//a')
   [ <a href="http://www.iana.org/domains/example">More
information...</a> ]
$x('//div/a')
   [ ]
```

You can also select attributes. The only attribute on http://example.com/ is the href of the link, which you can access using the character @ as follows:

```
$x('//a/@href')
   [ href="http://www.iana.org/domains/example" ]
```

 Apparently, in recent chrome versions, @href doesn't return the URLs but empty strings instead. Don't worry, your XPath expression is still correct.

You can also select just the text by using the text() function:

```
$x('//a/text()')
   [ "More information..." ]
```

You can use the * character to select all elements at a specific hierarchy level. For example:

```
$x('//div/*')
   [ <h1>Example Domain</h1>, <p>...</p>, <p>...</p> ]
```

You will find it very useful to select elements that have a specific attribute, such as @class, or that have a specific value as an attribute. You can do it by using more advanced predicates than the numeric ones which we used on the p[1] and p[2] examples earlier. For example, //a[@href] selects link that contains href attribute, and //a[@href="http://www.iana.org/domains/example"] selects link that have an attribute href with the specified value.

Even more useful is the ability to find links whose href attribute starts with, or contains, a specific substring. The following are some examples:

```
$x('//a[@href]')
  [ <a href="http://www.iana.org/domains/example">More
information...</a> ]
$x('//a[@href="http://www.iana.org/domains/example"]')
  [ <a href="http://www.iana.org/domains/example">More
information...</a> ]
$x('//a[contains(@href, "iana")]')
  [ <a href="http://www.iana.org/domains/example">More
information...</a> ]
$x('//a[starts-with(@href, "http://www.")]')
  [ <a href="http://www.iana.org/domains/example">More
information...</a>]
$x('//a[not(contains(@href, "abc"))]')
  [ <a href="http://www.iana.org/domains/example">More
information...</a>]
```

There are tens of XPath functions like not(), contains(), and starts-with() that you can find in the online documentation (http://www.w3schools.com/xpath/xpath_functions.asp), but you can go quite far without using most of them.

I might be getting a bit ahead of myself right now, but you can use the same XPath expressions in a Scrapy shell. To open a page and access the Scrapy shell, you just have to type the following:

scrapy shell http://example.com

The shell gives you access to many variables that are typically available when you write spider code (see next chapter). The most important of them is response, which is an HtmlResponse in case of HTML documents - a class that allows you via it's xpath() method $x in chrome. The following are a few examples:

```
response.xpath('/html').extract()
  [u'<html><head><title>...</body></html>']
response.xpath('/html/body/div/h1').extract()
  [u'<h1>Example Domain</h1>']
```

```
response.xpath('/html/body/div/p').extract()
  [u'<p>This domain ... permission.</p>', u'<p><a href="http://www.
iana.org/domains/example">More information...</a></p>']
response.xpath('//html/head/title').extract()
  [u'<title>Example Domain</title>']
response.xpath('//a').extract()
  [u'<a href="http://www.iana.org/domains/example">More
information...</a>']
response.xpath('//a/@href').extract()
  [u'http://www.iana.org/domains/example']
response.xpath('//a/text()').extract()
  [u'More information...']
response.xpath('//a[starts-with(@href, "http://www.")]').extract()
  [u'<a href="http://www.iana.org/domains/example">More
information...</a>']
```

This means that you can use Chrome to develop XPath expressions, and then use them in your Scrapy crawler as we will see in the following chapter.

Using Chrome to get XPath expressions

Chrome acts even more developer-friendly by giving us basic XPath expressions. Start by inspecting an element as shown earlier: right-click on the desired element, and then choose **Inspect Element**. This opens **Developer Tools** and the HTML element in the tree representation will be highlighted. Now right-click on it, and select **Copy XPath** from the menu; the XPath expression will be copied to the clipboard.

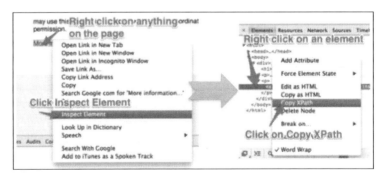

You can test the expression as always from the console:

```
$x('/html/body/div/p[2]/a')
  [ <a href="http://www.iana.org/domains/example">More
information...</a>]
```

Examples of common tasks

There are some uses for XPath expressions that you will probably encounter quite often. Let's see some examples that work (right now) for Wikipedia pages. Wikipedia has a very stable format, so I wouldn't expect them to break soon, but eventually they will. Consider those expressions as illustrative examples.

- Getting the `text` of the `span` under the `div` with id `"firstHeading"`:

  ```
  //h1[@id="firstHeading"]/span/text()
  ```

- Getting the URLs of links in an unordered list (`ul`) inside a `div` with `id` `"toc"`:

  ```
  //div[@id="toc"]/ul//a/@href
  ```

- Getting the text anywhere inside a header element (`h1`) inside any element with a `class` attribute containing `"ltr"` and a `class` attribute containing `"skin-vector"`. The two strings may be in the same class or different ones.

  ```
  //*[contains(@class,"ltr") and contains(@class,"skin-vector")]//
  h1//text()
  ```

Actually, you will often need to use classes in your XPath expressions. In these cases, you should remember that due to some styling elements called CSS, you will often see HTML elements having multiple classes stated on their `class` attribute. This means that you will see, for example, some of your divs with their `class` attribute set to `"link"` and some others to `"link active"` in a navigation system. The latter will be the links that are currently active, thus visible or highlighted with a special color (via CSS). When scraping, you will usually be interested in elements that contain a certain class, that is, both `"link"` and `"link active"` in the previous example. The `contains()` XPath function allows you to select all the elements that contain a certain class.

- To select the URL for the first image in the table that has a `class` attribute with value `"infobox"`, use the following:

  ```
  //table[@class="infobox"]//img[1]/@src
  ```

- To select all the URLs of the links under the `div` with a `class` attribute that starts with `"reflist"`:

  ```
  //div[starts-with(@class,"reflist")]//a/@href
  ```

- To select all the URLs of links under the `div` element following an element whose child element contains the text `"References"`:

  ```
  //*[text()="References"]/../following-sibling::div//a
  ```

Note that this is quite fragile and easy to break, because it makes many assumptions on the structure of the document.

- To get the URLs for every image on the page:

```
//img/@src
```

Anticipating changes

Scraping often targets pages on servers that are beyond our control. This means that if their HTML changes in a way that makes our XPath expressions invalid, we will have to go back to our spiders and correct them. This doesn't usually take long, because the changes are typically small. However, it's certainly something we would prefer to avoid. Some simple rules help us reduce the odds that your expressions will become invalid:

- Avoid array indexes (numbers)

  Chrome will often give you expressions with lots of constant numbers such as:

  ```
  //*[@id="myid"]/div/div/div[1]/div[2]/div/div[1]/div[1]/a/img
  ```

  This is quite fragile, because if something like an advertisement block adds an extra div somewhere in that hierarchy, those numbers will end up pointing to different elements. The solution in this case is to go as close as possible to the target img tag, and find an element with an id or a class attribute that you can use, such as:

  ```
  //div[@class="thumbnail"]/a/img
  ```

- Classes are not that good

  Using class attributes makes it easy to pinpoint elements, but they are often used to affect the looks of the page via CSS, and may thus change as a result of minor alterations to the website's layout. For example, the following class:

  ```
  //div[@class="thumbnail"]/a/img
  ```

  This might after a while, turn to:

  ```
  //div[@class="preview green"]/a/img
  ```

- Meaningful data-oriented classes are better than specific or layout-oriented ones

  In the previous example, both `"thumbnail"` and `"green"` are examples of bad class names to rely on. The name `"thumbnail"` is certainly better than `"green"`, but both are inferior to something like `"departure-time"`. The first two are used for layout, whereas `"departure-time"` is something meaningful, related to the contents of the `div`. As a result, the latter is more likely to remain valid even when the layout changes. It might also indicate that the developers of the site are aware of the benefits of annotating their data with meaningful and consistent ways.

- IDs are often the most reliable

  The `id` attributes are usually the best choice for a target, as long as they are meaningful and data-related. Partially, this is because JavaScript and external link anchors often use them to reference specific parts of the document. For example, the following XPath is quite robust:

  ```
  //*[@id="more_info"]//text()
  ```

  Exceptions to this are programmatically generated IDs that include unique references. Those render them useless for scraping. For example:

  ```
  //[@id="order-F4982322"]
  ```

  The above is a very bad XPath expression despite being an `id`. Also keep in mind that, even though IDs should be unique, you will find many HTML documents where they are not.

Summary

The quality of markup continuously improves, and it's now much easier to create robust XPath expressions that extract data from HTML documents. In this chapter, you learned the basics of HTML documents and XPath expressions. You saw how to use Google Chrome to automatically get some XPath expressions as a starting point that we can later optimize. You also learned how to create such expressions directly by inspecting the HTML document, and how to tell a robust XPath expression from a less robust one. We are now ready to use all this knowledge to write our first few spiders with Scrapy in *Chapter 3, Basic Crawling*.

3
Basic Crawling

This is a very important chapter, which you will probably read several times, and return to often for finding solutions. We are going to start by explaining how to install Scrapy, and then move on to the methodology of developing Scrapy crawlers along with numerous examples and alternative implementations. Before we start, let's take a look at some important notions.

Since we are quickly moving to the fun coding part, it's important to be able to use the code segments you find in this book. When you see the following:

```
$ echo hello world
hello world
```

it means you are to type echo hello world on a terminal (skip the dollar sign). The line(s) that follow are the output as seen on your terminal.

 We will use the terms 'terminal', 'console', and 'command line' interchangeably. They don't make much difference in the context of this book. Please Google a bit to find out how to start the console on your platform (Windows, OS X, or others). You will also find detailed instructions in *Appendix A, Installing Prerequisites*.

When you see the following:

```
>>> print 'hi'
hi
```

it means you have to type print 'hi' on a Python or Scrapy shell prompt (skip >>>). Again, the line(s) that follow are the output of the command as seen on your terminal.

For this book, you will also need to edit files. The tools you're going to use depend heavily on your environment. If you use Vagrant (highly recommended), you will be able to edit files with editors like Notepad, Notepad++, Sublime Text, TextMate, Eclipse, or PyCharm on your PC/laptop. If you are more experienced with Linux/Unix, you might also like to edit files directly from the console with vim or emacs. Both of them are powerful, but have a learning curve. If you are a beginner, and you have to edit something in the console, you might also like to try the more beginner-friendly nano editor.

Installing Scrapy

The installation of Scrapy is relatively easy, but it all depends on where you're starting from. To be able to support as many people as possible, the "official" way of running/installing Scrapy as well as all the examples in this book is through Vagrant—a software that allows you to run a standard Linux box with all the tools that we've set up for you inside your computer, no matter what operating system it runs on. We provide instructions for Vagrant, and a few instructions for some popular operating systems in the following sections.

MacOS

To easily follow this book, please follow the instructions on Vagrant given later. If you want to install Scrapy natively for MacOS, that's quite easy. Just type in the following command:

```
$ easy_install scrapy
```

and everything should be taken care of for you. It might, in the process, ask you for your password or installing Xcode. That's perfectly fine, and you can safely accept the same.

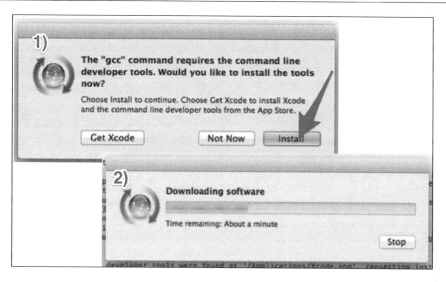

Windows

Installing Scrapy natively on Windows is somewhat advanced, and frankly, a bit of a pain. Additionally, installing all the software that you need to enjoy this book requires a significant degree of courage and determination. We have you covered though. Vagrant with Virtualbox runs great on every Windows 64-bit platform. Jump to the relevant section given further in this chapter, and you will be up and running in minutes. If you really need to install Scrapy natively on Windows, consult the resources on this book's website http://scrapybook.com

Linux

As with the previous two operating systems, Vagrant is the recommended way to go as far as following this book is your goal.

You will likely need to install Scrapy in many cases on Linux servers, so a few more detailed instructions might be beneficial.

 The exact dependencies change quite often. The Scrapy version we are installing at the time of writing is 1.0.3, and the following are indicative instructions for different major distributions.

Ubuntu or Debian Linux

In order to install Scrapy on Ubuntu (tested with Ubuntu 14.04 Trusty Tahr - 64 bit) or other distributions that use `apt`, the following three commands should be enough:

```
$ sudo apt-get update
$ sudo apt-get install python-pip python-lxml python-crypto python-
cssselect python-openssl python-w3lib python-twisted python-dev libxml2-
dev libxslt1-dev zlib1g-dev libffi-dev libssl-dev
$ sudo pip install scrapy
```

This preceding process requires some compilation, and might break every now and then, but it will give you the most recent version of Scrapy available on PyPI (that is, quite recent). If you want to avoid any complication, and are okay with a potentially less up-to-date version, google for "install Scrapy Ubuntu packages", and follow the instructions given in the official Scrapy documentation.

Red Hat or CentOS Linux

It's equally easy to install Scrapy on Red Hat or other distributions (tested with Ubuntu 14.04 Trusty Tahr - 64 bit) that use `yum`. All you need is the following three lines:

```
sudo yum update
sudo yum -y install libxslt-devel pyOpenSSL python-lxml python-devel gcc
sudo easy_install scrapy
```

From the latest source

If you have followed the preceding instructions, you have all the dependencies that Scrapy currently needs. Scrapy is 100 percent Python, so if you like hacking the source code or test-driving the latest features, you can easily clone the latest version from `https://github.com/scrapy/scrapy`. To install Scrapy on your system just type in the following commands:

```
$ git clone https://github.com/scrapy/scrapy.git
$ cd scrapy
$ python setup.py install
```

I guess if you belong to this class of Scrapy users, it's unnecessary for me to mention `virtualenv`.

Upgrading Scrapy

Scrapy gets upgraded rather often. You will find yourself needing to upgrade within no time, and you can do it with `pip`, `easy_install`, or `aptitude`:

```
$ sudo pip install --upgrade Scrapy
```

or

```
$ sudo easy_install --upgrade scrapy
```

If you need to downgrade or choose a specific version, you can do it by specifying the version you want, for example:

```
$ sudo pip install Scrapy==1.0.0
```

or

```
$ sudo easy_install scrapy==1.0.0
```

Vagrant: this book's official way to run examples

This book has some complex interesting examples some of which use many services. No matter how beginner or advanced you are, you will be able to run the examples in this book, because a program called Vagrant allows us to set up this complex system with a single command.

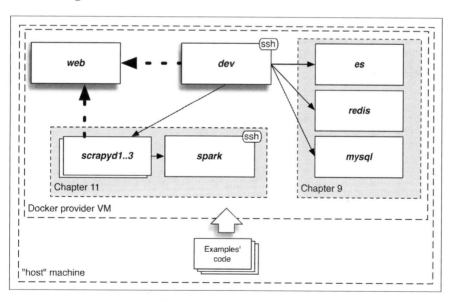

The system used in this book

Your PC or laptop in Vagrant terminology is called the "host" machine. Vagrant uses our host machine to run a docker provider **VM (virtual machine)**. These technologies allow us to have an isolated system with its own private network where this book's examples run regardless of the software and hardware of your host machine.

Most chapters use just two services - the "dev" machine and the "web" machine. We log-in to the dev machine and run Scrapy crawls that scrape pages from the web machine. Later chapters use more services including databases and big data processing engines.

Follow the instructions in *Appendix A, Installing Prerequisites*, to install Vagrant on your operating system. By the end of that chapter you will have `git` and `Vagrant` installed on your computer. You have your console/terminal/command prompt open and you can now get the code of this book by doing:

```
$ git clone https://github.com/scalingexcellence/scrapybook.git
$ cd scrapybook
```

You can then start the Vagrant system by typing:

```
$ vagrant up --no-parallel
```

This will take some time the first time you run it - depending on your internet connection. After the first time, `vagrant up` should be instantaneous. As soon as your system is up, you can log in to your virtual dev machine with:

```
$ vagrant ssh
```

You are now on the dev console where you can follow the rest of the instructions in this book. The code has been cloned from your host machine to the dev machine and you can find it on the book directory:

```
$ cd book
$ ls
```

```
ch03 ch04 ch05 ch07 ch08 ch09 ch10 ch11 ...
```

Open a few consoles and do `vagrant ssh` to have multiple dev terminals to play with. You can use `vagrant halt` to shut the system down and `vagrant status` to check their status. Note that `vagrant halt` won't turn off the VM. If that's a problem open VirtualBox and stop it manually or use `vagrant global-status` to find its id (name "docker-provider") and halt it with `vagrant halt <ID>`. Most of the examples will be able to run even if you are offline which is a great side effect of using Vagrant.

Now that we have set up the system properly, we are ready to start learning Scrapy.

UR²IM – the fundamental scraping process

Every website is different, and you will certainly need to do some extra study, or ask some questions on the Scrapy mailing list if something is unusual. However, what is important in order to know where and how to search is to have an overview of the process, and know the related terminology. While working with Scrapy, the general process that you most often follow is the UR²IM process.

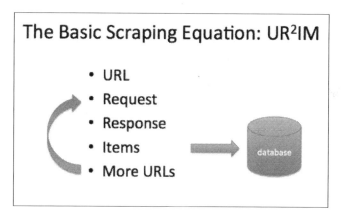

The UR²IM process

The URL

It all starts with a URL. You will need a few example URLs from the site you want to scrape. I'm going to demonstrate this using the Gumtree classifieds site (`https://www.gumtree.com/`) as an example.

By visiting, for example, the London properties index page of Gumtree on `http://www.gumtree.com/flats-houses/london`, you will be able to find numerous examples of URLs of properties. You can copy them by right clicking on the classifieds' listings, and clicking **Copy Link Address** or the equivalent for your browser. One of them, for example, might look like this: `https://www.gumtree.com/p/studios-bedsits-rent/split-level`. It's okay for you to play with a few URLs on the real site. Unfortunately, XPath expressions will likely stop working on the real Gumtree site after some time as their website changes. Gumtree also doesn't reply, unless you set a "user-agent header". More on this a bit later, but for now, if you want to load one of their pages, you can use the Scrapy shell, as follows:

```
scrapy shell -s USER_AGENT="Mozilla/5.0" <your url here  e.g. http://www.gumtree.com/p/studios-bedsits-rent/...>
```

To debug problems while using scrapy shell, add the `--pdb` argument to enable interactive debugging in case of exceptions. For example:

```
scrapy shell --pdb https://gumtree.com
```

 The Scrapy shell is an invaluable tool that helps us develop with Scrapy.

Obviously, we don't encourage you hitting Gumtree's website while learning with this book, and we don't want the examples of this book to break anytime soon. We also want you to be able to develop and play with our examples even if you aren't connected to the Internet. That's why your Vagrant development environment contains a web server that provides generated pages similar to those of Gumtree. They might not look as nice as the real site, but from a scraper's perspective, they are exactly the same. That said, we still prefer all the screenshots of the chapter to come from the real Gumtree site. From your Vagrant dev machine, you can hit the web server at `http://web:9312/`, and also from your web browser at `http://localhost:9312/`.

Let's open a page from that server with the Scrapy shell, and play a bit by typing the following on our dev machine:

```
$ scrapy shell http://web:9312/properties/property_000000.html
...
[s] Available Scrapy objects:
[s]    crawler      <scrapy.crawler.Crawler object at 0x2d4fb10>
[s]    item         {}
[s]    request      <GET http:// web:9312/.../property_000000.html>
[s]    response     <200 http://web:9312/.../property_000000.html>
[s]    settings     <scrapy.settings.Settings object at 0x2d4fa90>
[s]    spider       <DefaultSpider 'default' at 0x3ea0bd0>
[s] Useful shortcuts:

[s]    shelp()            Shell help (print this help)
[s]    fetch(req_or_url)  Fetch request (or URL) and update local...
[s]    view(response)     View response in a browser
>>>
```

We got some output, and now you are on a (Python) prompt that you can use to experiment with the page you just loaded (you can always exit with *Ctrl + D*).

The request and the response

What you might notice in the preceding log is that the Scrapy shell did some work for us by itself. We gave it a URL, and it performed a default GET request and got a response with the success code 200. This means that the information from this page is already loaded and ready to be used. If we try to print the first 50 characters of response.body, we get the following:

```
>>> response.body[:50]
'<!DOCTYPE html>\n<html>\n<head>\n<meta charset="UTF-8'
```

> What is this [:50]? It's the Python way of extracting the first 50 characters (if available) from a textual variable (in this case, response.body). If you haven't seen Python before, just keep calm and follow along. Soon you will be familiar with and enjoy all these syntax tricks.

This is the HTML content of the given page on Gumtree. The request and response part didn't cause us too much trouble. However, there are many cases where you will need to do some work to get those right. We will see a few of those in *Chapter 5, Quick Spider Recipes*. For now, we keep things simple, and move to the next part—the Item.

The Items

The next step is to try and extract data from the response into the fields of the Item. Since the format of this page is HTML, we use XPath expressions to do so. Let's first have a look at the page:

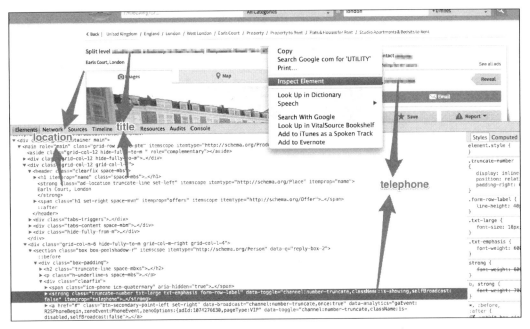

The page, the fields we are interested in, and their HTML code

As you can see in the preceding screenshot, there's lots of information here, but most of it is layout: logos, search boxes, buttons, and so on. It is great, but not very interesting from the scraping perspective. The fields we might be interested in might be, for example, the title of the listing, the location, or the agent's telephone number. Those have a corresponding HTML element, and we will need to locate it, and extract data with the process we described in the previous chapter. Let's start with the title.

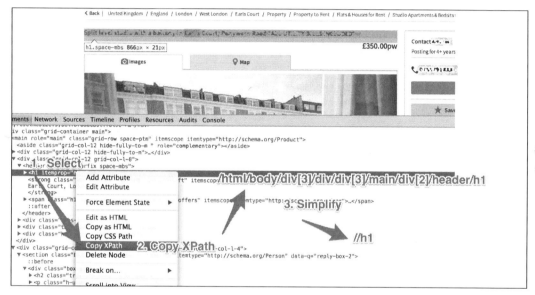

Extracting the title

Right-click on the title on the page, and select **Inspect Element**. This takes us to the relevant HTML code. Now, try to extract the XPath expression of this title by right-clicking and selecting **Copy XPath**. You will notice that Chrome gives us an XPath expression that is accurate, but it's very complicated, and thus, fragile. We will simplify it a bit. We will just use the last part of it and select H1 elements wherever we see them in the page by using the expression: //h1. This is the cheat's method, because we don't really want every H1 in the page, but just the one that is used as a title; however, it is considered good SEO practice to have a single H1 element in every page, and most websites will have only one.

 SEO is the acronym for Search Engine Optimization: the process of optimizing a website's coding, content, and inbound and outbound links in order to promote it in the best possible way to search engines.

Let's check to see if this XPath expression works with the Scrapy shell:

```
>>> response.xpath('//h1/text()').extract()
[u'set unique family well']
```

Excellent, it works fine. What you will notice is that I appended /text() at the end of the //h1 expression. This is necessary in order to extract just the text contained in H1, and not the H1 element itself. We will almost always use /text() for textual fields. If we skip it, we get the text for the whole element including markup, which is not what we want:

```
>>> response.xpath('//h1').extract()
[u'<h1 itemprop="name" class="space-mbs">set unique family well</h1>']
```

At this point, we have the code to extract the first interesting property of this page—the title—but if you take a better look, you will notice an easier and better way of doing so.

Gumtree has microdata markup

Gumtree has annotated their HTML with microdata markup. We can see, for example, that there is an `itemprop="name"` attribute in their header. This is great. It allows us to use a simpler XPath expression that doesn't include any visual elements: `//*[@itemprop="name"][1]/text()`. You might wonder why we select the first element with `itemprop="name"`.

 Wait—did you say first? If you are a seasoned programmer, you've probably been used to `array[1]` being the second element of an array. Surprisingly, XPath is 1-based (!) thus `array[1]` is the first element of the array.

We do so, not only because `itemprop="name"` is used in many different contexts in microdata but also because Gumtree has nested information for other properties in the "You may also like…" section of their page in a way that prevents us from easily distinguishing them. Nevertheless, this is not a big problem. We just select the first one, and we will do the same for all the other fields.

Let's have a look at price. Price is contained in the following HTML structure:

```
<strong class="ad-price txt-xlarge txt-emphasis" itemprop="price">
£334.39pw</strong>
```

Again we see `itemprop="name"`, which is brilliant. Our XPath will be `//*[@itemprop="price"][1]/text()`. Let's try it:

```
>>> response.xpath('//*[@itemprop="price"][1]/text()').extract()
[u'\xa3334.39pw']
```

We notice some Unicode characters (the pound sign £), and then the `350.00pw` price. It is indicative that data isn't always as clean as we would wish, and we might need to clean them a bit more. In this case, for example, we might want to use a regular expression to select just the numbers and the decimal dot. We can do so by using the `re()` method and a simple regular expression instead of `extract()`:

```
>>> response.xpath('//*[@itemprop="price"][1]/text()').re('[.0-9]+')
[u'334.39']
```

We use a `response` object, and call its `xpath()` method to extract interesting values. But what are the values `xpath()` returns us? If we don't use the `.extract()` method with a trivial XPath, we get the following indicative output:

```
>>> response.xpath('.')
[<Selector xpath='.' data=u'<html>\n<head>\n<meta
charse'>]
```

`xpath()` returns `Selector` objects preloaded with the contents of the page. We just used the `xpath()` method, but it has another useful method: `css()`. Both `xpath()` and `css()` return selectors, and only when we call the `extract()` or `re()` method we get actual arrays of text. This is brilliant, because it allows us to chain the `xpath()` and `css()` operations. For example, we could use `css()` to extract the right HTML element quickly:

```
>>> response.css('.ad-price')
[<Selector xpath=u"descendant-or-self::*[@class and
contains(concat(' ', normalize-space(@class), ' '), '
ad-price ')]" data=u'<strong class="ad-price txt-xlarge
txt-e'>]
```

Notice that behind the scenes, `css()` actually compiles an `xpath()` expression, but what we type is simpler than the XPath itself. Then we can chain `xpath()` to extract just the text.

```
>>> response.css('.ad-price').xpath('text()')
[<Selector xpath='text()' data=u'\xa3334.39pw'>]
```

Finally, we might chain our regular expression with `re()` to extract our value:

```
>>> response.css('.ad-price').xpath('text()').re('[.0-
9]+')
[u'334.39']
```

This expression is, practically speaking, no better or worse than our original expression. Consider this as a thought-provoking illustrative example. In this book, we will keep things as simple as possible, and we will use old good XPath as much as we can. The key point to remember is that `xpath()` and `css()` return `Selector` objects that might be chained. In order to get actual values, use either `extract()` or `re()`. With each new version of Scrapy there are new exciting and high-value features added around those classes. The relevant Scrapy documentation section - http://doc.scrapy.org/en/latest/topics/selectors.html - is excellent and make sure you have a good look at it to find the most efficient way to extract your data..

The story for the description text is similar. There is an `itemprop="description"` property that indicates description. The XPath expression is: `//*[@itemprop="description"][1]/text()`. Similarly, the address is annotated with `itemtype="http://schema.org/Place"`; thus, the XPath expression is: `//*[@itemtype="http://schema.org/Place"][1]/text()`.

Similarly, the image has an `itemprop="image"`. We thus use `//img[@itemprop="image"][1]/@src`. Notice that we won't use `/text()` in this case, because we don't want any text but just the `src` attribute that contains the URL for this image.

Assuming that this is all the information we want to extract, we can summarize it in the following table:

Primary fields	XPath expression
title	`//*[@itemprop="name"][1]/text()`
	Example value: `[u'set unique family well']`
price	`//*[@itemprop="price"][1]/text()`
	Example value (using `re()`): `[u'334.39']`
description	`//*[@itemprop="description"][1]/text()`
	Example value: `[u'website court warehouse\r\npool...']`
address	`//*[@itemtype="http://schema.org/Place"][1]/text()`
	Example value: `[u'Angel, London']`
image_urls	`//*[@itemprop="image"][1]/@src`
	Example value: `[u'../images/i01.jpg']`

Now this table is important, because if we had many websites with similar information, we would most likely need to create many similar spiders where only the preceding expressions may need to be different. Additionally, if we wanted to scrape tens of websites, we could use such a table to split the workload.

Up to this point, we used mostly HTML and XPath. From this point on, we will write some real Python.

A Scrapy project

Up to now, we were "playing" with Scrapy shell. Now we have all the necessary ingredients to start our first Scrapy project, and we can quit Scrapy shell by hitting *Ctrl + D*. Notice that everything you might have typed up to now gets lost. Obviously, we don't want to type the code each time we want to crawl something, so it's important to remember that the Scrapy shell is just a utility to help us play with pages, XPath expressions, and Scrapy objects. Don't invest much time in writing complicated code there, because it's bound to get lost as soon as you exit. In order to write real Scrapy code, we use projects. Let's create a Scrapy project and name it "properties", since we are scraping real estate properties.

```
$ scrapy startproject properties
$ cd properties
$ tree
.
├── properties
│   ├── __init__.py
│   ├── items.py
│   ├── pipelines.py
│   ├── settings.py
│   └── spiders
│       └── __init__.py
└── scrapy.cfg

2 directories, 6 files
```

> Just to remind you that you can get all the source code of this book from GitHub. To download this code, use the following command:
>
> ```
> git clone https://github.com/scalingexcellence/
> scrapybook
> ```
>
> The code from this chapter is available in the ch03 directory, and for this example in particular, in the ch03/properties directory.

We can see the directory structure for this Scrapy project. The `scrapy startproject properties` command created a directory with the name of the project with three interesting files: `items.py`, `pipelines.py`, and `settings.py`. There is also a subdirectory named `spiders`, which is empty right now. In this chapter, we will work mostly with `items.py` and files in the `spiders` directory. In later chapters, we will explore more settings, pipelines, and the `scrapy.cfg` file.

Defining items

Let's open `items.py` with a file editor. There is already some template code in there, but we will modify it for our use case. We will redefine the `PropertiesItem class` to add the fields that we summarized in the previous table.

We will also add a few fields that we will use later for our application (so that we won't have to touch this file again). We will explain them in depth later in this book. An important thing to notice is that the fact that we declare a field doesn't mean we are going to fill it in on every spider, or even use it altogether. Feel free to add whatever fields you feel appropriate—you can always correct them later.

Calculated fields	Python expressions
images	The images pipeline will fill this in automatically based on `image_urls`. More on this in a later chapter.
location	Our geocoding pipeline will fill this in later. More on this in a later chapter.

We will also add a few housekeeping fields. Those are not application-specific, but are just fields that I personally find interesting and think that might help me debug my spider in the future. You might or might not choose to have some of them for your projects. If you have a look at them, you'll understand that they allow me to find out where (server, url), when (date), and how (spider) an item got scraped. They might let me automate tasks like expiring items and scheduling new scrape iterations, or to drop items that came from a buggy spider. Don't worry if you don't understand all those expressions, especially the server one. Things will become clear as we move on to later chapters.

Housekeeping fields	Python expressions
url	`response.url` Example value: `'http://web.../property_000000.html'`
project	`self.settings.get('BOT_NAME')` Example value: `'properties'`
spider	`self.name` Example value: `'basic'`
server	`socket.gethostname()` Example value: `'scrapyserver1'`
date	`datetime.datetime.now()` Example value: `datetime.datetime(2015, 6, 25...)`

Given the list of fields, it's easy to modify and customize the `PropertiesItem` class that `scrapy startproject` created for us. With our text editor, we modify the `properties/items.py` file until it contains the following:

```python
from scrapy.item import Item, Field

class PropertiesItem(Item):
    # Primary fields
    title = Field()
    price = Field()
    description = Field()
    address = Field()
    image_urls = Field()

    # Calculated fields
    images = Field()
    location = Field()

    # Housekeeping fields
    url = Field()
    project = Field()
    spider = Field()
    server = Field()
    date = Field()
```

Since this is essentially the first Python code we write in a file, it's important to mention that Python uses indentation as part of its syntax. At the beginning of each field, there are exactly four spaces or one tab. This is important. If you start one line with four spaces and another with three you will get a syntax error. If you have four spaces in one and a tab in another, that too will be a syntax error. Those spaces group the field definitions under the `PropertiesItem` class. Other languages use curly braces ({ }) or special keywords like `begin - end` to group code, but Python uses spaces.

Writing spiders

We are halfway there. Now we need to write a spider. Typically, there will be one spider per website or a section of website if it's very large. A spider's code implements the whole UR^{2}IM process, as we will see in a moment.

When do you use a spider and when do you use a project? A project groups Items and spiders. If you have many websites from which you extract the same type of Items, for example: properties, then all those can be on a single project, and likely have one spider for each source/website. On the other hand, you would have different projects for sources with books and sources with properties.

Of course, you can create a new spider from scratch with a text editor, but it's better to save some typing by using the scrapy genspider command as follows:

```
$ scrapy genspider basic web
Created spider 'basic' using template 'basic' in module:
  properties.spiders.basic
```

Now if you rerun the tree command, you will notice that the only thing that changed is that a new file basic.py was added in your properties/spiders directory. What the preceding command did was to create a "default" spider with the name "basic" that is restricted to crawl URLs on the web domain. We can remove this restriction easily if we want, but for now it's fine. This spider was created using the "basic" template. You can see the other available templates by typing in scrapy genspider -l, and then creating spiders using any of those templates by using the -t parameter while doing scrapy genspider. We will see an example later in this chapter.

 Scrapy has many subdirectories. We will always assume that you are on the directory that contains a scrapy.cfg file. This is the "top level" directory for your project. Now whenever we refer to Python "packages" and "modules", they are set in such a way as to map the directory structure. For example, the output mentions properties.spiders. basic. This is the basic.py file in the properties/ spiders directory. The class PropertiesItem that we defined earlier is on the properties.items module, which corresponds to items.py file inside the properties directory.

If we have a look at the properties/spiders/basic.py file, we will see the following code:

```
import scrapy

class BasicSpider(scrapy.Spider):
    name = "basic"
    allowed_domains = ["web"]
```

```
    start_urls = (
        'http://www.web/',
    )


    def parse(self, response):
        pass
```

The `import` statement allows us to use the existing Scrapy framework classes. After this, it's the definition of a `BasicSpider` class that extends `scrapy.Spider`. By 'extends' we mean that despite the fact that we didn't write any code, this class already "inherits" quite some functionality from the Scrapy framework `Spider` class. This allows us to write very few extra lines of code and yet have a fully working spider. Then we see some parameters of the spider like its name and the domains that we are allowed to crawl. Finally, we have the definition of an empty function `parse()` that has a `self` and a `response` object as arguments. By using the `self` reference, we can use interesting functionality of our spider. However, the other object—`response` should be well familiar. It's exactly the same `response` object that we used to play with in the Scrapy shell.

This is your code—your spider. Don't be afraid to modify it; you won't really break anything very badly. In the worst case, you can always remove the file with `rm properties/spiders/basic.py*` and regenerate it. Feel free to play.

Okay, let's start hacking. First we will use the URL that we used with Scrapy shell by setting `start_urls` accordingly. Then we will use spider's predefined method `log()` to output everything that we summarized in the primary fields table. The modified code of `properties/spiders/basic.py` will be as follows:

```
import scrapy

class BasicSpider(scrapy.Spider):
    name = "basic"
    allowed_domains = ["web"]
    start_urls = (
        'http://web:9312/properties/property_000000.html',
    )

    def parse(self, response):
        self.log("title: %s" % response.xpath(
            '//*[@itemprop="name"][1]/text()').extract())
        self.log("price: %s" % response.xpath(
            '//*[@itemprop="price"][1]/text()').re('[.0-9]+'))
        self.log("description: %s" % response.xpath(
```

```
            '//*[@itemprop="description"][1]/text()').extract())
        self.log("address: %s" % response.xpath(
            '//*[@itemtype="http://schema.org/'
            'Place"][1]/text()').extract())
        self.log("image_urls: %s" % response.xpath(
            '//*[@itemprop="image"][1]/@src').extract())
```

 I'm going to modify the formatting every now and then to make it fit nicely on the screen and on paper. It doesn't mean that it has some particular meaning.

After all this wait, it's high time we run our spider. We can do so using the command `scrapy crawl` followed by the name of the spider:

```
$ scrapy crawl basic
INFO: Scrapy 1.0.3 started (bot: properties)
...
INFO: Spider opened
DEBUG: Crawled (200) <GET http://...000.html>
DEBUG: title: [u'set unique family well']
DEBUG: price: [u'334.39']
DEBUG: description: [u'website...']
DEBUG: address: [u'Angel, London']
DEBUG: image_urls: [u'../images/i01.jpg']
INFO: Closing spider (finished)
...
```

Excellent! Don't get overwhelmed by the large number of log lines. We will examine some of them more closely in a later chapter, but for now, just notice that all the data that was collected using the XPath expressions actually got extracted with this simple spider code.

Let's also play with another command—`scrapy parse`. It allows us to use the "most suitable" spider to parse any URL given as an argument. I don't like to leave things to chance, so let's use it in conjunction with the `--spider` parameter to set the spider:

```
$ scrapy parse --spider=basic http://web:9312/properties/property_000001.
html
```

You will see output similar to the previous one, but now for another property.

 `scrapy parse` is also a tool for debugging and quite a handy one. In any case, the main command if you need to do "serious" scrapping is `scrapy crawl`.

Populating an item

We will slightly modify the preceding code to populate `PropertiesItem` items. As you will see, the modification is going to be only slight, but it's going to "unlock" tons of new functionalities.

First of all, we need to import the `PropertiesItem` class. As we said earlier, this lies in the `items.py` file in the properties directory, and thus, in the `properties.items` module. We go back to our `properties/spiders/basic.py` file and import it with the following command:

```
from properties.items import PropertiesItem
```

Then we need to instantiate and return one. That's fairly simple. Inside our `parse()` method, we add an `item = PropertiesItem()` statement which creates a new item, and then we can assign expressions to its fields as follows:

```
item['title'] =
response.xpath('//*[@itemprop="name"][1]/text()').extract()
```

Finally, we return the item with `return item`. The updated code of `properties/spiders/basic.py` looks like the following:

```
import scrapy
from properties.items import PropertiesItem

class BasicSpider(scrapy.Spider):
    name = "basic"
    allowed_domains = ["web"]
    start_urls = (
        'http://web:9312/properties/property_000000.html',
    )

    def parse(self, response):
        item = PropertiesItem()
        item['title'] = response.xpath(
            '//*[@itemprop="name"][1]/text()').extract()
        item['price'] = response.xpath(
            '//*[@itemprop="price"][1]/text()').re('[.0-9]+')
        item['description'] = response.xpath(
            '//*[@itemprop="description"][1]/text()').extract()
```

```
item['address'] = response.xpath(
    '//*[@itemtype="http://schema.org/'
    'Place"][1]/text()').extract()
item['image_urls'] = response.xpath(
    '//*[@itemprop="image"][1]/@src').extract()
return item
```

Now if your run a `scrapy crawl basic` as before, you will notice a slight but important difference. We are no longer logging the scraped values (so no DEBUG: lines with field values). Instead, you will see the following line:

```
DEBUG: Scraped from <200
http://...000.html>
    {'address': [u'Angel, London'],
     'description': [u'website ... offered'],
     'image_urls': [u'../images/i01.jpg'],
     'price': [u'334.39'],
     'title': [u'set unique family well']}
```

This is a `PropertiesItem` that got scraped from this page. This is great, because Scrapy is built around the concept of `Items`, which means that you can now use the pipelines we will present in later chapters to filter and enrich them, and "Feed exports" to export and save them on different formats and places.

Saving to files

Try, for example, the following crawls:

```
$ scrapy crawl basic -o items.json
$ cat items.json
[{"price": ["334.39"], "address": ["Angel, London"], "description":
["website court ... offered"], "image_urls": ["../images/i01.jpg"],
"title": ["set unique family well"]}]


$ scrapy crawl basic -o items.jl
$ cat items.jl
{"price": ["334.39"], "address": ["Angel, London"], "description":
["website court ... offered"], "image_urls": ["../images/i01.jpg"],
"title": ["set unique family well"]}


$ scrapy crawl basic -o items.csv
$ cat items.csv
description,title,url,price,spider,image_urls...
"...offered",set unique family well,,334.39,,../images/i01.jpg
```

```
$ scrapy crawl basic -o items.xml
$ cat items.xml
<?xml version="1.0" encoding="utf-8"?>
<items><item><price><value>334.39</value></price>...</item></items>
```

Without us writing any extra code, we can save on all those different formats. What happens behind the scenes is that Scrapy recognizes the file extension that you want to output, and exports the file in the appropriate format. The preceding formats cover some of the most common use cases. CSV and XML files are very popular, because spreadsheet programs like Microsoft Excel can open them directly. JSON files are very popular on the Web due to their expressiveness and close relationship to JavaScript. The slight difference between the JSON and the JSON Line format is that the .json files store the JSON objects in a large array. This means that if you have such a file of 1 GB, you might have to store it all in the memory before you parse it with a typical parser. The .jl files on the other hand have one JSON object per line, so they can be read more efficiently.

It is also trivial to save your generated files in places other than your filesystem. By using the following, for example, you will have Scrapy automatically upload the files for you on an FTP or an S3 bucket:

```
$ scrapy crawl basic -o "ftp://user:pass@ftp.scrapybook.com/items.json "
$ scrapy crawl basic -o "s3://aws_key:aws_secret@scrapybook/items.json"
```

Note that this example won't work unless the credentials and URLs are updated to correspond to your valid hosting/S3 provider.

Where is my MySQL driver? I was originally surprised by the lack of built-in support by Scrapy for MySQL or other databases. The fact is that there is nothing built-in, because it's fundamentally wrong for Scrapy's way of thinking. Scrapy is meant to be fast and scalable. It uses very little CPU and as much inbound bandwidth as possible. Inserting to most relational databases would be a disaster from the perspective of performance. When you need to insert your items to a database, you have to store them in files, and then import them using bulk load mechanisms. That said, in *Chapter 9, Pipeline Recipes,* we will see many efficient ways of importing individual items in databases.

One more thing to notice is that if you try to use scrapy parse now, it will show you the scraped items and new requests (none in this case) that your crawl generated:

```
$ scrapy parse --spider=basic http://web:9312/properties/property_000001.html
```

```
INFO: Scrapy 1.0.3 started (bot: properties)
...
INFO: Spider closed (finished)

>>> STATUS DEPTH LEVEL 1 <<<
# Scraped Items  ------------------------------------------------
[{'address': [u'Plaistow, London'],
  'description': [u'features'],
  'image_urls': [u'../images/i02.jpg'],
  'price': [u'388.03'],
  'title': [u'belsize marylebone...deal']}]
# Requests  ------------------------------------------------
[]
```

You will appreciate `scrapy parse` even more while debugging URLs that give unexpected results.

Cleaning up – item loaders and housekeeping fields

Congratulations, you have done a great job in creating a basic spider! Let's make it a bit more professional-looking.

We start by using a great utility class, `ItemLoader`, in order to replace all those messy looking `extract()` and `xpath()` operations. By using it, our `parse()` method changes to the following:

```
def parse(self, response):
    l = ItemLoader(item=PropertiesItem(), response=response)

    l.add_xpath('title', '//*[@itemprop="name"][1]/text()')
    l.add_xpath('price', './/*[@itemprop="price"]'
            '[1]/text()', re='[,.0-9]+')
    l.add_xpath('description', '//*[@itemprop="description"]'
            '[1]/text()')
    l.add_xpath('address', '//*[@itemtype='
            '"http://schema.org/Place"][1]/text()')
    l.add_xpath('image_urls', '//*[@itemprop="image"][1]/@src')

    return l.load_item()
```

Much better, isn't it? But it's actually a bit more than just being visually more pleasant. It declares very clearly the intention of what we are trying to do without messing it up with the details of implementation. This makes the code more maintainable and self-documenting.

`ItemLoaders` provide many interesting ways of combining data, formatting them, and cleaning them up. Note that they are very actively developed so check the excellent documentation in `http://doc.scrapy.org/en/latest/topics/loaders.html` to find the most efficient ways to use them. `ItemLoaders` pass values from XPath/CSS expressions through different processor classes. Processors are fast yet simple functions. An example of a processor is `Join()`. This processor, assuming that you have selected multiple paragraphs with some XPath expression like `//p`, will join their text together in a single entry. Another particularly interesting processor is `MapCompose()`. You can use it with any Python function or chain of Python functions to implement complex functionality. For example, `MapCompose(float)` converts string data to numbers, and `MapCompose(unicode.strip, unicode.title)` gets rid of any excessive spaces and format strings with the first letter of each word capitalized. Let's take a look at some examples of these processors:

Processor	Functionality
`Join()`	Concatenates multiple results into one.
`MapCompose(unicode.strip)`	Removes leading and trailing whitespace characters.
`MapCompose(unicode.strip, unicode.title)`	Same as `Mapcompose`, but also gives title cased results.
`MapCompose(float)`	Converts strings to numbers.
`MapCompose(lambda i: i.replace(',', ''), float)`	Converts strings to numbers, ignoring possible ',' characters.
`MapCompose(lambda i: urlparse.urljoin(response.url, i))`	Converts relative URLs to absolute URLs using `response.url` as base.

You can use any Python expression as a processor. As you can see, it's easy to chain them one after the other as we do, for example, with the strip and title-case example given previously. `unicode.strip()` and `unicode.title()` are simple in the sense that they take a single argument and return a single result. We can use them directly in our `MapCompose` processors. Other functions such as `replace()` or `urljoin()` are slightly more complex, and require multiple arguments. For those, we can use Python "lambda expressions". Lambda expressions are compact functions. For example, the following compact lambda:

```
myFunction = lambda i: i.replace(',', '')
```

can be used instead of:

```
def myFunction(i):
    return i.replace(',', '')
```

By using lambdas, we wrap functions like `replace()` and `urljoin()` to functions that take a single argument and return a single result. To understand the processors of the previous table a little bit better, let's see a few examples of their usage. Open any URL with a `scrapy shell`, and try the following:

```
>>> from scrapy.loader.processors import MapCompose, Join
>>> Join()(['hi','John'])
u'hi John'
>>> MapCompose(unicode.strip)([u'  I',u' am\n'])
[u'I', u'am']
>>> MapCompose(unicode.strip, unicode.title)([u'nIce cODe'])
[u'Nice Code']
>>> MapCompose(float)(['3.14'])
[3.14]
>>> MapCompose(lambda i: i.replace(',', ''), float)(['1,400.23'])
[1400.23]
>>> import urlparse
>>> mc = MapCompose(lambda i: urlparse.urljoin('http://my.com/test/abc',
i))
>>> mc(['example.html#check'])
['http://my.com/test/example.html#check']
>>> mc(['http://absolute/url#help'])
['http://absolute/url#help']
```

The key thing to take away is that processors are just simple and small functions that post-process our XPath/CSS results. Let's use a few such processors in our spider to shape its output exactly as we want:

```
def parse(self, response):
    l.add_xpath('title', '//*[@itemprop="name"][1]/text()',
                MapCompose(unicode.strip, unicode.title))
    l.add_xpath('price', './//*[@itemprop="price"][1]/text()',
                MapCompose(lambda i: i.replace(',', ''), float),
                re='[,.0-9]+')
    l.add_xpath('description', '//*[@itemprop="description"]'
                '[1]/text()', MapCompose(unicode.strip), Join())
    l.add_xpath('address',
```

```
                            '//*[@itemtype="http://schema.org/Place"][1]/text()',
                        MapCompose(unicode.strip))
        l.add_xpath('image_urls', '//*[@itemprop="image"][1]/@src',
                        MapCompose(
                        lambda i: urlparse.urljoin(response.url, i)))
```

The full listing is given a bit later in this chapter. If you run `scrapy crawl basic` with the code that we've developed up to now, you'll get far cleaner output values:

```
'price': [334.39],

'title': [u'Set Unique Family Well']
```

Finally, we can add single values that we calculate with Python (instead of XPath/CSS expressions) by using the `add_value()` method. We can use it to set our "housekeeping fields"—things like the URL, the spider name, timestamp, and so on. We directly use the expressions summarized in the housekeeping fields table, as follows:

```
    l.add_value('url', response.url)
    l.add_value('project', self.settings.get('BOT_NAME'))
    l.add_value('spider', self.name)
    l.add_value('server', socket.gethostname())
    l.add_value('date', datetime.datetime.now())
```

Remember to `import datetime` and `socket` in order to use some of those functions.

That's it! We have perfectly good looking `Items`. Now, I know that your first feeling might be that this is all very complicated and you might be wondering if it's worth the effort. The answer is yes—this is because more or less, this is all you need to know in order to scrape everything in terms of extracting data from pages and storing them into items. This code typically, if written from scratch or in other languages, looks really ugly, and soon becomes unmaintainable. With Scrapy, it's just 25 lines of code and that's it. The code is clean, and indicates the intention instead of implementation details. You know exactly what each line does, and it's straightforward to modify, reuse, and maintain.

Another feeling you might have is that all those processors and `ItemLoaders` aren't worth the effort. If you are an experienced Python developer, it might feel a bit uncomfortable that you have to learn to use new classes for things you would typically do with string operations, lambda expressions, and list comprehensions. Still, this was a brief introduction to `ItemLoader` and its capabilities. If you dive a bit deeper, you will never look back. `ItemLoaders` and processors are toolkits that were developed based on the scraping needs of people who wrote and supported thousands of spiders. If you are planning to develop more than just a few spiders, it's worth learning how to use them.

Creating contracts

Contracts are a bit like unit tests for spiders. They allow you to quickly know if something is broken. For example, let's assume that you wrote a scraper a few weeks ago, and it had several spiders. You want to quickly check if everything is okay today. Contracts are included in the comments just after the name of a function (docstring), and they start with @. Let's look at the following contract for example:

```
def parse(self, response):
    """ This function parses a property page.

    @url http://web:9312/properties/property_000000.html
    @returns items 1
    @scrapes title price description address image_urls
    @scrapes url project spider server date
    """
```

The preceding code says, "check this URL and you should find one item with values on those fields I enlist". Now if you run `scrapy check`, it will go and check whether the contracts are satisfied:

```
$ scrapy check basic

----------------------------------------------------------------

Ran 3 contracts in 1.640s

OK
```

If it happens to leave the `url` field empty (by commenting out the line that sets it), you get a descriptive failure:

```
FAIL: [basic] parse (@scrapes post-hook)

----------------------------------------------------------------

ContractFail: 'url' field is missing
```

A contract might fail because either the spider code is broken, or some of the XPath expressions are out-of-date with the URL you are checking against. Certainly, they aren't exhaustive, but it's a very neat first line of defence against broken code.

Overall, the following is the code for our first basic spider:

```
from scrapy.loader.processors import MapCompose, Join
from scrapy.loader import ItemLoader
from properties.items import PropertiesItem
import datetime
import urlparse
import socket
```

```
import scrapy

class BasicSpider(scrapy.Spider):
    name = "basic"
    allowed_domains = ["web"]

    # Start on a property page
    start_urls = (
        'http://web:9312/properties/property_000000.html',
    )

    def parse(self, response):
        """ This function parses a property page.
        @url http://web:9312/properties/property_000000.html
        @returns items 1
        @scrapes title price description address image_urls
        @scrapes url project spider server date
        """
        # Create the loader using the response
        l = ItemLoader(item=PropertiesItem(), response=response)

        # Load fields using XPath expressions
        l.add_xpath('title', '//*[@itemprop="name"][1]/text()',
                    MapCompose(unicode.strip, unicode.title))
        l.add_xpath('price', './/*[@itemprop="price"][1]/text()',
                    MapCompose(lambda i: i.replace(',', ''),
                    float),
                    re='[,.0-9]+')
        l.add_xpath('description', '//*[@itemprop="description"]'
                    '[1]/text()',
                    MapCompose(unicode.strip), Join())
        l.add_xpath('address',
                    '//*[@itemtype="http://schema.org/Place"]'
                    '[1]/text()',
                    MapCompose(unicode.strip))
        l.add_xpath('image_urls', '//*[@itemprop="image"]'
                    '[1]/@src', MapCompose(
                    lambda i: urlparse.urljoin(response.url, i)))

        # Housekeeping fields
        l.add_value('url', response.url)
        l.add_value('project', self.settings.get('BOT_NAME'))
        l.add_value('spider', self.name)
        l.add_value('server', socket.gethostname())
        l.add_value('date', datetime.datetime.now())

        return l.load_item()
```

Extracting more URLs

Up to now, we have been working with a single URL that we set in the spider's `start_urls` property. Since that's a tuple, we can hardcode multiple URLs, for example:

```
start_urls = (
    'http://web:9312/properties/property_000000.html',
    'http://web:9312/properties/property_000001.html',
    'http://web:9312/properties/property_000002.html',
)
```

Not that exciting. We might also use a file as the source of those URLs as follows:

```
start_urls = [i.strip() for i in
open('todo.urls.txt').readlines()]
```

This is not very exciting either, but it certainly works. What will happen more often that not is that the website of interest will have some index pages and some listing pages. For example, Gumtree has the following index pages: `http://www.gumtree.com/flats-houses/london`:

Gumtree's index page

A typical index page will have links to many listing pages, and a pagination system that allows you to move from one index page to the other.

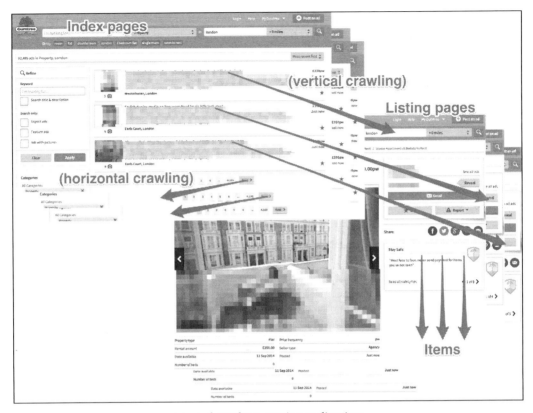

A typical crawler moves in two directions

As a result, a typical crawler moves in two directions:

- Horizontally—from an index page to another
- Vertically—from an index page to the listing pages to extract Items

In this book, we call the former **horizontal crawling**, since it crawls pages at the same hierarchical level (for example, indices), and the latter **vertical crawling**, since it moves from a higher hierarchical level (for example, indices) to a lower one (for example, listings).

It's all easier than it sounds. All we need is two more XPath expressions. For the first expression, we right-click on the **Next page** button, and we notice that the URL is contained in a link inside a `li` that has the class name `next`. As a result, the convenient XPath expression `//*[contains(@class,"next")]//@href` will work like a charm.

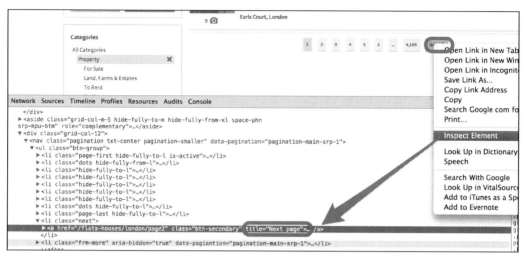

Finding the next index page URL XPath expression

For the second expression, we right-click and **Inspect Element** on the title of a listing in the page:

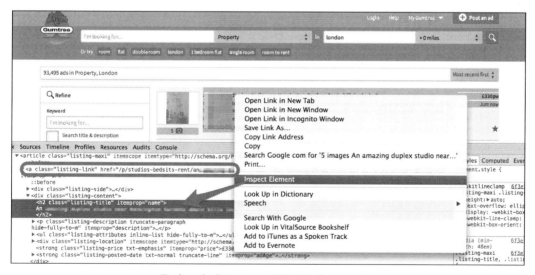

Finding the listing page URL XPath expression

Notice that the URL has an interesting `itemprop="url"` attribute. As a result, `//*[@itemprop="url"]/@href` should work. Let's open a `scrapy shell` to confirm both:

```
$ scrapy shell http://web:9312/properties/index_00000.html
>>> urls = response.xpath('//*[contains(@class,"next")]//@href').
extract()
>>> urls
[u'index_00001.html']
>>> import urlparse
>>> [urlparse.urljoin(response.url, i) for i in urls]
[u'http://web:9312/scrapybook/properties/index_00001.html']
>>> urls = response.xpath('//*[@itemprop="url"]/@href').extract()
>>> urls
[u'property_000000.html', ... u'property_000029.html']
>>> len(urls)
30
>>> [urlparse.urljoin(response.url, i) for i in urls]
[u'http://..._000000.html', ... /property_000029.html']
```

Excellent! We can see that by using what we have already learned and the two XPath expressions, we are able to extract the URLs that we need to do both horizontal and vertical crawling.

Two-direction crawling with a spider

We will copy our previous spider to a new one named `manual.py`:

```
$ ls
properties   scrapy.cfg
$ cp properties/spiders/basic.py properties/spiders/manual.py
```

In `properties/spiders/manual.py`, we import `Request` by adding `from scrapy.http import Request`, change the spider's name to `'manual'`, change `start_urls` to use our first index page, and rename the `parse()` method to `parse_item()`. Great! We are now ready to write a new `parse()` method that will perform both horizontal and vertical crawling:

```
def parse(self, response):
    # Get the next index URLs and yield Requests
    next_selector = response.xpath('//*[contains(@class,'
                                  '"next")]//@href')
    for url in next_selector.extract():
```

```
        yield Request(urlparse.urljoin(response.url, url))

    # Get item URLs and yield Requests
    item_selector = response.xpath('//*[@itemprop="url"]/@href')
    for url in item_selector.extract():
        yield Request(urlparse.urljoin(response.url, url),
                    callback=self.parse_item)
```

You might have noticed the `yield` statement in the previous example. The `yield` is a bit like `return` in the sense that it returns values to the caller. However, in contrast to `return`, it doesn't exit the function, but continues with the `for` loop instead. Functionally, the preceding example is roughly equivalent to the following:

```
next_requests = []
for url in...
    next_requests.append(Request(...))
for url in...
    next_requests.append(Request(...))
return next_requests
```

The `yield` is a piece of Python "magic" that makes coding efficient routines easy.

We are now ready to run it. If you let this spider run though, it's going to scrape the entire 50k pages of the website. In order to avoid running for too long, we can tell the spider to stop after a specific (for example, 90) number of items by using this command line parameter: `-s CLOSESPIDER_ITEMCOUNT=90` (more details on those settings are given in *Chapter 7, Configuration and Management*). We can now run it:

```
$ scrapy crawl manual -s CLOSESPIDER_ITEMCOUNT=90
INFO: Scrapy 1.0.3 started (bot: properties)
...
DEBUG: Crawled (200) <...index_00000.html> (referer: None)
DEBUG: Crawled (200) <...property_000029.html> (referer: ...index_00000.
html)
DEBUG: Scraped from <200 ...property_000029.html>
  {'address': [u'Clapham, London'],
   'date': [datetime.datetime(2015, 10, 4, 21, 25, 22, 801098)],
   'description': [u'situated camden facilities corner'],
   'image_urls': [u'http://web:9312/images/i10.jpg'],
   'price': [223.88],
   'project': ['properties'],
```

```
    'server': ['scrapyserver1'],
    'spider': ['manual'],
    'title': [u'Portered Mile'],
    'url': ['http://.../property_000029.html']}
DEBUG: Crawled (200) <...property_000028.html> (referer: ...index_00000.
html)
...
DEBUG: Crawled (200) <...index_00001.html> (referer: ...)
DEBUG: Crawled (200) <...property_000059.html> (referer: ...)
...
INFO: Dumping Scrapy stats: ...
    'downloader/request_count': 94, ...
    'item_scraped_count': 90,
```

If you take a look at the preceding output, you will observe that we get both horizontal and vertical crawling. First index_00000.html is read, and then it spawns many Requests. As they get executed, the debug messages indicate who initiated the Request with the referer URL. We can see, for example, that property_000029. html, property_000028.html ... and index_00001.html have the same referer (index_00000.html). Then, property_000059.html and others get index_00001. html as referer, and the process continues.

As we observed in the example, Scrapy uses a **last in, first out** (LIFO) strategy for processing requests (depth first crawl). The last request you submit will be processed first. This default is convenient for most of our cases. For example, we like processing each listing page before moving to the next index page. Otherwise, we would fill a huge queue of pending listing page URLs that would just consume memory. Additionally, in many cases you might need auxiliary Requests to complete a single Request, as we will see in a later chapter. You need those auxiliary Requests to be completed as soon as possible to free up the resources and have a steady flow of scraped items.

We can modify the default order by setting the priority Request() argument to a value greater than 0 to indicate a higher-than-default priority, or less than 0 to indicate a lower-than-default priority. In general, the Scrapy scheduler will execute higher priority requests first, but don't spend much time thinking about the exact request that should be executed first. Its highly likely that you won't use more than one or two request priority levels in most of your applications. Notice also that URLs are subject to duplication filtering, which is most often what we want. If we need to perform a request to the same URL more than once, we can set the dont_filter Request() argument to true.

Two-direction crawling with a CrawlSpider

If you felt that this two-direction crawling was a bit too tedious, then you are really getting it. Scrapy tries to simplify all those very common cases, and makes them easier to code. The easiest way to achieve the same results is by using a CrawlSpider, a class that allows easier implementation of such crawls. To do so, we will use the genspider command, setting a -t crawl parameter in order to create a spider using the crawl spider template:

```
$ scrapy genspider -t crawl easy web
Created spider 'crawl' using template 'crawl' in module:
  properties.spiders.easy
```

Now the file properties/spiders/easy.py contains the following:

```
...
class EasySpider(CrawlSpider):
    name = 'easy'
    allowed_domains = ['web']
    start_urls = ['http://www.web/']

    rules = (
        Rule(LinkExtractor(allow=r'Items/'),
callback='parse_item', follow=True),
    )

    def parse_item(self, response):
        ...
```

If you see the auto-generated code, it looks similar to the previous spiders but in this case in the class definition, this spider derives from CrawlSpider instead of Spider. CrawlSpider provides an implementation of the parse() method that uses the rules variable to do exactly what we did manually in the previous example.

 You might be wondering why I provided the manual version first instead of the shortcut. What you learned on the manual example, yield'ing Requests with callbacks, is such a useful and fundamental technique that we will use again and again in the following chapters, so understanding it is well worth the effort.

We will now set start_urls to our first index page, and replace the predefined parse_item() method with our previous implementation. We won't implement any parse() method this time. We will replace the predefined rules variable instead with two rules, one for horizontal and one for vertical crawling:

```
rules = (
```

```
    Rule(LinkExtractor(restrict_xpaths='//*[contains(@class,"next")]')),
    Rule(LinkExtractor(restrict_xpaths='//*[@itemprop="url"]'),
          callback='parse_item')
)
```

Those two rules use the same XPath expressions we used in the manual example, but without the a or `href` constraints. As their name implies, LinkExtractors are specialized in extracting links, so by default, they are looking for the a (and `area`) `href` attributes. You can customize this by setting the `tags` and `attrs` `LinkExtractor()`'s arguments. Also note that callbacks are now strings containing the callback method name (for example `'parse_item'`) in contrast to method references, as was the case for `Requests(self.parse_item)`. Finally, unless `callback` is set, a `Rule` will follow the extracted URLs, which means that it will scan target pages for extra links and follow them. If a `callback` is set, the `Rule` won't follow the links from target pages. If you would like it to follow links, you should either `return/yield` them from your `callback` method, or set the `follow` argument of `Rule()` to `true`. This might be useful when your listing pages contain both `Items` and extra useful navigation links.

You can run this spider and get exactly the same results as with the manual one, but now with an even simpler source code:

```
$ scrapy crawl easy -s CLOSESPIDER_ITEMCOUNT=90
```

Summary

This is probably the most important chapter for everyone starting with Scrapy. You just learned the basic methodology of developing spiders: UR²IM. You learned how to define custom `Items` that fit our needs, use `ItemLoaders`, XPath expressions and processors to load `Items`, and how to `yield Requests`. We used `Requests` to navigate horizontally across multiple index pages and vertically towards listing pages to extract `Items`. Finally, we saw how `CrawlSpider` and `Rules` can be used to create very powerful spiders with even less lines of codes. Please feel free to read this chapter as many times as you want to get a deeper understanding of the concepts, and of course, use it as a reference as you develop your own spiders.

We just got some information out of a website. Why is it such a big deal? I think the answer will become obvious in the next chapter where in just a few pages, we are going to develop a simple mobile app, and use Scrapy to populate it with data. The result, I think, is impressive.

4
From Scrapy to a Mobile App

I can hear people screaming, "What does Appery.io, a proprietary platform for mobile applications, have to do with Scrapy?" Well, seeing is believing. Showing someone (a friend, manager, or customer) your data on an Excel spreadsheet may have impressed them a few years ago. Nowadays, unless your audience is quite sophisticated, their expectations will likely be quite different. In the next few pages, you will see a simple mobile app, a minimum viable product, being built with just a few clicks. Its aim is to communicate clearly to your stakeholders the power of the data that you are extracting, and to demonstrate bringing value back to the ecosystem in the form of web traffic for the source website.

I will try to keep the motivating examples short, and they are here to show you ways to make the most out of your data. Unless you have a specific application that will consume your data, in which case you can safely skip this chapter, this chapter will show you how to make your data available to the public in the most popular way today—a mobile application.

Choosing a mobile application framework

Feeding data into a mobile application is quite easy if you use the appropriate tools. There are many good frameworks for cross-platform mobile application development, such as PhoneGap, Appcelerator with Appcelerator Cloud Services, jQuery Mobile, and Sencha Touch.

In this chapter, we will use Appery.io because it allows us to build iOS, Android, Windows Phone, and HTML5 mobile apps quickly using PhoneGap and jQuery Mobile. There is no affiliation between me or Scrapy and Appery.io. I encourage you to conduct your own independent research to see whether it fits your needs beyond what I present in this chapter. Keep in mind that it's a paid service with a 14-day trial but with a price that, in my opinion, makes it a no-brainer to develop a quick prototype, especially for someone who isn't a web expert. The main reason that I chose this service is because it provides both mobile and backend services, which means that we won't have to configure databases, write REST APIs, or have to use potentially different languages for the server and the mobile application. As you will see, we won't have to write any code at all! We will use their online tools; but at any point, you can download the app as a PhoneGap project and use the full range of PhoneGap features.

You will need an Internet connection in order to use Appery.io in this chapter. Also, please note that the layout of their website may change in the future. Use our screenshots as a guide but don't be surprised if their site doesn't look identical.

Creating a database and a collection

The first step is to sign up to the free Appery.io plan by clicking on the **Sign-Up** button on Appery.io and choosing the free plan. You will need to provide a name, e-mail address, and a password after which your new account is created. Give it a few seconds until the account gets activated. Then you will be able to log in to the Appery.io dashboard. You are ready to create a new database and collection:

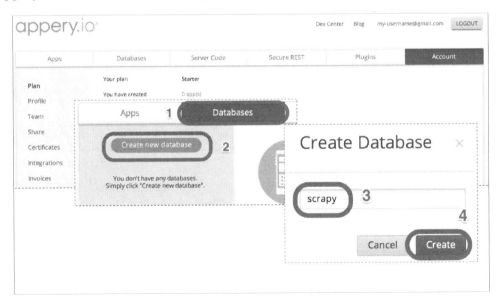

Creating a new database and collection with Appery.io

In order to do so, please follow these steps:

1. Click on the **Databases** tab (1).
2. Then click the green **Create new database** (2) button. Name the new database `scrapy` (3).
3. Now, click the **Create** button (4). This opens the Scrapy database's dashboard automatically, and here, you can create a new collection.

A database is a set of collections in Appery.io terminology. An application, roughly speaking, uses a single database (at least initially), which will have many collections, for example users, properties, messages, and so on. Appery.io already has a **Users** collection for us that holds usernames and passwords (they power lots of its built-in functionality).

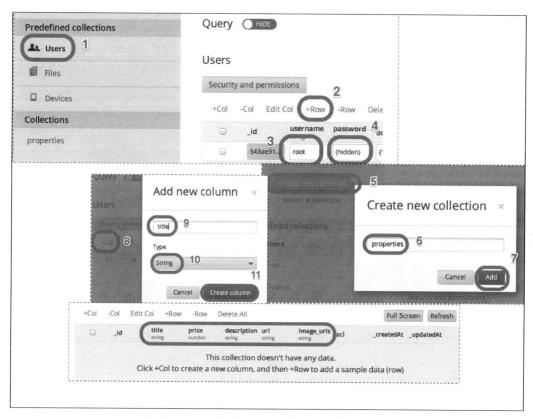

Creating a new database and collection with Appery.io

Let's add a user with the username, root, and a password, pass. Obviously, feel free to choose something more secure. You can do that by clicking on the **Users** collection on the sidebar (1), and then add a user/row by clicking **+Row** (2). You fill in the username and password on the two fields that just appeared (3, 4).

We will also create a new collection for the properties that we scrape with Scrapy, and we will name it properties. We create a new collection by clicking on the green **Create new collection** button (5), name it `properties` (6), and click the **Add** button (7). Now, we have to customize this collection a bit. We click on **+Col** to add columns (8). Columns have types that help validate values. Most of our fields are simple strings with the exception of price that is a number. We will add a few columns by clicking on **+Col** (8), filling in the name of the column (9), the type if it's not string (10), and then clicking on the **Create column** button (11). We will repeat this process five times to create the table that in shown in the following image:

Column	title	price	description	url	image_urls
Type	string	number	string	string	string

By the end of this collection, you should have the columns that you require, and it will look like the preceding image. We are now ready to import some data from Scrapy.

Populating the database with Scrapy

First of all, we will need one single number and that's the API key. We can find it in the **Settings** tab (1). We can copy it (2) and then go back to our properties collection by clicking on the **Collections** tab (3):

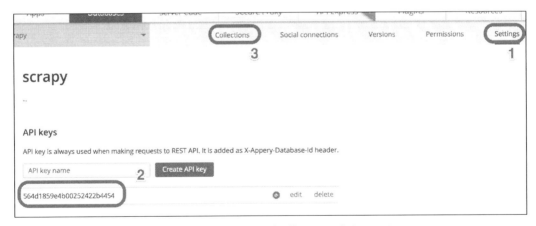

Creating a new database and collection with Appery.io

Great! Now, let's modify the application that we created in the previous chapter to import the data in Appery.io. We start by copying our project and our spider named easy (easy.py) to a spider named tomobile (tomobile.py). We also edit the file to set its name to tomobile:

```
$ ls
properties   scrapy.cfg
$ cat properties/spiders/tomobile.py
...
class ToMobileSpider(CrawlSpider):
    name = 'tomobile'
    allowed_domains = ["scrapybook.s3.amazonaws.com"]

    # Start on the first index page
    start_urls = (
        'http://scrapybook.s3.amazonaws.com/properties/'
        'index_00000.html',
    )
...
```

 The code from this chapter is in the ch04 directory on GitHub.

One caveat you may have just noticed is that we don't use our web server (http://web:9312) as we did in the previous chapter. We use a publicly available copy of the site that I keep on http://scrapybook.s3.amazonaws.com. Using it, exceptionally in this chapter, our images and URLs are publicly available, which allows us to share our app effortlessly.

We will use an Appery.io pipeline to insert the data. Scrapy pipelines are typically small Python classes that postprocess, clean, and store Scrapy items. We will discuss them in depth in *Chapter 8, Programming Scrapy*. For now, you can install it with easy_install or pip, but if you use our Vagrant dev machine, you don't need to do anything because it's already installed:

```
$ sudo easy_install -U scrapyapperyio
```

or

```
$ sudo pip install --upgrade scrapyapperyio
```

At this point, you will have to modify a little bit of the main Scrapy settings file to add the API key that you copied earlier. We are going to discuss settings in depth in *Chapter 7, Configuration and Management*. For now, all we need to do is append the following lines in `properties/settings.py`:

```
ITEM_PIPELINES = {'scrapyapperyio.ApperyIoPipeline': 300}

APPERYIO_DB_ID = '<<Your API KEY here>>'
APPERYIO_USERNAME = 'root'
APPERYIO_PASSWORD = 'pass'
APPERYIO_COLLECTION_NAME = 'properties'
```

Don't forget to replace the `APPERYIO_DB_ID` with the API key. Also make sure that your settings have the same username and password as the one that you used when you created a database user in Appery.io. To start filling up Appery.io's database with data, start a Scrapy crawl as usual:

```
$ scrapy crawl tomobile -s CLOSESPIDER_ITEMCOUNT=90
INFO: Scrapy 1.0.3 started (bot: properties)
...
INFO: Enabled item pipelines: ApperyIoPipeline
INFO: Spider opened
...
DEBUG: Crawled (200) <GET https://api.appery.io/rest/1/db/login?username=
root&password=pass>
...
DEBUG: Crawled (200) <POST https://api.appery.io/rest/1/db/collections/
properties>
...
INFO: Dumping Scrapy stats:
  {'downloader/response_count': 215,
   'item_scraped_count': 105,
   ...}
INFO: Spider closed (closespider_itemcount)
```

The output this time is slightly different. You can see the `ApperyIoPipeline` item pipeline getting enabled in one of the first few lines; but most notably, you will notice that for about 100 items scrapped, there were about 200 requests/responses. This is because the Appery.io pipeline makes an extra request per item to the Appery.io servers in order to write each item. These requests also appear in the logs with an `api.appery.io` URL.

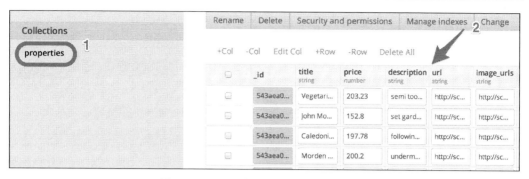

The properties collection is filled in with data

If we head back to Appery.io, we will see the **properties** collection (1) filled in with data (2).

Creating a mobile application

Staring a new mobile application is trivial. We just click on the **Apps** tab (1) and then the **Create new app** green button (2). We will name this application **properties** (3) and click the **Create** button (4) to create it:

Creating a new mobile application and a database connection

Creating a database access service

The number of options when you start the new application may be a bit overwhelming. Using the Appery.io application editor, one can write complex applications, but for our purposes, we will keep things simple. What we are looking for, to start with, is creating a service that gives us access to the Scrapy database from our application. In order to do this, we click on the square green **CREATE NEW** button (5), and then we select **Database Services** (6). A new dialog box appears that lets us chose where we want to connect to. We select the **scrapy** database (7). We won't use most of the options in this menu bar but just click to expand the **properties** section (8) and then select **List** (9). Behind the scenes, this writes code for us that makes the data that we crawled with Scrapy available on the web. We finish by clicking the **Import selected services** button (10).

Setting up the user interface

Take a deep breath. We are now going to create all the visual elements of our app. We will work within the **DESIGN** tab of their editor:

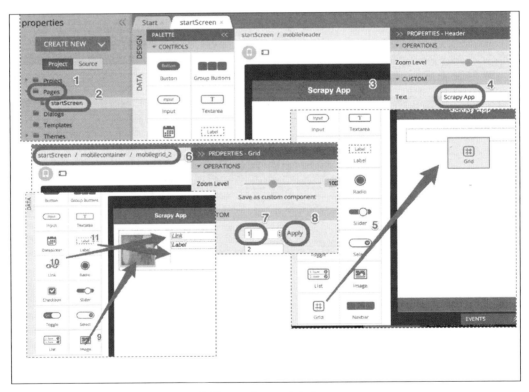

Setting up the user interface

From the tree on the left of the page, we expand the **Pages** folder (1) and then click on **startScreen** (2). The UI editor will open this page, and we can add a few controls. Let's edit the title to familiarize ourselves a bit with the editor. Click on the caption header (3), and then you will notice that the properties section on the right of the screen is being updated to show the header's properties, among which is the **Text** property. Change that to **Scrapy App**. You will see the header in the middle screen updating accordingly.

Then, we will add a grid component. To do this, drag and drop a **Grid** control from the left palette (5). You will notice that it has two rows. We only need one row for our purposes; select the grid that we just added. You will know that the grid is selected when it's gray on the thumbnails section at the top of the mobile view (6). If it isn't, click on it in order to select it. Then the properties on the right side will be updated with grid's properties. Just edit the **Rows** property and set it to **1** and then click **Apply** (7, 8). Now, the grid will be updated to have only one row.

Finally drag and drop a few more controls inside the grid. First add an image control on the left side of the grid (9), then a link on the right side of the grid (10), and finally, a label just under the link (11).

That's more than enough in terms of layout. We will now feed data from the database to the user interface.

Mapping data to the User Interface

Until now, we've spent most of our time in the **DESIGN** tab setting up the visuals of our application. In order to link available data to controls, we switch to the **DATA** tab (1):

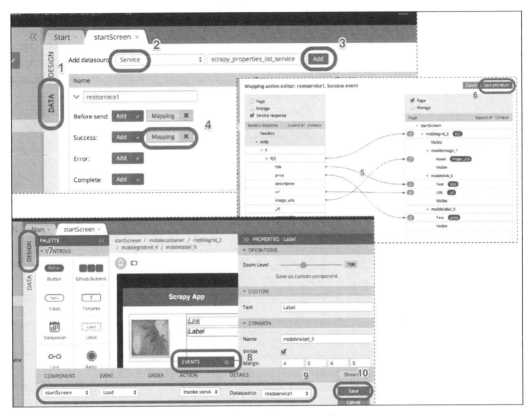

Mapping data to the user interface

We select **Service** (2) as the data source type. The service that we created previously is the only one available and gets automatically selected. so we can proceed to clicking the **Add** button (3). The service properties will be listed just below it. As soon as you press the **Add** button, you will notice events, such as **Before send** and **Success**. We will customize what happens when a call to the service succeeds by clicking on the **Mapping** button that is next to **Success**.

The **Mapping action editor** opens, and this is where we will do all our wiring. This editor has two sides. On the left are the fields available in the service's responses. On the right, you will find the properties for the UI controls that we added in the previous step. You will notice an **Expand all** link on both sides. Click on it to see all the data and controls that are available. You then need to perform the following five mappings (5) by dragging and dropping from the left side to the right:

Response	Component	Property	Notes
$[i]	mobilegrid_2		This makes a for loop that creates and sets up each row.
title	mobilelink_8	Text	This sets the text for the link.
price	mobilelabel_9	Text	This sets the price on the text field.
image_urls	mobileimage_7	Asset	This loads the image from the URL on the image container.
url	mobilelink_8	URL	This sets the URL for a link. When the user clicks on it, the associated page loads.

Mappings between database fields and User Interface controls

The numbers on the preceding table may be slightly different in your case, but as there's only one of each type of control, the odds of something going wrong are minimal. By setting these mappings, we tell Appery.io to write all the code behind the scenes that will load the controls with values when the database query succeeds. You can then click on **Save and return** (6) to continue.

This gets us back to the **DATA** tab. We need to return to the UI editor, so we click on the **DESIGN** tab (7). On the lower part of the screen, you will notice an **EVENTS** section (8) that was always there but has just been expanded. With the **EVENTS** section, we make Appery.io do things as responses to UI events. This brings us to the final step that we need to perform. This is to make our app call the service and retrieve data as soon as the UI loads. In order to do so, we choose **startScreen** as a component; we keep the default **Load** option for the event. We then select **Invoke service** as an **action** and leave **Datasource** as the default **restservice1** option (9). We click **Save** (10), and that's all we had to do for this mobile application.

Testing, sharing, and exporting your mobile app

We are now ready to test our app. All we have to do is click on the **TEST** button at the top of the UI builder (1):

This is the application running in your browser

The mobile application runs in your browser. The links are active (2) and ready to navigate. You can preview different mobile screen resolutions and device orientations. You can also click on the **View on Phone** button to display a QR code that you can scan with your mobile device and preview the application there. You just share the link that will be provided, and others are able to play with the app in their browsers.

With just a few clicks, we organized and presented the data we scraped with Scrapy on a mobile application. You may want to further customize this application by following the Appery.io tutorials at `http://devcenter.appery.io/tutorials/`. When you are ready, Appery.io also gives you lots of export options via the **EXPORT** button:

You can export your application for most major mobile platforms

You can export project files to perform further development on your favorite IDE or get a binary that you can publish on each platform's mobile marketplace.

Summary

Using these two tools, Scrapy and Appery.io, we have a system that scrapes a website and inserts data to a database. We also have a RESTful API and a simple mobile application for Android and iOS. For advanced features and further development, you can dive deeper into these platforms, outsource part of the development to field experts, or research alternatives. At this point, you have a little product to demonstrate application concepts with minimal coding.

You will notice that our app looks quite good given its extremely short development time. It has realistic data instead of Lorem Ipsum placeholders, and the links work and do something meaningful. We successfully built a minimum viable product that respects its ecosystem (source websites) and returns value back to it in the form of traffic.

We are now ready to find out how to use Scrapy spiders to extract data under more complex scenarios.

5
Quick Spider Recipes

In *Chapter 3, Basic Crawling,* we focused on how to extract information from pages and store them into Items. What we learned covers the most common Scrapy use cases, and it should be enough to get you up and running. In this chapter, we will examine more specialized cases in order to become more familiar with the two most important Scrapy classes — Request and Response — the two R's on the UR²IM scraping model we presented in *Chapter 3, Basic Crawling.*

A spider that logs in

Quite often, you may find yourself wanting to extract data from websites that have a login mechanism. In the most common case, a website will require you to provide a username and a password in order to log in. We are going to use the example that you can find in: `http://web:9312/dynamic` (from our dev machine) or `http://localhost:9312/dynamic` (from your host's web browser). If you use the username, "user", and password, "pass", you will get access to a page with three links of property pages. The question now is how do you perform the same operation with Scrapy?

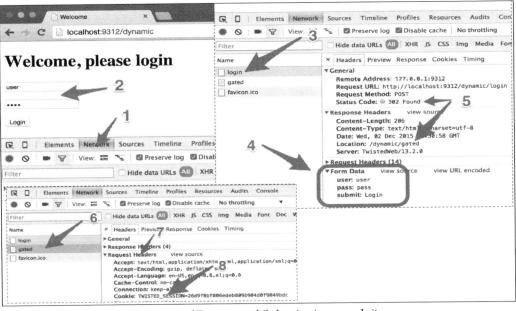

Requests and Responses while logging in on a website

Let's use the Google Chrome debugger and try to understand how login works. First of all, we go to the **Network** tab (1). Then, we fill in the username and password and click **Login** (2). If the username and password are correct, you will see a page with three links. If there was a mistake, you will see an error page.

As soon as you push the **Login** button, on the Google Chrome debugger **Network** tab, you will see a request with **Request Method: POST** to `http://localhost:9312/dynamic/login`.

> Previous chapters' requests were GET-type requests, which are most often used to retrieve data that doesn't change, such as simple web pages, and images. POST-type requests are typically used when we want to retrieve data that depends on the data that we sent to the server, such as the username and password in this example.

If you click on it (3), you can inspect the data that was sent to the server, including **Form Data** (4), which will have the username and the password that you entered. All this data was sent as text to the server. Chrome just groups them nicely and shows them to us. The server responds with **302 Found** (5) that redirects us to a new page: `/dynamic/gated`. This page has links that appear only after a successful login. If you try to visit `http://localhost:9312/dynamic/gated` directly without entering the correct username and password, the server would find out that you cheated and redirect you to an error page: `http://localhost:9312/dynamic/error`. How does the server know you and your password? If you click on **gated** on the left of the debugger (6), you will notice a **Cookie** value (8) that is set under the **Request Headers** section (7).

> HTTP cookies are some, usually short, pieces of text or numbers that servers send to browsers. In turn, browsers send them back to servers in every subsequent request in order to identify you, the user, and your session. This allows you to perform complex operations that require server-side state information, such as the contents of your basket or your username and password.

Summarizing, a single operation, such as logging in, may involve several server round-trips, including POST-requests, and HTTP redirects. Scrapy handles most of these operations automatically, and the code that we need to write is simple.

We start with the spider named easy from *Chapter 3, Basic Crawling,* and we create a new spider named login by renaming the file and changing the name property inside the spider (it should look like this):

```
class LoginSpider(CrawlSpider):
    name = 'login'
```

The code from this chapter is in ch05 directory in github. this example in particular will be in ch05/properties.

We need to send the initial request that logs in by performing a POST request on `http://localhost:9312/dynamic/login`. We do this with Scrapy's `FormRequest` class. This class is similar to `Request` from *Chapter 3, Basic Crawling,* but with an extra `formdata` argument that we use to pass form data (`user` and `pass`). To use this class, we have to import it first with:

```
from scrapy.http import FormRequest
```

We then replace the `start_urls` statement with a `start_requests()` method. We do this because in this case, we need to start with something a bit more custom than just a few URLs. More specifically, we create and return a `FormRequest` from this function:

```
# Start with a login request
def start_requests(self):
  return [
    FormRequest(
      "http://web:9312/dynamic/login",
      formdata={"user": "user", "pass": "pass"}
      )]
```

That's it really. The default `parse()` of `CrawlSpider` (the base class of our `LoginSpider`) handles `Response` and uses our `Rules` and `LinkExtractors` exactly as it did in *Chapter 3, Basic Crawling.* We have so little extra code because Scrapy handles cookies transparently for us, and as soon as we log in, it passes them on to subsequent requests in exactly the same manner as a browser. We can run this using `scrapy crawl` as usual:

```
$ scrapy crawl login
INFO: Scrapy 1.0.3 started (bot: properties)
...
DEBUG: Redirecting (302) to <GET .../gated> from <POST .../login >
DEBUG: Crawled (200) <GET .../data.php>
DEBUG: Crawled (200) <GET .../property_000001.html> (referer: .../data.
php)
DEBUG: Scraped from <200 .../property_000001.html>
```

```
  {'address': [u'Plaistow, London'],
   'date': [datetime.datetime(2015, 11, 25, 12, 7, 27, 120119)],
   'description': [u'features'],
   'image_urls': [u'http://web:9312/images/i02.jpg'],
...
INFO: Closing spider (finished)
INFO: Dumping Scrapy stats:
  {...
   'downloader/request_method_count/GET': 4,
   'downloader/request_method_count/POST': 1,
...
   'item_scraped_count': 3,
```

We can notice the redirection from dynamic/login to dynamic/gated on the log and then a scrape of Items as usual. In the statistics, we see one POST request and four GET requests; one for dynamic/gated index and three for property pages.

 In this example, we don't protect the property pages themselves but just the links to these pages. The code would be the same in either case.

If we used the wrong user/pass, we would get a redirect to a page with no item URLs and the process would terminate at that point, as you can see in the following run:

```
$ scrapy crawl login
INFO: Scrapy 1.0.3 started (bot: properties)
...
DEBUG: Redirecting (302) to <GET .../dynamic/error > from <POST .../
dynamic/login>
DEBUG: Crawled (200) <GET .../dynamic/error>
...
INFO: Spider closed (closespider_itemcount)
```

This was a simple login example that demonstrates essential login mechanisms. Most websites will likely have slightly more complex mechanisms that Scrapy also handles with ease. Some sites, for example, require you to pass some form variables from the form page to the login page while performing the POST request in order to confirm that cookies are enabled, and also to make it a bit more difficult for you to try to check with brute-force thousands of user/pass combinations.

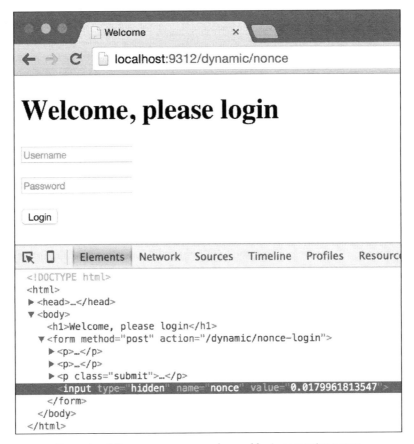

Request and Response on a more advanced login case using nonce

For example, if you visit `http://localhost:9312/dynamic/nonce`, you will see a page that looks identical, but if you use Chrome's Debugger, you will notice that the form in this page has a hidden field called **nonce**. When you submit this form (to `http://localhost:9312/dynamic/nonce-login`), the login won't be successful unless you pass not only the correct user/pass, but also the exact `nonce` value that server gave you when you visited this login page. There is no way for you to guess that value as it typically will be random and single-use. This means that in order to successfully log in, you now need two requests. You have to visit the form page and then the login page and pass through some data. As usual, Scrapy has built-in functionality that helps.

We create a `NonceLoginSpider` spider that is similar to the previous one. Now, in `start_requests()`, we are going to return a simple `Request` (don't forget to import it) to our form page, and will manually handle the response by setting its `callback` property to our handler method named `parse_welcome()`. In `parse_welcome()`, we use the helper `from_response()` method of the `FormRequest` object to create `FormRequest` that is pre-populated with all the fields and values from the original form. `FormRequest.from_response()` roughly emulates a submit click on the first form on the page with all the fields left blank.

 It's worth spending some time familiarizing yourself with the documentation of `from_response()`. It has many useful features like `formname` and `formnumber` that helps you select the form you want if there's more than one in a page.

What makes this very useful to us is that it effortlessly includes, verbatim, all the hidden fields of that form. All we need to do is to use the `formdata` argument to fill in the `user` and `pass` fields and return the `FormRequest`. Here is the relevant code:

```
# Start on the welcome page
def start_requests(self):
    return [
        Request(
            "http://web:9312/dynamic/nonce",
            callback=self.parse_welcome)
    ]

# Post welcome page's first form with the given user/pass
def parse_welcome(self, response):
    return FormRequest.from_response(
        response,
        formdata={"user": "user", "pass": "pass"}
    )
```

We can run this spider as usual:

```
$ scrapy crawl noncelogin
INFO: Scrapy 1.0.3 started (bot: properties)
...
DEBUG: Crawled (200) <GET .../dynamic/nonce>
DEBUG: Redirecting (302) to <GET .../dynamic/gated > from <POST .../
dynamic/login-nonce>
DEBUG: Crawled (200) <GET .../dynamic/gated>
...
INFO: Dumping Scrapy stats:
  {...
    'downloader/request_method_count/GET': 5,
    'downloader/request_method_count/POST': 1,
...
    'item_scraped_count': 3,
```

We can see the first GET request to /dynamic/nonce page, and then POST, and redirection on the /dynamic/nonce-login page that leads us to /dynamic/gated as it did before. This concludes our login discussion. This example used two steps to log in. With enough patience, one can form arbitrary long chains that are able to perform almost every login operation.

A spider that uses JSON APIs and AJAX pages

Sometimes, you will find yourself exploring pages with data that you'll be unable to find on the HTML of the page. For example, if you visit http://localhost:9312/static/ and right-click **inspect element** (1, 2) somewhere in the page you will see the DOM tree with all the usual HTML elements. On the other hand, if you use scrapy shell or right-click on **View Page Source** (3, 4) in Chrome, you will see that the HTML code for this page doesn't contain any information relevant to properties. Where does this data come from?

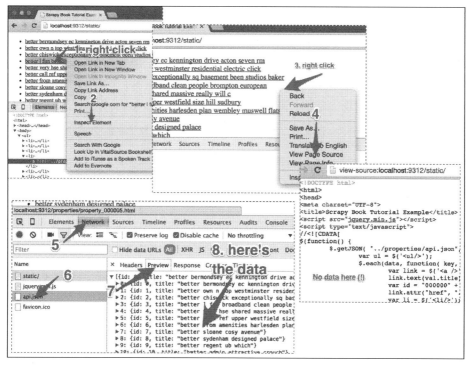

Request and Response on pages that load JSON objects dynamically

In these cases your next step is, as usual, to open the **Network** tab of Chrome's debugger (5) to find out what's going on. In the list on the left, we can see all the requests that Chrome performed to load this page. In this simple page, there are only three requests: **static/** that we already checked, **jquery.min.js** that retrieves the code for a popular Javascript framework, and **api.json** which seems interesting. If we click on it (6) and we then click the **Preview** tab on the right (7), we will notice that it contains the data we have been looking for. Indeed `http://localhost:9312/` `properties/api.json` contains property IDs and names (8), as follows:

```
[{
    "id": 0,
    "title": "better set unique family well"
},
... {
    "id": 29,
    "title": "better portered mile"
}]
```

This is a very simple example of a JSON API. More complex APIs may require you to log in, use POST requests, or return more interesting data structures. In any case, JSON is one of the easiest formats to parse because you don't have to write any XPath expressions to extract data from it.

Python provides a great JSON parsing library. When we `import json`, we can use `json.loads(response.body)` to parse JSON and convert it to an equivalent Python object consisting of Python primitives, lists, and dicts.

Let's do this by copying `manual.py` from *Chapter 3, Basic Crawling*. This is the best option to start with in this case as we need to manually build property URLs and `Request` objects from IDs that we find in the JSON object. We rename the file to `api.py`, rename the spider class to `ApiSpider` and name it `api`. Our new `start_urls` should be the JSON API URL:

```
start_urls = (
    'http://web:9312/properties/api.json',
)
```

If you need to do POST requests or more complex operations, you can use the `start_requests()` method and the techniques we saw in previous sections. At this point, Scrapy will open this URL and call our `parse()` method with `Response` as an argument. We can `import json` and use the following code to parse the JSON object:

```
def parse(self, response):
    base_url = "http://web:9312/properties/"
    js = json.loads(response.body)
    for item in js:
        id = item["id"]
        url = base_url + "property_%06d.html" % id
        yield Request(url, callback=self.parse_item)
```

The preceding code uses `json.loads(response.body)` to parse the `Response` JSON object to a Python list that then it iterates through. For each item in the list, we put together a URL consisting of three parts: `base_url`, `property_%06d` and `.html`. `base_url` is a URL prefix that was defined previously. `%06d` is a very useful piece of Python syntax that allows us to create new strings by combining Python variables. In this case, `%06d` will be replaced with the value of the `id` variable (the one after the `%` at the end of the line). `id` will be treated as a number (`%d` means treat it as a number) and it will be extended to six characters by prepending 0's if necessary. If `id` has, for example, the value 5, `%06d` will be replaced with 000005, whereas if `id` happens to be 34322, `%06d` will be replaced with 034322. The end result is perfectly valid URLs for our properties. We use this URL to form a new `Request` object that we `yield` exactly as we did in *Chapter 3, Basic Crawling*. We can run this example as usual with `scrapy crawl`:

```
$ scrapy crawl api
INFO: Scrapy 1.0.3 started (bot: properties)
...
DEBUG: Crawled (200) <GET ...properties/api.json>
```

```
DEBUG: Crawled (200) <GET .../property_000029.html>
...
INFO: Closing spider (finished)
INFO: Dumping Scrapy stats:
...
    'downloader/request_count': 31, ...
    'item_scraped_count': 30,
```

You might notice in the stats at the end, 31 Requests—one for each item as well as an initial one for `api.json`.

Passing arguments between responses

In many cases, you will have interesting information on your JSON APIs that you will want to store to your `Item`. To demonstrate this case, in our example, for a given property, the JSON API returns its title prepended with "better". If property's title is "Covent Garden" for example, the API will have "Better Covent Garden" as its title. Let's assume that we want to store these "better" titles in our `Items`. How do we pass information from our `parse()` to our `parse_item()` method?

You won't be surprised to hear that we can do this by setting something in the `Request` that `parse()` generates. We can then retrieve this from the `Response` that `parse_item()` receives. `Request` has a dict named `meta` that is directly accessible on `Response`. For our example, let's set a title value on this dict to store the title from the JSON object:

```
title = item["title"]
yield Request(url, meta={"title": title},callback=self.parse_item)
```

Inside `parse_item()`, we can use this value instead of the XPath expression that we used to have:

```
l.add_value('title', response.meta['title'],
            MapCompose(unicode.strip, unicode.title))
```

You will notice that we switched from calling `add_xpath()` to `add_value()` because we don't need to use any XPath for that field any more. We can now run the new spider with `scrapy crawl`, and we will see titles from `api.json` on our `PropertyItems`.

A 30-times faster property spider

There is a tendency when you start with a framework to use, maybe, the most sophisticated and, typically, the most complex way for anything you do. You will likely find yourself doing that with Scrapy too. Just before you go crazy with XPath and technology, it is worth to pause for a moment and wonder; is the way I chose the easiest way to extract data from this website?

You can have orders-of-magnitude savings if you avoid scraping every single listing page if you can extract about the same information from index pages.

 Please keep in mind that many websites offer a different number of items on their index pages. For example, a website might be able to give you 10, 50 or 100 listings per index page by tuning a parameter, such as &show=50. If so, obviously, set it to the maximum value available.

For example, in our properties case, all the information we need exists in the index pages. They contain the title, the description, the price and the image. This means that we can scrape a single index page and extract 30 items and a link to the next index page. By crawling 100 index pages, we get 3000 items with just 100 requests instead of 3000. That's just great!

In the actual Gumtree website, the description on the index pages is shorter than the full description on the listing page. This may be okay or even desirable.

 In many cases, you will have to trade off data quality with number of requests. Many sources throttle the number of requests heavily (more on that in later chapter), so hitting indices might help you solve an otherwise hard problem.

In our example, if we have a look at the HTML of one of the index pages, we will notice that each listing in the index page has its own node indicated by `itemtype="http://schema.org/Product"`. Within this node, we have all the information for each property annotated in exactly the same way as in the detail pages:

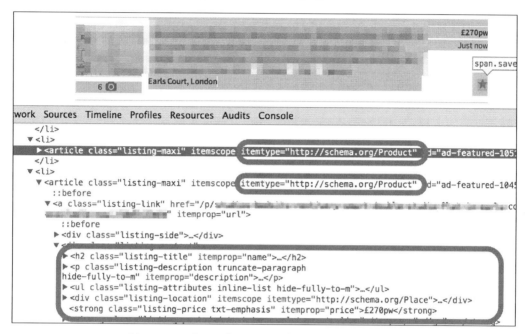

Many properties can be extracted from a single index page

Let's load the first index page in Scrapy shell and play a bit with XPath expressions:

```
$ scrapy shell http://web:9312/properties/index_00000.html
```

While within the Scrapy shell, let's try to select everything with the `Product` tag:

```
>>> p=response.xpath('//*[@itemtype="http://schema.org/Product"]')
>>> len(p)
30
>>> p
[<Selector xpath='//*[@itemtype="http://schema.org/Product"]' data=u'<li
class="listing-maxi" itemscopeitemt'...]
```

We notice that we get a list of 30 `Selector` objects, each pointing to one of our listings. The `Selector` objects are similar to the `Response` objects in the sense that we can use XPath expression on them and get information only from within whatever they point to. The only caveat is that those expressions should be relevant XPath expressions. Relevant XPath expressions are identical to the ones that we've seen already but with a '.' dot prepended to them. Let's see how this works by extracting a title from, for example, the fourth listing using the `.//*[@itemprop="name"][1]/text()` relevant XPath expression:

```
>>> selector = p[3]
>>> selector
<Selector xpath='//*[@itemtype="http://schema.org/Product"]' ... '>
>>> selector.xpath('.//*[@itemprop="name"][1]/text()').extract()
[u'1 fun broadband clean people brompton european']
```

We can use a for loop on the list of `Selector` objects to extract information for all 30 items of an index page.

To do so, we start again from our `manual.py` file from *Chapter 3, Basic Crawling,* and name the new spider "fast" on a file named `fast.py`. We reuse most of the code with small changes in the `parse()` and `parse_item()` methods. The updated methods are as follows:

```
def parse(self, response):
    # Get the next index URLs and yield Requests
    next_sel = response.xpath('//*[contains(@class,"next")]//@href')
    for url in next_sel.extract():
        yield Request(urlparse.urljoin(response.url, url))

    # Iterate through products and create PropertiesItems
    selectors = response.xpath(
        '//*[@itemtype="http://schema.org/Product"]')
    for selector in selectors:
        yield self.parse_item(selector, response)
```

There are no changes in the first part of the code that yields the next index `Request`. The only difference lies in the second part where instead of using `yield` to create `Requests` for the detail pages, we iterate through selectors and call our `parse_item()`. This is also quite similar to our original code, as follows:

```
def parse_item(self, selector, response):
    # Create the loader using the selector
    l = ItemLoader(item=PropertiesItem(), selector=selector)

    # Load fields using XPath expressions
```

```
l.add_xpath('title', './/*[@itemprop="name"][1]/text()',
        MapCompose(unicode.strip, unicode.title))
l.add_xpath('price', './/*[@itemprop="price"][1]/text()',
        MapCompose(lambda i: i.replace(',', ''), float),
        re='[,.0-9]+')
l.add_xpath('description',
            './/*[@itemprop="description"][1]/text()',
        MapCompose(unicode.strip), Join())
l.add_xpath('address',
            './/*[@itemtype="http://schema.org/Place"]'
            '[1]/*/text()',
        MapCompose(unicode.strip))
make_url = lambda i: urlparse.urljoin(response.url, i)
l.add_xpath('image_urls', './/*[@itemprop="image"][1]/@src',
        MapCompose(make_url))


# Housekeeping fields
l.add_xpath('url', './/*[@itemprop="url"][1]/@href',
        MapCompose(make_url))
l.add_value('project', self.settings.get('BOT_NAME'))
l.add_value('spider', self.name)
l.add_value('server', socket.gethostname())
l.add_value('date', datetime.datetime.now())

return l.load_item()
```

The slight changes that we made are as follows:

- **ItemLoader** now uses `selector` as a source rather than `Response`. This is a very convenient feature of the `ItemLoader` API, allowing us to extract from the currently selected segment instead of the entire page.

- XPath expressions turned to relative XPath by prepending the dot (.).

 It so happened that in our case, our XPath expressions were identical in the detail and the index pages. This won't always be the case and you may have to redevelop your XPath expressions to match the structure of your index pages.

- We have to compile the URL of `Item` ourselves. Before `response.url` was giving us the URL for the listing page. Now, it gives the URL of the index page because this was the page that we crawled. We have to extract the URL of the listing using our familiar `.//*[@itemprop="url"][1]/@href` XPath expression and then convert it to an absolute URL with our usual `MapCompose` processor.

Small changes have generated huge savings. Now, we can run this spider with the following code:

```
$ scrapy crawl fast -s CLOSESPIDER_PAGECOUNT=3
...
INFO: Dumping Scrapy stats:
    'downloader/request_count': 3, ...
    'item_scraped_count': 90,...
```

As promised, with just three requests, we scraped 90 items. We would need 93 requests to do the same if we didn't hit the index. This is brilliant!

If you want to use `scrapy parse` to debug, you would now have to set the `spider` argument, as follows:

```
$ scrapy parse --spider=fast http://web:9312/properties/index_00000.html
...
>>> STATUS DEPTH LEVEL 1 <<<
# Scraped Items  ------------------------------------------------
[{'address': [u'Angel, London'],
... 30 items...
# Requests  -----------------------------------------------------
[<GET http://web:9312/properties/index_00001.html>]
```

Exactly as we expected, `parse()` returns 30 `Items` and one `Request` to the next index page. Feel free to experiment with `scrapy parse` by, for example, passing `--depth=2`.

A spider that crawls based on an Excel file

Most of the time you have one spider per source web-site, but there are cases where you want to scrape data from many websites and the only thing that changes between them is the XPath expressions you use. In these cases, it feels like overkill to have a spider for every site. Can you crawl through them all with a single spider? The answer is yes.

Let's create a new project for this experiment as the items that we crawl are very different (actually we won't define any in this project!). I assume that we were in the `properties` directory of `ch05`. Let's go one level up, as follows:

```
$ pwd
/root/book/ch05/properties
$ cd ..
$ pwd
/root/book/ch05
```

We can create a new project named `generic` and a spider named `fromcsv`:

```
$ scrapy startproject generic
$ cd generic
$ scrapy genspider fromcsv example.com
```

Now let's create a `.csv` file with what we want to extract. We can use a spreadsheet program, such as Microsoft Excel, to create this `.csv` file. Fill in a few URLs and XPath expressions as shown in the following figure and then save it as `todo.csv` in spider's directory (the one with `scrapy.cfg`). To save as `.csv`, chose CSV file (Windows) as file format on the save dialog:

	A	B	C
1	url	name	price
2	http://web:9312/static/a.html	//*[@id="itemTitle"]/text()	//*[@id="prcIsum"]/text()
3	http://web:9312/static/b.html	//h1/text()	//span/strong/text()
4	http://web:9312/static/c.html	//*[@id="product-desc"]/span/text()	

todo.csv contains URLs and XPath expressions

Great! If it all went fine, you should be able to see the file on your terminal:

```
$ cat todo.csv
url,name,price
a.html,"//*[@id=""itemTitle""]/text()","//*[@id=""prcIsum""]/text()"
b.html,//h1/text(),//span/strong/text()
c.html,"//*[@id=""product-desc""]/span/text()"
```

Python has built-in libraries for `.csv` files. We just have to `import csv`, and we can then use the following straightforward code to read the lines one by one as `dict`. If we open a Python prompt on the current directory, we can try the following:

```
$ pwd
/root/book/ch05/generic2
$ python
>>> import csv
>>> with open("todo.csv", "rU") as f:
        reader = csv.DictReader(f)
        for line in reader:
            print line
```

The first line from the file will be treated automatically as a header and from that the names of the keys for the dict will be deduced. For each subsequent line, we get a dict containing the data. We iterate each row with a for loop. If we run the preceding code, we get the following output:

```
{'url': ' http://a.html', 'price': '//*[@id="prcIsum"]/text()',
'name': '//*[@id="itemTitle"]/text()'}
{'url': ' http://b.html', 'price': '//span/strong/text()', 'name': '//
h1/text()'}
{'url': ' http://c.html', 'price': '', 'name': '//*[@id="product-
desc"]/span/text()'}
```

This is great. Let's now edit our `generic/spiders/fromcsv.py` spider. We will use the URLs from the `.csv` file, and we don't want any domain restrictions. Thus, the first thing to do is to remove `start_urls` and `allowed_domains`. Then we will read the `.csv` file.

Since we want to start with URLs that we don't know in advance but we read from a file instead, we will implement a `start_requests()` method. For each row, we will create `Request` and yield it. We will also store field names and XPaths from `csv` in `request.meta` in order to use them in our `parse()` function. Then, we use an `Item` and an `ItemLoader` to populate `Item`'s fields. Here's the full code:

```
import csv
import scrapy
from scrapy.http import Request
from scrapy.loader import ItemLoader
from scrapy.item import Item, Field

class FromcsvSpider(scrapy.Spider):
    name = "fromcsv"

def start_requests(self):
    with open("todo.csv", "rU") as f:
        reader = csv.DictReader(f)
        for line in reader:
            request = Request(line.pop('url'))
            request.meta['fields'] = line
            yield request

def parse(self, response):
    item = Item()
    l = ItemLoader(item=item, response=response)
    for name, xpath in response.meta['fields'].iteritems():
        if xpath:
```

```
                    item.fields[name] = Field()
                    l.add_xpath(name, xpath)
              return l.load_item()
```

Let's crawl and save the output to an out.csv file:

```
$ scrapy crawl fromcsv -o out.csv
INFO: Scrapy 0.0.3 started (bot: generic)
...
DEBUG: Scraped from <200 a.html>
{'name': [u'My item'], 'price': [u'128']}
DEBUG: Scraped from <200 b.html>
{'name': [u'Getting interesting'], 'price': [u'300']}
DEBUG: Scraped from <200 c.html>
{'name': [u'Buy this now']}
...
INFO: Spider closed (finished)
$ cat out.csv
price,name
128,My item
300,Getting interesting
,Buy this now
```

This is as neat and straightforward as it gets!

There are some things you may have noticed in the code. Since we don't define project-wide Items for this project, we have to provide one to ItemLoader manually as follows:

```
item = Item()
l = ItemLoader(item=item, response=response)
```

We also add fields dynamically using the fields member variable of Item. To add a new field dynamically and have it populated by our ItemLoader, all we have to do is the following:

```
item.fields[name] = Field()
l.add_xpath(name, xpath)
```

We can finally make our code a bit nicer. Hardcoding `todo.csv` isn't very good practice. Scrapy gives us a very convenient way to pass arguments to spiders. If we pass an `-a` command-line argument, for example, `-a variable=value`, a spider property is set for us and we are able to retrieve it with `self.variable`. In order to check for the variable and use a default if it isn't provided, we use the `getattr()` Python method: `getattr(self, 'variable', 'default')`. Overall, we replace our original `with open...` statement with the following one:

```
with open(getattr(self, "file", "todo.csv"), "rU") as f:
```

Now, `todo.csv` is the default value unless it's overridden by setting a source file explicitly with an `-a` argument. Given a second file, `another_todo.csv`, we can run the following:

```
$ scrapy crawl fromcsv -a file=another_todo.csv -o out.csv
```

Summary

In this chapter, we dived a bit deeper into the internals of Scrapy spiders. We used `FormRequest` to log in, passed variables around with `meta` of `Request`/`Response`, used relevant XPaths and `Selectors`, used `.csv` files as sources, and much more.

We are now ready to see how we can deploy our spiders in the Scrapinghub cloud in the brief *Chapter 6, Deploying to Scrapinghub* before we move onto reviewing the wealth of Scrapy settings in *Chapter 7, Configuration and Management*.

6
Deploying to Scrapinghub

In the last few chapters, we took a look at how to develop Scrapy spiders. As soon as we're satisfied with their functionality, we have two options. If all we want is to use them for a single scrape, we may be okay with letting them run for some time on our dev machine. On the other hand, quite often, we need to run scraping jobs periodically. We may use cloud servers from Amazon, RackSpace, or any other provider, but this requires some setup, configuration and maintenance. This is where Scrapinghub comes into play.

Scapinghub is the Amazon of Scrapy hosting — a cloud Scrapy infrastructure provider that is built by lead Scrapy developers. It is a paid service, but they provide a free tier with no need for a credit card. If you want to have your Scrapy crawler running on a professionally set up and maintained infrastructure within minutes, then this chapter is for you.

Signing up, signing in, and starting a project

The first step is to open an account on http://scrapinghub.com/. All we need is an e-mail address and a password. After clicking on the link in the confirmation e-mail, we can log in to the service. The first page that we see is our profile dashboard. We don't have any projects, so we click on the **+ Service** button (1) to create one:

Creating a new project with scrapinghub

We can name our project properties (2) and click on the **Create** button (3). Then, we click on the **new** link in the homepage (4) to open the project.

The main menu

The project dashboard is the most important screen for our project. In the menu, on the left, we can see several sections. **Jobs** and **Spiders** sections provide information about our runs and spiders, respectively. **Periodic Jobs** enables us to schedule recurrent crawls. The other four sections are not that useful for us right now.

Spider deployment settings

We can go directly to the **Settings** section (1). In contrast to many websites' settings, Scrapinghub's setting provide lots of functionality one should really be aware of. Right now, we are mostly interested in the **Scrapy Deploy** section (2).

Deploying our spiders and scheduling runs

We will deploy directly from our dev machine. In order to do so, we just have to copy the lines from the **Scrapy Deploy** page (3) and put them on `scrapy.cfg` of our project, replacing the default `[deploy]` section. You will note that we don't need to set a password. As an example, we will use the properties project from *Chapter 4, From Scrapy to a Mobile App*. The reason that we use that spider is that we need our target data to be accessible from the Web exactly as we used to back in that chapter. Before we use it, we restore the original `settings.py` file by removing any references to the Appery.io pipeline:

 The code from this chapter is in the `ch06` directory. This example in particular is in the `ch06/properties` directory.

```
$ pwd
/root/book/ch06/properties
$ ls
properties   scrapy.cfg
$ cat scrapy.cfg
...

[settings]
default = properties.settings

# Project: properties
[deploy]
url = http://dash.scrapinghub.com/api/scrapyd/
username = 180128bc7a0.....50e8290dbf3b0
password =
project = 28814
```

In order to deploy the spider, we will use the `shub` tool provided by Scrapinghub. We can install it with `pip install shub`, and it is already installed on our dev machine. We can log in to Scrapinghub using `shub login`, as follows:

```
$ shub login
Insert your Scrapinghub API key : 180128bc7a0.....50e8290dbf3b0
Success.
```

We already copied and pasted our API key on the `scrapy.cfg` file, but we can also find it by clicking on our username on the upper-right side on Scrapinghub's website and then **API Key**. In any case, we are now ready to deploy the spider using `shub deploy`:

```
$ shub deploy
Packing version 1449092838
Deploying to project "28814" in {"status": "ok", "project": 28814,
"version": "1449092838", "spiders": 1}
Run your spiders at: https://dash.scrapinghub.com/p/28814/
```

Scrapy packs all the spiders from this project and uploads them to Scrapinghub. We will notice two new directories and a file. These are auxiliary, and we can safely delete them if we wish although typically I don't mind them:

```
$ ls
build project.egg-info properties scrapy.cfgsetup.py
$ rm -rf build project.egg-info setup.py
```

Now, if we click on the **Spiders** section (1) in Scrapinghub, we will find the **tomobile** spider that we've just deployed:

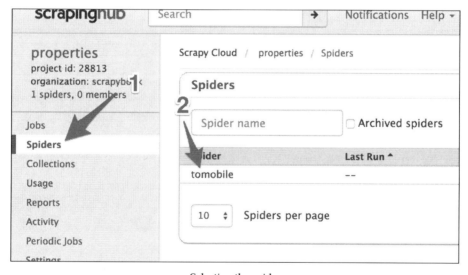

Selecting the spider

If we click on it (2), we get to the spider dashboard. This has lots of information, but all we need to do is click the green **Schedule** button (3) on the top-right corner, and then the second **Schedule** button (4) on the popup.

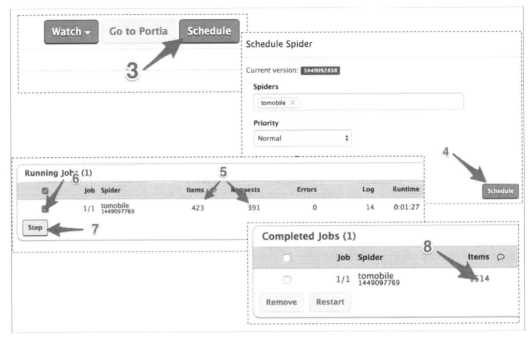

Scheduling a spider run

After a few seconds, we will notice a new row on the **Running Jobs** section of the page and a bit later the number of **Requests** and **Items** increasing (5).

 You will likely not reduce scraping speed compared to your dev runs. Scrapyhub uses an algorithm to estimate the number of requests per second that you can perform without getting banned.

Let it run for a while, and then select the checkbox of this job (6) and click **Stop** (7).

After a few more seconds our job will end up on the **Completed Jobs** section. In order to inspect scraped items, we can click on the number of items link (8).

Accessing our items

This takes us to the job dashboard page. From this page we can inspect our items (9) and make sure that they look okay. We can also filter them with the controls above those items. As we scroll down the page, more items get automatically loaded.

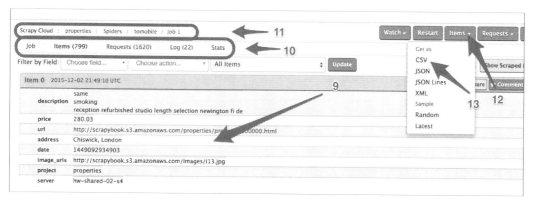

Inspecting and exporting items

If something went wrong, we can find useful information on our **Requests** and **Log** just above **Items** (10). We can navigate back to the spider or project using the breadcrumbs at the top (11). Of course, we can download our items in the usual CSV, JSON, and JSON Lines formats by clicking on the green **Items** button on the top left (12) and then selecting the appropriate option (13).

Another way to access our items is through Scrapinghub's Items API. All we need to do is have a look at the URL of this job's or items' page. It will look similar to this:

`https://dash.scrapinghub.com/p/28814/job/1/1/`

On this URL, **28814** is the project number (we have also set this in the `scrapy.cfg` file before) then the first `1` is the number/ID of this spider (the one named "**tomobile**"), and the second `1` is the number of the job. Using these three numbers in this order, we can use `curl` from our console to retrieve our items by making a request to `https://storage.scrapinghub.com/items/<project id>/<spider id>/<job id>` and using our username/API key to authenticate, as follows:

```
$ curl -u 180128bc7a0.....50e8290dbf3b0: https://storage.scrapinghub.com/
items/28814/1/1
{"_type":"PropertiesItem","description":["same\r\nsmoking\r\nr...
{"_type":"PropertiesItem","description":["british bit keep eve...
...
```

If it asks for a password, we can leave it blank. Having programmatic access to our data allows us to write applications that use Scrapinghub as a data storage backend. Please keep in mind though that data won't be stored indefinitely but for a limited time depending on our subscription plan (seven days for the free plan).

Scheduling recurring crawls

I guess that by now you won't be surprised to hear that scheduling recurrent crawls is a matter of just a few clicks.

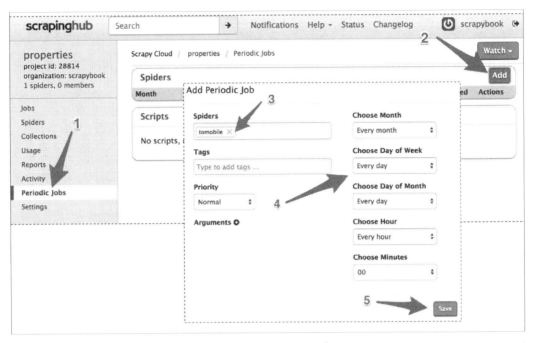

Scheduling recurrent crawls

We just go to the **Periodic Jobs** section (1), click **Add** (2), set the spider (3), adjust the crawling frequency (4), and finally click **Save** (5).

Summary

In this chapter, we had our first experience with deploying a Scrapy project to the cloud using Scrapinghub. We scheduled a run and collected thousands of items that we were able to browse and extract easily by using the API. In the following chapters, we will keep building our knowledge up to the level of setting up a small Scrapinghub-like server for ourselves. We start in the next chapter by exploring configuration and management.

7
Configuration and Management

We just saw how easy it is to develop a simple spider with Scrapy and use it to extract data from the Web. Scrapy comes with lots of utilities and functionality that is made available through its settings. For many software frameworks, settings are the "geeky stuff" that fine tune how the system works. For Scrapy, settings are one of the most fundamental mechanisms, which, beyond tuning and configuration, enable functionality and allow us to extend the framework. We don't aim to compete with the excellent Scrapy documentation but supplement it by helping you navigate the settings landscape faster and find the ones that are most relevant to you. Please read the details on the documentation before you move your changes to production.

Using Scrapy settings

With Scrapy, you can modify settings in five levels of increasing priority. We will see each of them in turn. The first level is the default settings. You wouldn't typically need to modify the default settings but `scrapy/settings/default_settings.py` (in your system's Scrapy source code or Scrapy's GitHub) is certainly an interesting read. The default settings get refined at command level. Practically speaking, you shouldn't ever have to worry about this unless you are implementing custom commands. More often than not, we modify settings just after the command level on our project's `<project_name>/settings.py` file. Those settings apply on our current project only. This level is the most convenient because `settings.py` gets packaged when we deploy the project in a cloud service, and since it's a file, we can adjust tens of settings easily with our favourite text editor. The next level is its per-spider settings level. By using a `custom_settings` attribute in our spider definitions, we can easily customize settings per spider. This would allow us, for example, to enable or disable Item Pipelines for a given spider. Finally, for some last-minute modifications, we can pass settings on the command line using the `-s` command-line parameter. We have already done this several times by setting, for example `-s CLOSESPIDER_PAGECOUNT=3`, which enables the close spider extension and closes the spider early. In this level, we may want to set API secrets, passwords, and so on. Don't store these things in `settings.py` because most likely, you don't want them to accidentally end up checked in to some public repository.

Throughout this section, we will examine some very important commonly-used settings. To get a feeling of different types, try the following with any random project:

```
$ scrapy settings --get CONCURRENT_REQUESTS
16
```

What you get is the default value. Then, modify your project's `<project_name>/settings.py` file and set a value for CONCURRENT_REQUESTS, for example, 14. The preceding `scrapy settings` command will give you the value that you just set—don't forget to revert it. Then, by setting the argument explicitly from the command line you get the following:

```
$ scrapy settings --get CONCURRENT_REQUESTS -s CONCURRENT_REQUESTS=19
19
```

The preceding output hints at an interesting thing. `scrapy crawl` and `scrapy settings` are just commands. Every command uses the methodology that we just described to load settings. An example of this is as follows:

```
$ scrapy shell -s CONCURRENT_REQUESTS=19
>>> settings.getint('CONCURRENT_REQUESTS')
19
```

Whenever you need to find out what the effective value for a setting is within your project, use one of the preceding methods. We will now have a closer look at Scrapy's settings.

Essential settings

Scrapy has so many settings that categorizing them becomes an urgent necessity. We start with the most essential settings that we summarize in the following diagram. They give you awareness of the important system features and you may find yourself adjusting them somewhat frequently.

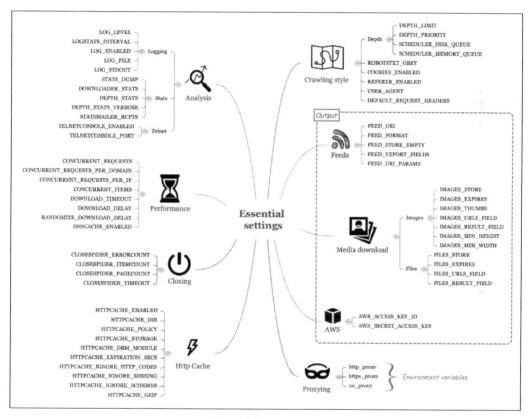

Essential Scrapy settings

Analysis

By using those settings you can configure the way Scrapy provides performance and debugging information via logs, statistics, and the telnet facility.

Logging

Scrapy has different levels of logs based on their severity: DEBUG (lowest level), INFO, WARNING, ERROR, and CRITICAL (highest level). Beyond that, there's a SILENT level that you can use to get no logging whatsoever. You can restrict the log file to only accept logs above a certain level by setting LOG_LEVEL to the minimum desired level. We often set this value to INFO because DEBUG is a bit too verbose. One very useful Scrapy extension is the Log Stats extension, which prints the number of items and pages scraped per minute. Logging frequency is set with the LOGSTATS_INTERVAL setting to a default value of 60 seconds. This may be a bit too infrequent. While developing, I like to set that to five seconds because most runs are short. Logs are written to the file that is set in LOG_FILE. Unless set, the output will go to the standard error except if logging gets explicitly disabled by setting the LOG_ENABLED setting to False. Finally, you can tell Scrapy to record all of its standard output (for example, "print" messages) to the log by setting LOG_STDOUT to true.

Stats

STATS_DUMP is enabled by default, and it dumps values from the Stats Collector to the log once the spider is finished. You can control whether stats are recorded for the downloader by setting DOWNLOADER_STATS to False. You can also control whether stats are collected for site depth through the DEPTH_STATS setting. For more detailed information on depth, set DEPTH_STATS_VERBOSE to True. STATSMAILER_RCPTS is a list (for example, set to ['my@mail.com']) of e-mails to send stats to when a crawl finishes. You won't adjust these settings that often but they can occasionally help with debugging.

Telnet

Scrapy includes a built-in telnet console that gives you a Python shell to the running Scrapy process. TELNETCONSOLE_ENABLED is enabled by default, while TELNETCONSOLE_PORT determines the port(s) that is used to connect to the console. You may need to alter them in case of a conflict.

Example 1 – using telnet

There will be cases where you would like to have a look on the internal status of Scrapy while it is running. Let's see how we can do that with the telnet console:

The code from this chapter is in the ch07 directory. This example in particular is in the ch07/properties directory.

```
$ pwd
/root/book/ch07/properties
$ ls
properties   scrapy.cfg
```

Start a crawl as follows:

```
$ scrapy crawl fast
...
[scrapy] DEBUG: Telnet console listening on 127.0.0.1:6023:6023
```

The preceding message means that telnet is activated and listening in port 6023. Now on another terminal, use the telnet command to connect to it:

```
$ telnet localhost 6023
>>>
```

Now, this console gives you a Python console inside Scrapy. You can inspect several components, such as the engine using the engine variable, but in order to get a quick overview of the status, you can use the est() command:

```
>>> est()
Execution engine status

time()-engine.start_time                    : 5.73892092705
engine.has_capacity()                       : False
len(engine.downloader.active)               : 8
...
len(engine.slot.inprogress)                 : 10
...
len(engine.scraper.slot.active)             : 2
```

We will explore a few of the metrics there in *Chapter 10, Understanding Scrapy's Performance*. You will notice that you are still running this inside the Scrapy engine. Let's assume that you use the following command:

```
>>> import time
>>> time.sleep(1) # Don't do this!
```

You will notice a short pause in the other terminal. Certainly this console isn't the right place to calculate the first million digits of Pi. Some other interesting things you can do in the console are to pause, continue, and stop the crawl. You may find these and the terminal in general very useful while working with Scrapy sessions in remote machines:

```
>>> engine.pause()
>>> engine.unpause()
>>> engine.stop()
Connection closed by foreign host.
```

Performance

We will have a detailed look at these settings in *Chapter 10, Understanding Scrapy's Performance*, but here is a little summary. Performance settings let you adjust the performance characteristics of Scrapy to your particular workload. CONCURRENT_REQUESTS sets the maximum number of requests to be performed simultaneously. This mostly protects your server's outbound capacity in case you are crawling many different websites (domains/IPs). Unless that's the case, you will typically find CONCURRENT_REQUESTS_PER_DOMAIN and CONCURRENT_REQUESTS_PER_IP more restrictive. These two protect remote servers by limiting the number of simultaneous requests for each unique domain or IP address, respectively. If CONCURRENT_REQUESTS_PER_IP is non-zero, CONCURRENT_REQUESTS_PER_DOMAIN gets ignored. These settings are not per second. If CONCURRENT_REQUESTS = 16 and the average request takes a quarter of a second, your limit is $16 / 0.25 = 64$ requests per second. CONCURRENT_ITEMS sets the maximum number of items from each response that can be processed simultaneously. You may find this setting way less useful than it seems because quite often there's a single Item per page/request. The default value of 100 is also quite arbitrary. If you reduce it to, for example, 10 or 1 you might even see performance gains depending on the number of Items/request as well as how complex your pipelines are. You will also note that as this value is per request, if you have a limit of CONCURRENT_REQUESTS = 16, CONCURRENT_ITEMS = 100 might mean up to 1600 items concurrently trying to be written in your databases, and so on. I would prefer a little bit more conservative value for this setting in general.

For downloads, DOWNLOAD_TIMEOUT determines the amount of time the downloader will wait before canceling a request. This is 180 seconds by default, which by all means seems excessive (with 16 concurrent requests this would mean five pages/minute for a site that is down). I would recommend reducing it to, for example, 10 seconds if you have timeout issues. By default, Scrapy sets the delay between downloads to zero to maximize scraping speed. You can modify this to apply a more conservative download speed using the DOWNLOAD_DELAY setting. There are websites that measure the frequency of requests as an indication of "bot" behavior. By setting DOWNLOAD_DELAY, you also enable a ±50% randomizer on download delay. You can disable this feature by setting RANDOMIZE_DOWNLOAD_DELAY to False.

Finally, for faster DNS lookups, an in-memory DNS cache is enabled by default via the DNSCACHE_ENABLED setting.

Stopping crawls early

Scrapy's CloseSpider extension automatically stops a spider crawl when a condition is met. You can configure the spider to close after a period of time, after a number of items have been scraped, after a number of responses have been received, or after a number of errors have occurred using the CLOSESPIDER_TIMEOUT (in seconds), CLOSESPIDER_ITEMCOUNT, CLOSESPIDER_PAGECOUNT, and CLOSESPIDER_ERRORCOUNT settings, respectively. You will usually set them from the command line while running the spider as we've done a few times in previous chapters:

```
$ scrapy crawl fast -s CLOSESPIDER_ITEMCOUNT=10

$ scrapy crawl fast -s CLOSESPIDER_PAGECOUNT=10

$ scrapy crawl fast -s CLOSESPIDER_TIMEOUT=10
```

HTTP caching and working offline

Scrapy's HttpCacheMiddleware component (deactivated by default) provides a low-level cache for HTTP requests and responses. If enabled, the cache stores every request and its corresponding response. By setting HTTPCACHE_POLICY to scrapy. contrib.httpcache.RFC2616Policy, we can enable a way more sophisticated caching policy that respects website's hints according to RFC2616. To enable this cache, set HTTPCACHE_ENABLED to True and HTTPCACHE_DIR to a directory on the filesystem (using a relative path will create the directory in the project's data folder).

You can optionally specify a database backend for your cached files by setting the storage backend class HTTPCACHE_STORAGE to scrapy.contrib.httpcache. DbmCacheStorage and, optionally, adjusting the HTTPCACHE_DBM_MODULE setting (defaults to anydbm). There are a few more settings that fine-tune cache's behavior but the defaults are likely to serve you fine.

Example 2 – working offline by using the cache

Let's assume that you run the following code:

```
$ scrapy crawl fast -s LOG_LEVEL=INFO -s CLOSESPIDER_ITEMCOUNT=5000
```

You will notice that it takes about a minute to complete. If you didn't have access to the web server though, you would be unable to crawl anything. Let's assume that you now run the crawl again as follows:

```
$ scrapy crawl fast -s LOG_LEVEL=INFO -s CLOSESPIDER_ITEMCOUNT=5000 -s
HTTPCACHE_ENABLED=1

...

INFO: Enabled downloader middlewares:...*HttpCacheMiddleware*
```

You will notice that `HttpCacheMiddleware` got enabled, and if you look into the hidden directories on your current directory you will find a new `.scrapy` directory as follows:

```
$ tree .scrapy | head
.scrapy
└── httpcache
    └── easy
        ├── 00
        │   ├── 002054968919f13763a7292c1907caf06d5a4810
        │   │   ├── meta
        │   │   ├── pickled_meta
        │   │   ├── request_body
        │   │   ├── request_headers
        │   │   ├── response_body
...
```

Now if you rerun your scrape even in the case when you don't have access to the web server for a bit fewer items, you will notice it finishing faster:

```
$ scrapy crawl fast -s LOG_LEVEL=INFO -s CLOSESPIDER_ITEMCOUNT=4500 -s HTTPCACHE_ENABLED=1
```

We use a bit fewer items as a limit because when stopping using CLOSESPIDER_ITEMCOUNT, we often read a few more pages before the crawler stops completely, and we wouldn't like to hit ones not available in our cache. To clean the cache, just delete the cache directory:

```
$ rm -rf .scrapy
```

Crawling style

Scrapy lets you adjust how it chooses which pages to crawl first. You can set a maximum depth in the DEPTH_LIMIT setting, with 0 meaning no limit. Requests can be assigned priorities based on their depth through the DEPTH_PRIORITY setting. Most notably this allows you to perform a Breadth First Crawl by setting this value to a positive number and switching scheduler's queues from LIFO to FIFO:

```
DEPTH_PRIORITY = 1
SCHEDULER_DISK_QUEUE = 'scrapy.squeue.PickleFifoDiskQueue'
SCHEDULER_MEMORY_QUEUE = 'scrapy.squeue.FifoMemoryQueue'
```

This is useful when you crawl, for example, a news portal that has the most recent news closer to the home page while each news page has links to other related news. The default Scrapy behavior would be to go as deeply as possible in the first few news stories in the home page and only after that continue with subsequent front-page news. BFO order would crawl top-level news before proceeding further, and when combined with a DEPTH_LIMIT, such as 3, it might allow you to quickly scan the latest news on a portal.

Sites declare their crawler policies and hint at uninteresting parts of their structure with a web-standard robots.txt file in their root directory. Scrapy can take it into consideration if you set the ROBOTSTXT_OBEY setting to True. If you enable it, keep it in mind while debugging in case you notice any unexpected behavior.

The CookiesMiddleware transparently takes care of all cookie-related operations, enabling among others, session tracking, which allows you to log in, and so on. If you want to have more "stealth" crawling, you can disable this by setting COOKIES_ENABLED to False. Disabling cookies also slightly reduces the bandwidth that you use and might speed up your crawling a little bit depending on the website. Similarly, the REFERER_ENABLED setting is True by default, enabling RefererMiddleware, which populates Referer headers. You can define custom headers using DEFAULT_REQUEST_HEADERS. You may find this useful for weird sites that ban you unless you have particular request headers. Finally, the automatically generated settings.py file recommends that we set USER_AGENT. This defaults to the Scrapy version, but we should change it to something that allows website owners to be able to contact us.

Feeds

Feeds let you export the data that is scraped by Scrapy to the local filesystem or to a remote server. The location of the feed is determined by FEED_URI.FEED_URI and may have named parameters. For example, scrapy crawl fast -o "%(name)s_%(time)s.jl" will automatically have the current time and spider name (fast) filled in on the output file. If you needed a custom parameter, such as %(foo)s, feed exporter will expect you to provide a foo attribute in your spider. The storage of the feed, such as S3, FTP, or local filesystem is defined in the URI as well. For example, FEED_URI='s3://mybucket/file.json' will upload your file to Amazon's S3 using your Amazon credentials (AWS_ACCESS_KEY_ID and AWS_SECRET_ACCESS_KEY). The format of the feed—JSON, JSON Lines, CSV, and XML—is determined by FEED_FORMAT. If it is not set, Scrapy will guess it according to the extension of FEED_URI. You can choose to export empty feeds by setting FEED_STORE_EMPTY to true. You can also choose to export only certain fields using the FEED_EXPORT_FIELDS setting. This is particularly useful for .csv files that feature fixed header columns. Finally, FEED_URI_PARAMS is used to define a function to postprocess any parameters to FEED_URI.

Downloading media

Scrapy can download media content using the Image Pipeline, which can also convert images to different formats, generate thumbnails, and filter images based on size.

The IMAGES_STORE setting sets the directory where images are stored (using a relative path will create a directory in the project's root folder). The URLs for the images for each Item should be in its image_urls field (this can be overridden by the IMAGES_URLS_FIELD setting) and filenames for the downloaded images will be set to a new images field (this can be overridden by the IMAGES_RESULT_FIELD setting). You can filter out smaller images by setting IMAGES_MIN_WIDTH and IMAGES_MIN_HEIGHT. IMAGES_EXPIRES determines the number of days that images will be kept in the cache before they expire. For thumbnail generation, the IMAGES_THUMBS setting lets you define one or more thumbnails to generate along with their dimensions. For instance, you could have Scrapy generate one icon-sized thumbnail and one medium thumbnail for each downloaded image.

Other media

You can download other media files using the Files Pipeline. Similarly to images, FILES_STORE determines where files get downloaded and FILES_EXPIRES determines the number of days that files are retained. The FILES_URLS_FIELD and FILES_RESULT_FIELD settings have similar functionality to their IMAGES_* counterparts. Both the files and image pipelines can be active at the same time without conflict.

Example 3 – downloading images

In order to use image functions, we have to install the image package with sudo pip install image. In our dev machine, this has already been done for us. To enable the Image Pipeline, you just have to edit your project's settings.py file and add a few settings. The first one is including scrapy.pipelines.images.ImagesPipeline on your ITEM_PIPELINES. Also, set IMAGES_STORE to a relative path "images", and optionally a description for some thumbnails by setting IMAGES_THUMBS, as follows:

```
ITEM_PIPELINES = {
...
    'scrapy.pipelines.images.ImagesPipeline': 1,
}
IMAGES_STORE = 'images'
IMAGES_THUMBS = { 'small': (30, 30) }
```

We already have an image_urls field set appropriately for our Item, so we are ready to run it as follows:

```
$ scrapy crawl fast -s CLOSESPIDER_ITEMCOUNT=90
...
DEBUG: Scraped from <200 http://http://web:9312/.../index_00003.html/
property_000001.html>{
    'image_urls': [u'http://web:9312/images/i02.jpg'],
    'images': [{'checksum': 'c5b29f4b223218e5b5beece79fe31510',
                'path': 'full/705a3112e67...a1f.jpg',
                'url': 'http://web:9312/images/i02.jpg'}],
...
$ tree images
images
├── full
│   ├── 0abf072604df23b3be3ac51c9509999fa92ea311.jpg
│   ├── 1520131b5cc5f656bc683ddf5eab9b63e12c45b2.jpg
...
└── thumbs
    └── small
        ├── 0abf072604df23b3be3ac51c9509999fa92ea311.jpg
        ├── 1520131b5cc5f656bc683ddf5eab9b63e12c45b2.jpg
...
```

We see that the images were successfully downloaded and thumbnails were created. The JPG names for the main files get stored in the images field as expected. It's easy to infer thumbnails' paths. To clean the images we can use rm -rf images.

Amazon Web Services

Scrapy has built-in support to access Amazon web services. You can store your AWS access key in the AWS_ACCESS_KEY_ID setting, and you can store your secret key in the AWS_SECRET_ACCESS_KEY setting. Both of these settings are empty by default. They are used as follows:

- When you download URLs that start with s3:// (that instead of http://, and so on)

- When you use s3:// paths to store files or thumbnails with the media pipelines

- When you store your output Item feed on an s3:// directory

It's a good idea to NOT store these settings in your settings.py file in case it becomes public one day for any reason.

Using proxies and crawlers

Scrapy's `HttpProxyMiddleware` component lets you use the proxy settings that are defined by the `http_proxy`, `https_proxy`, and `no_proxy` environment variables in accordance with the Unix convention. This component is enabled by default.

Example 4 – using proxies and Crawlera's clever proxy

DynDNS (or any similar service) provides a free online tool to check your current IP address. Using a Scrapy shell, we'll make a request to `checkip.dyndns.org` and examine the response to find our current IP address:

```
$ scrapy shell http://checkip.dyndns.org
>>> response.body
'<html><head><title>Current IP Check</title></head><body>Current IP
Address: xxx.xxx.xxx.xxx</body></html>\r\n'
>>> exit()
```

To start proxying requests, exit the shell and use the `export` command to set a new proxy. You can test a free proxy by searching through HMA's public proxy list (`http://proxylist.hidemyass.com/`). For example, let's assume that from this list, we chose the proxy with IP `10.10.1.1` and port `80` (not a real one—replace it with your own), we have the following:

```
$ # First check if you already use a proxy
$ env | grep http_proxy
$ # We should have nothing. Now let's set a proxy
$ export http_proxy=http://10.10.1.1:80
```

Rerun the Scrapy shell, as we just did, and you will see that the request was performed using a different IP. You will also notice that it will typically be quite slower, and in some cases it won't be successful, in which case you could try another proxy. To disable the proxy, exit the Scrapy shell and `unset http_proxy` (or restore its previous value).

Crawlera is a service by Scrapinghub and lead developers of Scrapy that acts like a very clever proxy. Apart from using a large pool of IPs behind the scenes to route your requests, it also adjusts the delays and retries failures to give you a stable stream of successful responses as much as possible while remaining as fast as possible. It's essentially a scraper's dream come true, and you can use it just by setting the `http_proxy` environment variable as before:

```
$ export http_proxy=myusername:mypassword@proxy.crawlera.com:8010
```

Beyond HTTP proxy, Crawlera can also be used via its own middleware component for Scrapy.

Further settings

We will now explore some less common aspects of Scrapy and settings related to extending Scrapy, which we will see in more detail in later chapters.

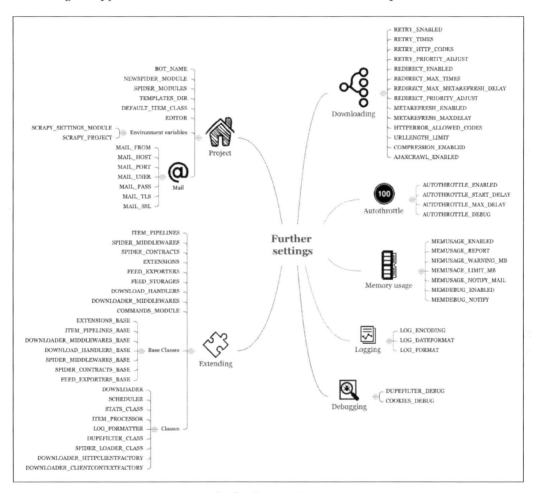

Further Scrapy settings

Project-related settings

Under this umbrella, you will find housekeeping settings related to a specific project, such as BOT_NAME, SPIDER_MODULES, and so on. It's good to have a quick look at them in the documentation because they may increase your productivity for specific use cases, but typically, Scrapy's startproject and genspider commands provide sensible defaults and you may be okay without ever explicitly changing them. Mail-related settings, such as MAIL_FROM, allow you to configure the MailSender class, which is currently used to mail stats (see also: STATSMAILER_RCPTS) and memory usage (see also: MEMUSAGE_NOTIFY_MAIL). There are also two environment variables, SCRAPY_SETTINGS_MODULE and SCRAPY_PROJECT, that allow you to fine tune the way a Scrapy project integrates within, for example, a Django project. scrapy.cfg also allows you to adjust the name of your settings module.

Extending Scrapy settings

These are settings that allow you to extend and modify almost every aspect of Scrapy. The king of these settings is definitely ITEM_PIPELINES. It allows you to use Item Processing Pipelines on your projects. We will see many such examples in *Chapter 9, Pipeline Recipies*. Beyond pipelines, we can extend Scrapy in various ways, some of them are summarized in *Chapter 8, Programming Scrapy*. COMMANDS_MODULE allows us to add custom commands. For example, let's assume that we add in a properties/hi.py file to the following:

```
from scrapy.commands import ScrapyCommand
class Command(ScrapyCommand):
    default_settings = {'LOG_ENABLED': False}
    def run(self, args, opts):
        print("hello")
```

As soon as we add COMMANDS_MODULE='properties.hi' on our settings.py file, we activate this trivial command making it show up in Scrapy's help and run with scrapy hi. The settings that are defined in a command's default_settings get merged into a project's settings overriding the defaults but with lower priority to settings that defined on your settings.py file or set in the command line.

Scrapy uses the -_BASE dictionaries (for example, FEED_EXPORTERS_BASE) to store default values for various framework extensions and then allows us to customize them in our settings.py file and command line by setting their non-_BASE versions of them (for example, FEED_EXPORTERS).

Finally, Scrapy uses settings, such as DOWNLOADER or SCHEDULER, which hold package/class names for essential components of the system. We could potentially inherit from the default downloader (scrapy.core.downloader.Downloader), overload a few methods, and then set our custom class on the DOWNLOADER setting. This allows developers to experiment wildly with experimental features and eases automated testing, but you shouldn't ever have to modify them unless you really know what you're doing.

Fine-tuning downloading

The RETRY_*, REDIRECT_*, and METAREFRESH_* settings configure the Retry, Redirect and Meta-Refresh middleware, respectively. For example, REDIRECT_PRIORITY_ADJUST set to 2 means that every time there's a redirect, the new request will be scheduled after all non-redirected requests get served, and REDIRECT_MAX_TIMES set to 20 means that after 20 redirects the downloader will give up and return whatever it has. It's nice to be aware of these settings in case you crawl some ill-cased websites, but the default values will serve you fine in most cases. The same applies to HTTPERROR_ALLOWED_CODES and URLLENGTH_LIMIT.

Autothrottle extension settings

The AUTOTHROTTLE_* settings enable and configure the autothrottle extension. This comes with a great promise, but in practice, I find that it tends to be somewhat conservative and difficult to tune. It uses download latencies to get a feeling of how loaded our and the target server are and adjusts downloader's delay accordingly. If you have a hard time finding the best value for DOWNLOAD_DELAY (defaults to 0), you should find this module useful.

Memory UsageExtension settings

The MEMUSAGE_* settings enable and configure the memory usage extension. This shuts down the spider when it exceeds a memory limit. This could be useful in a shared environment where processes have to be very polite. More often, you may find it useful to receive just its warning e-mail by disabling the shut down functionality by setting MEMUSAGE_LIMIT_MB to 0. This extension works only on Unix-like platforms.

MEMDEBUG_ENABLED and MEMDEBUG_NOTIFY enable and configure the memory debugger extension, printing the number of live references on spider close. Overall, I would say that chasing memory leaks isn't fun or easy (okay, it might be a bit fun). Read the excellent documentation on *Debugging memory leaks with trackref*, but most importantly, I would suggest keeping your crawls relatively short, batched, and in accordance with your server's capacity. I think there's no good reason to run batches of more than a few thousand pages or more than a few minutes long.

Logging and debugging

Finally, there are a few logging and debugging functions. LOG_ENCODING, LOG_DATEFORMAT and LOG_FORMAT let you fine tune your logging formats, which you may find useful if you intend to use log-management solutions, such as Splunk, or Logstash, and Kibana. DUPEFILTER_DEBUG and COOKIES_DEBUG will help you debug relatively complex situations where you get less than expected requests, or your sessions get lost unexpectedly.

Summary

By reading this chapter, I'm sure you appreciate the depth and breadth of the functionality that you get using Scrapy when compared with a crawler that you might write from scratch. If you need to fine-tune or extend Scrapy's functionality, you have plenty of options, as we will see in the following chapters.

8

Programming Scrapy

Up to this point, we wrote spiders whose main responsibility is to define the way we crawl data sources and how we extract information from them. Beyond spiders, Scrapy provides mechanisms that allow us to fine-tune most aspects of its functionality. For example, you may often find yourself dealing with some of the following problems:

1. You copy and paste lots of code among spiders of the same project. The repeated code is more related to data (for example, performing calculations on fields) rather than data sources.

2. You have to write scripts that postprocess Items doing things like dropping duplicate entries or postprocessing values.

3. You have repeated code across projects to deal with infrastructure. For example, you might need to log in and transfer files to proprietary repositories, add Items to databases, or trigger postprocessing operations when crawls complete.

4. You find aspects of Scrapy that are not exactly as you wish, and you need to apply customizations or workarounds on many of your projects.

Scrapy developers designed its architecture in a way that allows us to solve such recurrent problems. We will investigate this architecture later in this chapter. First though, let's start with an introduction to the engine that powers Scrapy. It's called **Twisted**.

Scrapy is a Twisted application

Scrapy is a scraping application built using the Twisted Python framework. Twisted is indeed somewhat unusual because it's event-driven and encourages us to write asynchronous code. Getting used to it takes some time, but we will make our task easier by studying only the parts of it that are relevant to Scrapy. We will also be a bit relaxed in terms of error handling. The full code on GitHub has more thorough error handling, but we will skip it for this book.

Let's start from the beginning. What makes Twisted different is its main mantra.

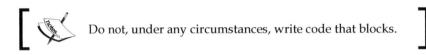 Do not, under any circumstances, write code that blocks.

The implications are severe. Code that might block includes:

- Code that accesses files, databases or the Web
- Code that spawns new processes and consumes their output, for example, running shell commands
- Code that performs hacky system-level operations, for example, waiting for system queues

Twisted provides us with methods that allow us to perform all these and many more without blocking code execution.

To showcase the difference, let's assume that we have a typical synchronous scrapping application. It has, for example, four threads, and at a given moment, three of them are blocked waiting for responses, and one of them is blocked performing a database write access to persist an Item. At any given moment, it's quite unlikely to find a general-purpose thread of a scrapping application doing anything else but waiting for some blocking operation to complete. When blocking operations complete, some computations may take place for a few microseconds and then threads block again on other blocking operations that likely last for at least a few milliseconds. Overall the server isn't idle because it runs tens of applications utilizing thousands of threads, thus, after some careful tuning, CPUs remain reasonably utilized.

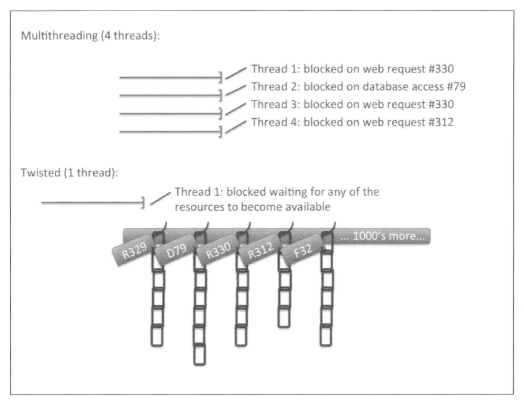

Multithreaded code versus Twisted asynchronous code

Twisted/Scrapy's approach favors using a single thread as much as possible. It uses modern Operating System's I/O multiplexing functions (see `select()`, `poll()`, and `epoll()`) as a "hanger". Where we would typically have a blocking operation, for example `result = i_block()`, Twisted provides us with an alternative implementation that returns immediately. However, it doesn't return the actual value but a hook, for example `deferred = i_dont_block()`, where we can hang whatever functionality we want to run whenever the value becomes available (for example, `deferred.addCallback(process_result)`). A Twisted application is made of chains of such deferred operations. The single main Twisted thread is called a Twisted Event Reactor thread and it monitors the hanger until some resource becomes available (for example, a server response to our `Request`s). When this happens, it fires the topmost deferred in the chain, which performs some computations and, in turn, fires the next one. Some of these deferreds might initiate further I/O operations, which will bring the chain of deferreds back to the hanger and free the CPU to perform other work, if available. Since we are single-threaded, we don't suffer the costs of context switches and save resources (like memory) that extra threads require. In other words, using this nonblocking infrastructure, we get performance that is similar to if we had thousands of threads, while using a single one.

To be perfectly honest, OS developers have been optimizing thread operations for decades making them very fast. The performance argument is not as strong as it used to be. One thing that everyone can agree on though, is that writing correct thread-safe code for complex applications is very difficult. After you get over the initial shock of having to think in terms of deferreds/callbacks, you will find Twisted code significantly simpler than threaded code. The `inlineCallbacks` generator utility makes code even simpler. We will explore them further in the following sections.

Arguably, the most successful nonblocking I/O system until now is Node.js, mainly because it started with high performance/ concurrency in mind, and nobody argued about whether that's a good or bad thing. Every Node.js application uses just nonblocking APIs. In the Java world, Netty is probably the most successful NIO framework powering applications, such as Apache Storm and Spark. C++11's `std::future` and `std::promise` (quite similar to deferreds) make it easier to write asynchronous code using libraries, such as libevent or plain POSIX.

Deferreds and deferred chains

Deferreds are the most essential mechanism that Twisted offers to help us write asynchronous code. Twisted APIs use deferreds to allow us to define sequences of actions that take place when certain events occur. Let's have a look at them.

You can get all the source code of this book from GitHub. To download this code go to git clone `https://github.com/ scalingexcellence/scrapybook`

The full code from this chapter will be in the `ch08` directory, and for this example in particular, in the `ch08/deferreds.py` file, and you can run it with `./deferreds.py 0`.

You can use a Python console to run the following experiments interactively:

```
$ python
>>> from twisted.internet import defer
>>> # Experiment 1
>>> d = defer.Deferred()
>>> d.called
False
>>> d.callback(3)
>>> d.called
True
```

```
>>> d.result
3
```

What we see is that Deferred is essentially a thing representing a value that we don't have immediately. When we fire d (call its callback method) it's called state becomes True, and the result attribute is set to the value that we set on the callback:

```
>>> # Experiment 2
>>> d = defer.Deferred()
>>> def foo(v):
...     print "foo called"
...     return v+1
...
>>> d.addCallback(foo)
<Deferred at 0x7f...>
>>> d.called
False
>>> d.callback(3)
foo called
>>> d.called
True
>>> d.result
4
```

The most powerful feature of deferreds is that we can chain other operations to be called when a value is set. In the last example, we add a foo() function as a callback for d. When we fire d by calling callback(3), function foo() gets called printing the message, and the value that it returns is set as the final result value for d:

```
>>> # Experiment 3
>>> def status(*ds):
...     return [(getattr(d, 'result', "N/A"), len(d.callbacks)) for d in
ds]
>>> def b_callback(arg):
...     print "b_callback called with arg =", arg
...     return b
>>> def on_done(arg):
...     print "on_done called with arg =", arg
...     return arg

>>> # Experiment 3.a
>>> a = defer.Deferred()
>>> b = defer.Deferred()
```

```
>>> a.addCallback(b_callback).addCallback(on_done)
>>> status(a, b)
[('N/A', 2), ('N/A', 0)]
>>> a.callback(3)
b_callback called with arg = 3
>>> status(a, b)
[(<Deferred at 0x10e7209e0>, 1), ('N/A', 1)]
>>> b.callback(4)
on_done called with arg = 4
>>> status(a, b)
[(4, 0), (None, 0)]
```

This example gets us to more complex deferred behaviors. We see a normal deferred, a, set up exactly as before, but now it has two callbacks. The first one is b_callback(), which returns a b deferred instead of a value. The second one is the on_done() printing function. We also have a little status() function that prints the status of deferreds. After the initial setup in both cases, we have the same state, [('N/A', 2), ('N/A', 0)], meaning that both deferreds haven't been fired, and the first one has two callbacks, while the second one has none. Then, if we fire a first, we get into a weird [(<Deferred at 0x10e7209e0>, 1), ('N/A', 1)] state, which shows that a now has a value, which is a deferred (the b deferred actually), and it also has a single callback, which is reasonable because b_callback() has already been called and only on_done() is left. The unexpected fact is that b now has a callback. Indeed a registered behind the scenes a callback, which will update its value as soon as b gets fired. Once this happens, on_done() also gets called and the final state is [(4, 0), (None, 0)], which is exactly what we expected:

```
>>> # Experiment 3.b
>>> a = defer.Deferred()
>>> b = defer.Deferred()
>>> a.addCallback(b_callback).addCallback(on_done)
>>> status(a, b)
[('N/A', 2), ('N/A', 0)]
>>> b.callback(4)
>>> status(a, b)
[('N/A', 2), (4, 0)]
>>> a.callback(3)
b_callback called with arg = 3
on_done called with arg = 4
>>> status(a, b)
[(4, 0), (None, 0)]
```

On the other hand, if b gets fired before a as experiment 3.b shows, the status becomes [('N/A', 2), (4, 0)], and then when a gets fired both callbacks get called and the final state ends up being the same as before. It's interesting to note that regardless of the order, the result is the same. The only difference between the two cases is that in the first case, the value of b value remains deferred for a bit longer because it gets fired second, while in the second example, b gets fired first and from that point on its value is used immediately when needed.

At this point, you have a quite good understanding of what deferreds are and how they can be chained and used to represent values that aren't yet available. We finish our exploration with a fourth example showing you how to fire something that depends on a number of other deferreds. This in Twisted is implemented using the defer.DeferredList class:

```
>>> # Experiment 4
>>> deferreds = [defer.Deferred() for i in xrange(5)]
>>> join = defer.DeferredList(deferreds)
>>> join.addCallback(on_done)
>>> for i in xrange(4):
...     deferreds[i].callback(i)
>>> deferreds[4].callback(4)
on_done called with arg = [(True, 0), (True, 1), (True, 2),
                           (True, 3), (True, 4)]
```

What we notice is that it doesn't matter that four out of five get fired with the for statement, on_done() doesn't get called until all the deferreds in the list get fired, that is, after our final deferreds[4].callback() call. The argument for on_done() is a list of tuples where each tuple corresponds to a deferred and contains True for success or False for failure and deferred's value.

Understanding Twisted and nonblocking I/O – a Python tale

Now that we have a grasp of the primitives, let me tell you a little Python story. All characters appearing in this work are fictitious. Any resemblance to real persons is purely coincidental:

```
# ~*~ Twisted - A Python tale ~*~

from time import sleep

# Hello, I'm a developer and I mainly setup Wordpress.
def install_wordpress(customer):
```

```
    # Our hosting company Threads Ltd. is bad. I start installation
and...
        print "Start installation for", customer
        # ...then wait till the installation finishes successfully. It is
        # boring and I'm spending most of my time waiting while consuming
        # resources (memory and some CPU cycles). It's because the process
        # is *blocking*.
        sleep(3)
        print "All done for", customer

    # I do this all day long for our customers
    def developer_day(customers):
        for customer in customers:
            install_wordpress(customer)

    developer_day(["Bill", "Elon", "Steve", "Mark"])
```

Let's run it:

```
$ ./deferreds.py 1
------ Running example 1 ------
Start installation for Bill
All done for Bill
Start installation
...
* Elapsed time: 12.03 seconds
```

What we get is sequential execution. Four customers with three seconds processing each means twelve seconds overall. This doesn't scale very well, so we add some threading in our second example:

```
import threading

# The company grew. We now have many customers and I can't handle
the
# workload. We are now 5 developers doing exactly the same thing.
def developers_day(customers):
    # But we now have to synchronize... a.k.a. bureaucracy
    lock = threading.Lock()
    #
    def dev_day(id):
        print "Goodmorning from developer", id
        # Yuck - I hate locks...
        lock.acquire()
        while customers:
            customer = customers.pop(0)
            lock.release()
```

```
            # My Python is less readable
            install_wordpress(customer)
            lock.acquire()
        lock.release()
        print "Bye from developer", id
    # We go to work in the morning
    devs = [threading.Thread(target=dev_day, args=(i,)) for i in
range(5)]
    [dev.start() for dev in devs]
    # We leave for the evening
    [dev.join() for dev in devs]

# We now get more done in the same time but our dev process got more
# complex. As we grew we spend more time managing queues than doing dev
# work. We even had occasional deadlocks when processes got extremely
# complex. The fact is that we are still mostly pressing buttons and
# waiting but now we also spend some time in meetings.
developers_day(["Customer %d" % i for i in xrange(15)])
```

Let's run it as follows:

```
$ ./deferreds.py 2
------ Running example 2 ------
Goodmorning from developer 0Goodmorning from developer
1Start installation forGoodmorning from developer 2
Goodmorning from developer 3Customer 0
...
from developerCustomer 13 3Bye from developer 2
* Elapsed time: 9.02 seconds
```

What you get is parallel execution using five worker threads. 15 customers with three seconds processing each means 45 seconds overall, but with five workers in parallel it ends up taking just nine seconds. The code got a bit ugly though. Instead of focusing on the algorithm or business logic, now a good fraction of the code is there just to manage concurrency. Additionally, output became something between messy and unreadable. It's quite hard to get even easy multithreaded code perfectly right, which leads us to Twisted:

```
# For years we thought this was all there was... We kept hiring more
# developers, more managers and buying servers. We were trying harder
# optimising processes and fire-fighting while getting mediocre
# performance in return. Till luckily one day our hosting
# company decided to increase their fees and we decided to
# switch to Twisted Ltd.!
```

```
from twisted.internet import reactor
from twisted.internet import defer
from twisted.internet import task

# Twisted has a slightly different approach
def schedule_install(customer):
    # They are calling us back when a Wordpress installation completes.
    # They connected the caller recognition system with our CRM and
    # we know exactly what a call is about and what has to be done
    # next.
    #
    # We now design processes of what has to happen on certain events.
    def schedule_install_wordpress():
        def on_done():
            print "Callback: Finished installation for", customer
        print "Scheduling: Installation for", customer
        return task.deferLater(reactor, 3, on_done)
    #
    def all_done(_):
        print "All done for", customer
    #
    # For each customer, we schedule these processes on the CRM
    # and that
    # is all our chief-Twisted developer has to do
    d = schedule_install_wordpress()
    d.addCallback(all_done)
    #
    return d

# Yes, we don't need many developers anymore or any synchronization.
# ~~ Super-powered Twisted developer ~~
def twisted_developer_day(customers):
    print "Goodmorning from Twisted developer"
    #
    # Here's what has to be done today
    work = [schedule_install(customer) for customer in customers]
    # Turn off the lights when done
    join = defer.DeferredList(work)
    join.addCallback(lambda _: reactor.stop())
    #
    print "Bye from Twisted developer!"
```

```
# Even his day is particularly short!
twisted_developer_day(["Customer %d" % i for i in xrange(15)])

# Reactor, our secretary uses the CRM and follows-up on events!
reactor.run()
```

Let's run it:

```
$ ./deferreds.py 3
------ Running example 3 ------
Goodmorning from Twisted developer
Scheduling: Installation for Customer 0
....
Scheduling: Installation for Customer 14
Bye from Twisted developer!
Callback: Finished installation for Customer 0
All done for Customer 0
Callback: Finished installation for Customer 1
All done for Customer 1
...
All done for Customer 14
* Elapsed time: 3.18 seconds
```

What we get is perfect working code and nicely looking output while using no threads. We process all 15 customers in parallel, that is, 45 seconds computation in just three seconds! The trick is that we replaced all blocking calls to sleep() with its Twisted counterpart task.deferLater() and callback functions. As processing now takes place somewhere else, we can effortlessly serve 15 customers simultaneously.

I mentioned that the preceding processing is now being done somewhere else. Is this cheating? The answer is no. Algorithmic computation still happens in CPUs but CPU operations are very fast nowadays when compared to disk and the network operations. As a result bringing data to CPUs and sending data from one CPUs or storage to another take most of the time. We save all this time for our CPUs using nonblocking I/O operations. They, exactly like task.deferLater(), use callbacks that get fired when data transfers complete.

Another very important thing to notice is the Goodmorning from Twisted developer and Bye from Twisted developer! messages. They are printed instantly when our code starts. If our code reaches that point so early, when does our application really run? The answer is that a Twisted application (including Scrapy) runs entirely within reactor.run()! By the time you call that method, you must have every possible deferred chain your application is expected to use in place (equivalent to setting up steps and processes in the CRM system in the preceding story). Your reactor.run() (the secretary) performs the event monitoring and fires callbacks.

[The main rule of the reactor is; I can do anything as long as it's a fast nonblocking operation.]

Excellent! The code doesn't have any threading nonsense but still these callback functions look a bit ugly. This leads us to the next example:

```python
# Twisted gave us utilities that make our code way more readable!
@defer.inlineCallbacks
def inline_install(customer):
    print "Scheduling: Installation for", customer
    yield task.deferLater(reactor, 3, lambda: None)
    print "Callback: Finished installation for", customer
    print "All done for", customer

def twisted_developer_day(customers):
    ... same as previously but using inline_install()
        instead of schedule_install()

twisted_developer_day(["Customer %d" % i for i in xrange(15)])
reactor.run()
```

Let's run it as follows:

```
$ ./deferreds.py 4
... exactly the same as before
```

The preceding code does exactly the same as the previous one but looks nicer. The inlineCallbacks generator makes the code of inline_install() pause and resume using a few Python mechanisms. inline_install() becomes a deferred and gets executed in parallel for every customer. Every time we yield, execution pauses on the current instance of inline_install() and resumes when the deferred that we yielded gets fired.

The only problem that we have now is that if instead of 15 customers, we had, for example 10000, this code would shamelessly start 10000 simultaneous sequences of processing (call it HTTP requests, database write operations, and so on). This may be okay or it could cause all sorts of failures. In massively concurrent applications such as Scrapy, we often have to limit the amount of concurrency to acceptable levels. In this example, we can do this using a `task.Cooperator()`. Scrapy uses the same mechanism to limit the amount of concurrency in item processing pipelines (the `CONCURRENT_ITEMS` setting):

```
@defer.inlineCallbacks
def inline_install(customer):
    ... same as above

# The new "problem" is that we have to manage all this concurrency to
# avoid causing problems to others, but this is a nice problem to have.
def twisted_developer_day(customers):
    print "Goodmorning from Twisted developer"
    work = (inline_install(customer) for customer in customers)
    #
    # We use the Cooperator mechanism to make the secretary not
    # service more than 5 customers simultaneously.
    coop = task.Cooperator()
    join = defer.DeferredList([coop.coiterate(work) for i in xrange(5)])
    #
    join.addCallback(lambda _: reactor.stop())
    print "Bye from Twisted developer!"

twisted_developer_day(["Customer %d" % i for i in xrange(15)])
reactor.run()

# We are now more lean than ever, our customers happy, our hosting
# bills ridiculously low and our performance stellar.

# ~*~ THE END ~*~
```

Let's run it:

```
$ ./deferreds.py 5
------ Running example 5 ------
Goodmorning from Twisted developer
Bye from Twisted developer!
Scheduling: Installation for Customer 0
...
Callback: Finished installation for Customer 4
```

```
All done for Customer 4
Scheduling: Installation for Customer 5
...
Callback: Finished installation for Customer 14
All done for Customer 14
* Elapsed time: 9.19 seconds
```

What we observe is that we now have something that is similar to five processing slots for customers. Processing for a new customer doesn't start unless there's an empty slot, which, effectively, in our case that customer processing time is always the same (three seconds), leads to batches of five customers at a time. We end up with the same performance with our threaded example but now using just one thread while enjoying simpler and more correct code.

Congratulations, you had a—frankly put—quite intense introduction to Twisted and nonblocking I/O programming.

Overview of Scrapy architecture

The following diagram summarizes Scrapy's architecture:

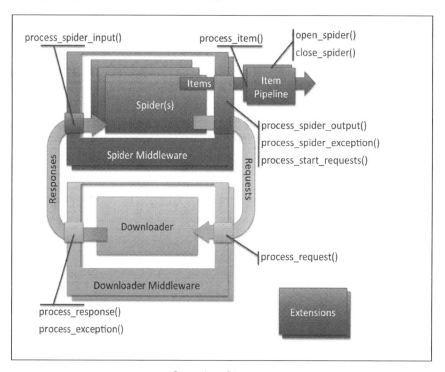

Scrapy's architecture

You may notice three familiar types of objects upon which this architecture operates; `Requests`, `Responses`, and `Items`. Our spiders lie right at the core of the architecture. They create `Requests`, process `Responses`, and generate `Items` and more `Requests`.

Each `Item` generated by a spider is postprocessed by a sequence of Item Pipelines using their `process_item()` method. Typically, `process_item()` modifies `Items` and passes them to the subsequent pipelines by returning them. Occasionally (for example, in the case of a duplicate or invalid data), we may need to drop an `Item`, and we do so by raising a `DropItem` exception. In this case, subsequent pipelines won't receive it. If we also provide an `open_spider()` and/or `close_spider()` method, it will get called on spider open and close, respectively. That's an opportunity for initializations and cleanups. Item Pipelines are typically used to perform problem domain or infrastructure operations, such as cleaning up data, or inserting `Items` into databases. You will also find yourself reusing them to great extent between projects, especially if they deal with your infrastructure's specifics. The Appery.io pipeline that we used in *Chapter 4, From Scrapy to a Mobile App*, is an example of an Item Pipeline that performs infrastructure work, that is, with minimal configuration it uploads `Items` to Appery.io.

We typically send `Requests` from our Spiders and get back `Responses` and it just works. Scrapy takes care of cookies, authentication, caching, and so on, in a transparent manner, and all we need to do is occasionally adjust a few settings. Most of this functionality is implemented in the form of downloader middlewares. They are often quite sophisticated and highly technical dealing with `Request`/`Response` internals. You may create custom ones to make Scrapy work exactly the way you want it to in terms of `Request` processing. A typical successful middleware will be reused across many projects and likely provide functionality that is useful to many Scrapy developers, thus, it would be nice to be shared with the community. You won't write a downloader middleware very often. If you want to have a look at the default downloader middlewares, check the `DOWNLOADER_MIDDLEWARES_BASE` setting in `settings/default_settings.py` in Scrapy's GitHub.

Downloader is the engine that performs the actual downloads. You will never have to modify this unless you are a Scrapy contributor.

Every now and then you might have to write Spider middlewares. They process `Requests` just after the spider and before any downloader middleware and `Responses` in the opposite order. With a downloader middleware you may, for example, decide to rewrite all your URLs to use HTTPS instead of HTTP regardless of what a spider extracts from pages. It implements functionality that is specific to your project's needs and shared across all spiders. The main thing that differentiates between downloader middlewares and spider middlewares is that when a downloader middleware gets a `Request`, it should return a single `Response`. On the other hand, it's okay for spider middleware to drop `Requests` if they don't like them or, for example, emit many `Requests` for each input `Request` if this serves your application's purpose. You could say that spider middlewares are for `Requests` and `Responses` what item pipelines are for `Items`. Spider middlewares receive `Items` as well but typically don't modify them because this can be done more easily with an item pipeline. If you want to have a look at the default spider middlewares, check the `SPIDER_MIDDLEWARES_BASE` setting in `settings/default_settings.py` in Scrapy's git.

Finally, there are extensions. Extensions are quite common—actually the next most common thing after Item Pipelines. They are plain classes that get loaded at crawl startup and can access settings, the crawler, register callbacks to signals, and define their own signals. Signals is an essential Scrapy API that allows callbacks to be called when something happens in the system, for example, an `Item` gets crawled, dropped, or when a spider opens. There are lots of useful predefined signals, and we will see some of them later. Extensions are a Jack of all trades in the sense that they allow you to write every utility you can possibly imagine but without really giving you any help(like, for example, the process_item() method of Item Pipelines). We have to hook to signals and implement the functionality we need ourselves. For example, stopping the crawl after a specific number of pages or `Items` is implemented with an extension. If you want to have a look at the default extensions, check the `EXTENSIONS_BASE` setting in `settings/default_settings.py` in Scrapy's git.

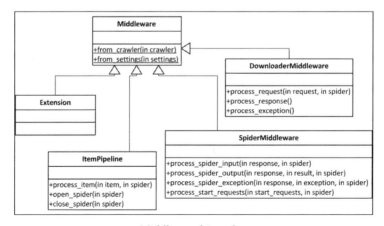

Middleware hierarchy

A bit more strictly speaking, Scrapy treats all these classes as middlewares (managed by decedents of the `MiddlewareManager` class) and allows us to initialize them from a `Crawler` or a `Settings` object by implementing the `from_crawler()` or `from_settings()` class-methods, respectively. Since one can get the `Settings` easily from `Crawler` (`crawler.settings`), `from_crawler()` is way more popular. If one doesn't need `Settings` or `Crawler`, it's fine not to implement them.

Here is a table that can help you decide what the best mechanism for a given problem is:

Problem	Solution
Something that is specific to the website that I'm crawling.	Modify your Spider.
Modifying or storing `Items`—domain-specific, may be reused across projects.	Write an Item Pipeline.
Modifying or dropping `Requests`/`Responses`—domain-specific, may be reused across projects.	Write a spider middleware.
Executing `Requests`/`Responses`—generic, for example, to support some custom login scheme or a special way to handle cookies.	Write a downloader middleware.
All other problems.	Write an extension.

Example 1 - a very simple pipeline

Let's assume that we have an application with several spiders, which provide the crawl date in the usual Python format. Our databases require it in string format in order to index it. We don't want to edit our spiders because there are many of them. How can we do it? A very simple pipeline can postprocess our items and perform the conversion we need. Let's see how this works:

```
from datetime import datetime

class TidyUp(object):
    def process_item(self, item, spider):
        item['date'] = map(datetime.isoformat, item['date'])
        return item
```

As you can see, this is nothing more than a simple class with a `process_item()` method. This is all we need for this simple pipeline. We can reuse the spiders from *Chapter 3*, *Basic Crawling*, and add the preceding code in a `tidyup.py` file inside a `pipelines` directory.

> We can put this item pipeline's code anywhere we want, but a separate directory is a good idea.

We now have to edit our project's `settings.py` file and set `ITEM_PIPELINES` to:

```
ITEM_PIPELINES = {'properties.pipelines.tidyup.TidyUp': 100 }
```

The number `100` on preceding `dict` defines the order in which pipelines are going to be connected. If another pipeline has a smaller number, it will process `Items` prior to this pipeline.

> The full code for this example is in the `ch08/properties` folder on GitHub.

We are now ready to run our spider:

```
$ scrapy crawl easy -s CLOSESPIDER_ITEMCOUNT=90
...
INFO: Enabled item pipelines: TidyUp
...
DEBUG: Scraped from <200 ...property_000060.html>
...
    'date': ['2015-11-08T14:47:04.148968'],
```

As we expected, the date is now formatted as an ISO string.

Signals

Signals provide a mechanism to add callbacks to events that happen in the system, such as when a spider opens, or when an `item` gets scraped. You can hook to them using the `crawler.signals.connect()` method (an example of using it can be found in the next section). There are just 11 of them and maybe the easiest way to understand them is to see them in action. I created a project where I created an extension that hooks to every available signal. I also created one Item Pipeline, one Downloader and one spider middleware, which also logs every method invocation. The spider it uses is very simple. It just yields two items and then raises an exception:

```
def parse(self, response):
    for i in range(2):
        item = HooksasyncItem()
        item['name'] = "Hello %d" % i
        yield item
    raise Exception("dead")
```

On the second item, I've configured the Item Pipeline to raise a DropItem exception.

 The full code for this example is in the ch08/hooksasync folder on GitHub.

Using this project, we can get a better understanding of when certain signals get sent. Take a look at the comments between the log lines of the following execution (lines have been omitted for brevity):

```
$ scrapy crawl test
... many lines ...
# First we get those two signals...
INFO: Extension, signals.spider_opened fired
INFO: Extension, signals.engine_started fired
# Then for each URL we get a request_scheduled signal
INFO: Extension, signals.request_scheduled fired
...# when download completes we get response_downloaded
INFO: Extension, signals.response_downloaded fired
INFO: DownloaderMiddlewareprocess_response called for example.com
# Work between response_downloaded and response_received
INFO: Extension, signals.response_received fired
INFO: SpiderMiddlewareprocess_spider_input called for example.com
# here our parse() method gets called... and then SpiderMiddleware used
INFO: SpiderMiddlewareprocess_spider_output called for example.com
# For every Item that goes through pipelines successfully...
INFO: Extension, signals.item_scraped fired
# For every Item that gets dropped using the DropItem exception...
INFO: Extension, signals.item_dropped fired
# If your spider throws something else...
INFO: Extension, signals.spider_error fired
# ... the above process repeats for each URL
# ... till we run out of them. then...
INFO: Extension, signals.spider_idle fired
# by hooking spider_idle you can schedule further Requests. If you don't
# the spider closes.
```

```
INFO: Closing spider (finished)
INFO: Extension, signals.spider_closed fired
# ... stats get printed
# and finally engine gets stopped.
INFO: Extension, signals.engine_stopped fired
```

It may feel a bit limited to have just 11 signals, but every Scrapy default middleware is implemented using just them, so they must be sufficient. Please note that from every signal except `spider_idle`, `spider_error`, `request_scheduled`, `response_received`, and `response_downloaded`, you can also return deferreds instead of actual values.

Example 2 - an extension that measures throughput and latencies

It's interesting to measure how throughput (in items per second) and latencies (time since schedule and time after download) change as we add pipelines in *Chapter 9, Pipeline Recipes*.

There is already a Scrapy extension that measures throughput, the Log Stats extension (`scrapy/extensions/logstats.py` in scrapy's GitHub), and we use it as a starting point. In order to measure latencies, we hook the `request_scheduled`, `response_received`, and `item_scraped` signals. We timestamp each and subtract the appropriate to calculate latencies that we accumulated to calculate averages. By observing the callback arguments that these signals provide, we notice something annoying. `item_scraped` gets just `Responses`, `request_scheduled` gets just the `Requests`, and `response_received` gets both. Luckily, we don't have to do any hacking to pass-through values. Every `Response` has a `Request` member, which points back to its `Request` and even better it has `meta dict` that we saw in *Chapter 5, Quick Spider Recipes*, which is the same as the original `Requests`' no matter if there were any redirects. Excellent, we can store our timestamps there!

> Actually, this wasn't my idea. The same mechanism is used by the AutoThrottle extension (`scrapy/extensions/throttle.py`)—using `request.meta.get('download_latency')` where `download_latency` is calculated by the `scrapy/core/downloader/webclient.py` downloader. The fastest way to improve at writing middlewares is by familiarizing yourself with Scrapy's default middlewares' code.

Here is the code for our extension:

```
class Latencies(object):
    @classmethod
    def from_crawler(cls, crawler):
        return cls(crawler)

    def __init__(self, crawler):
        self.crawler = crawler
        self.interval = crawler.settings.getfloat('LATENCIES_INTERVAL')
            if not self.interval:
                raise NotConfigured
        cs = crawler.signals
        cs.connect(self._spider_opened, signal=signals.spider_opened)
        cs.connect(self._spider_closed, signal=signals.spider_closed)
        cs.connect(self._request_scheduled, signal=signals.request_
scheduled)
        cs.connect(self._response_received, signal=signals.response_
received)
        cs.connect(self._item_scraped, signal=signals.item_scraped)
        self.latency, self.proc_latency, self.items = 0, 0, 0

    def _spider_opened(self, spider):
        self.task = task.LoopingCall(self._log, spider)
        self.task.start(self.interval)

    def _spider_closed(self, spider, reason):
        if self.task.running:
            self.task.stop()

    def _request_scheduled(self, request, spider):
        request.meta['schedule_time'] = time()
    def _response_received(self, response, request, spider):
        request.meta['received_time'] = time()
    def _item_scraped(self, item, response, spider):
        self.latency += time() - response.meta['schedule_time']
        self.proc_latency += time() - response.meta['received_time']
        self.items += 1
    def _log(self, spider):
        irate = float(self.items) / self.interval
        latency = self.latency / self.items if self.items else 0
```

```
      proc latency = self.proc_latency / self.items if self.items else 0
      spider.logger.info(("Scraped %d items at %.1f items/s, avg
  latency: "
          "%.2f s and avg time in pipelines: %.2f s") %
          (self.items, irate, latency, proc_latency))
      self.latency, self.proc_latency, self.items = 0, 0, 0
```

The first two methods are very important because they are very typical. They initialize the middleware using a `Crawler` object. You will find such code on almost every nontrivial middleware. `from_crawler(cls, crawler)` is the way of grabbing the `Crawler` object. Then, we notice in the __init__() method accessing `crawler.settings` and raise a `NotConfigured` exception if it isn't set. You will see many `FooBar` extensions checking the corresponding `FOOBAR_ENABLED` setting and raise if it isn't set or if it's `False`. This is a very common pattern allowing middleware to be included for convenience in the corresponding `settings.py` settings (for example, `ITEM PIPELINES`) but being disabled by default, unless explicitly enabled by their corresponding flag settings. Many default Scrapy middleware (for example, AutoThrottle or HttpCache) use this pattern. In our case, our extension remains disabled unless `LATENCIES_INTERVAL` is set.

A bit later in __init__(), we find ourselves registering callbacks for all the signals we are interested in using `crawler.signals.connect()`, and we initialize a few member variables. The rest of the class implements signal handlers. On _spider_opened(), we initialize a timer that calls our _log() method every `LATENCIES_INTERVAL` seconds, and on _spider_closed(), we stop that timer. In _request_scheduled() and _response_received(), we store timestamps in `request.meta`, and in _item_scraped(), we accumulate the two latencies (from scheduled/received until now) and increase the number of `Items` scraped. Our _log() method calculates a few averages, formats and prints a message, and resets the accumulators to start another sampling period.

Whoever has written something similar in a multithreaded context will appreciate the absence of mutexes in the preceding code. They may not be particularly complicated in this case, but still, writing single-threaded code is easier and scales well in more complex scenarios.

We can add this extension's code in a `latencies.py` module at the same level as `settings.py`. To enable it, we add two lines in our `settings.py`:

```
EXTENSIONS = { 'properties.latencies.Latencies': 500, }
LATENCIES_INTERVAL = 5
```

We can run it as usual:

```
$ pwd
/root/book/ch08/properties
$ scrapy crawl easy -s CLOSESPIDER_ITEMCOUNT=1000 -s LOG_LEVEL=INFO
...
INFO: Crawled 0 pages (at 0 pages/min), scraped 0 items (at 0 items/min)
INFO: Scraped 0 items at 0.0 items/sec, average latency: 0.00 sec and
average time in pipelines: 0.00 sec
INFO: Scraped 115 items at 23.0 items/s, avg latency: 0.84 s and avg time
in pipelines: 0.12 s
INFO: Scraped 125 items at 25.0 items/s, avg latency: 0.78 s and avg time
in pipelines: 0.12 s
```

The first log line comes from the Log Stats extension, while subsequent ones come from our extension. We can see a throughput of 24 items per second, an average overall latency of 0.78 sec, and that we are spending almost no time processing after download. Little's law gives the number of items in our system as $N = S \cdot T = 43 \cdot 0.45 \cong 19$. No matter what we set the CONCURRENT_REQUESTS and CONCURRENT_REQUESTS_PER_DOMAIN settings to, despite us not hitting 100% CPU, we don't seem to be able to make it go above 30 for some weird reason. More on this in *Chapter 10, Understanding Scrapy's Performance*.

Extending beyond middlewares

This section is here for the curious reader more than the practitioner. You certainly don't need to know these in order to write basic/intermediate Scrapy extensions.

If you have a look at `scrapy/settings/default_settings.py` you will see quite a few class names among the default settings. Scrapy extensively uses a dependency-injection-like mechanism that allows us to customize and extend many of its internal objects. For example, one may want to support more protocols for URLs beyond file, HTTP, HTTPS, S3, and FTP that are defined in the `DOWNLOAD_HANDLERS_BASE` setting. To do so, one has to just create a Download Handler class and add a mapping in the `DOWNLOAD_HANDLERS` setting. The most difficult part is to discover what the interface for your custom classes must be (that is, which methods to implement) because most interfaces aren't explicit. You have to read the source code and see how these classes get used. Your best bet is starting with an existing implementation and altering it to your satisfaction. That said, these interfaces become more and more stable with recent versions of Scrapy, and I attempt to document them along with some core Scrapy classes on the following diagram (I omit the middleware hierarchy that was presented earlier).

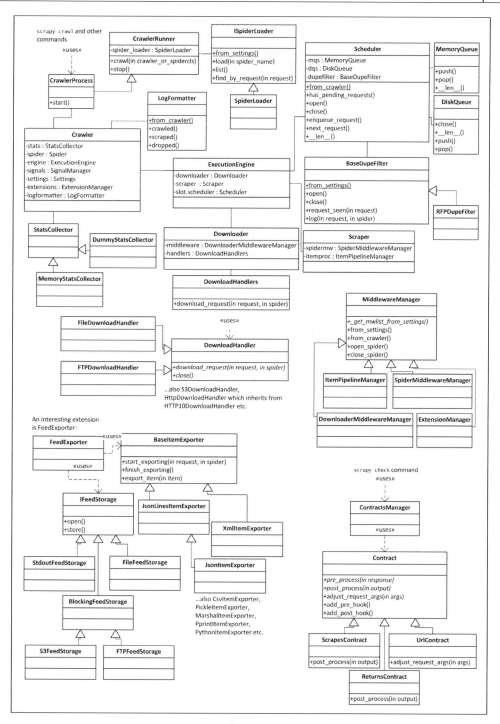

Scrapy interfaces and core objects

The core objects are in the upper-left corner. When someone uses `scrapy crawl`, a `CrawlerProcess` object is used to create our familiar `Crawler` object. The `Crawler` object is the most important Scrapy class. It holds `settings`, `signals`, and our `spider`. It also holds all the extensions in an `ExtensionManager` object named `extensions`. `crawler.engine` leads us to another very important class, `ExecutionEngine`. This holds `Scheduler`, `Downloader`, and `Scraper`. URLs get scheduled by `Scheduler`, downloaded by `Downloader`, and postprocessed by `Scraper`. It's no wonder that `Downloader` keeps `DownloaderMiddleware` and `DownloadHandler`, while `Scraper` holds both `SpiderMiddleware` and `ItemPipeline`. The four `MiddlewareManager` have their own little hierarchy. Output feeds in Scrapy are implemented as an extension; `FeedExporter`. It uses two independent hierarchies, one defining output formats and the other the storage types. This allows us, by adjusting output URLs, to export to anything from XML files in S3 to Pickle-encoded output on the console. Both hierarchies can also be extended independently using the `FEED_STORAGES` and `FEED_EXPORTERS` settings. Finally contracts that are used by the `scrapy check` command have their own hierarchy and can be extended using the `SPIDER_CONTRACTS` setting.

Summary

Congratulations, you just completed a quite in-depth introduction to Scrapy and Twisted programming. You will likely go through this chapter a few times and use it as a reference. By far, the most popular extension that one needs is Item Processing Pipelines. We will see how to solve many common problems using them in the next chapter.

9
Pipeline Recipes

In the previous chapter, we explored the programming techniques that we use to write Scrapy middlewares. In this chapter, we will focus on writing correct and efficient pipelines by showcasing various common use cases, including consuming REST APIs, interfacing with databases, performing CPU-intensive tasks, and interfacing with legacy services.

For this chapter, we will use several new servers that you can see on the right-hand side of the following diagram:

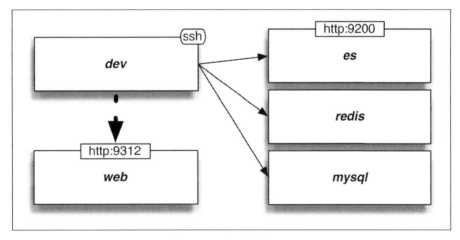

The system for this chapter

Vagrant should have already set them up for us, and we should be able to ping them from dev using their hostname, such as `ping es` or `ping mysql`. Without further ado, let's start exploring using REST APIs.

Using REST APIs

REST is a set of technologies that is used to create modern web services. Its main benefit is that it is simpler and more lightweight than SOAP or proprietary web-service mechanisms. Software designers observed a similarity between the **CRUD (Create, Read, Update, Delete)** functionality that web services often provide and basic HTTP operations (GET, POST, PUT, DELETE). They also observed that much of the information that is required for a typical web-service call could be compacted on a resource URL. For example, `http://api.mysite.com/customer/john` is a resource URL that allows us to identify the target server (`api.mysite.com`), the fact that I'm trying to perform operations related to `customers` (table) in that server, and more specifically something that has to do with someone named `john` (row — primary key). This, when combined with other web concepts, such as secure authentication, being stateless, caching, XML or JSON as payload, and so on, provides a powerful yet simple, familiar, and effortlessly cross-platform way to provide and consume web services. It's no wonder that REST took the software industry by storm.

It's quite common some of the functionality that we want to use in a Scrapy pipeline to be provided in the form of a REST API. In the following sections, we will understand how to access such functionality.

Using treq

`treq` is a Python package that tries to be the equivalent of the Python `requests` package for Twisted-based applications. It allows us to perform GET, POST, and other HTTP requests easily. To install it, we use `pip install treq`, but it's already preinstalled in our dev.

We prefer `treq` over Scrapy's `Request`/`crawler.engine.download()` API because it is equally simple, but it has performance benefits as we will see in *Chapter 10, Understanding Scrapy's Performance*.

A pipeline that writes to Elasticsearch

We will start with a spider that writes `Items` on an **ES (Elasticsearch)** server. You may feel that starting with ES — even before MySQL — as a persistence mechanism is a bit unusual, but it's actually the easiest thing one can do. ES can be schema-less, which means that we can use it without any configuration. `treq` is also sufficient for our (very simple) use case. If we need more advanced ES functionality, we should consider using `txes2` and other Python/Twisted ES packages.

With our vagrant machine, we already have an ES server running. Let's log in on our dev and verify that it's running fine:

```
$ curl http://es:9200
{
  "name" : "Living Brain",
  "cluster_name" : "elasticsearch",
  "version" : { ... },
  "tagline" : "You Know, for Search"
}
```

We should be able to see the same results by visiting `http://localhost:9200` in our host's browser. If we visit `http://localhost:9200/properties/property/_ search`, we will see a response indicating that ES globally tried but didn't find any index related to properties. Congratulations, we have just used ES's REST API.

> In the course of this chapter, we are going to insert properties in the properties collection. You will likely need to reset the properties collection, and you can do this with `curl` and a DELETE request:
>
> `$ curl -XDELETE http://es:9200/properties`

The full code of the pipeline implementations for this chapter have extra details such as more extensive error handling, but I will keep the code here simple by highlighting the key points.

> You can download the source code of this book from GitHub: `git clone https://github.com/scalingexcellence/scrapybook` This chapter is in the `ch09` directory and this example in particular is in `ch09/properties/properties/pipelines/es.py`.

In essence, this spider consists of just four lines of code:

```
@defer.inlineCallbacks
def process_item(self, item, spider):
    data = json.dumps(dict(item), ensure_ascii=False).encode("utf-
8")
    yield treq.post(self.es_url, data)
```

The first two lines define a standard `process_item()` method that is able to `yield` `Deferred`s (refer to *Chapter 8, Programming Scrapy*).

The third line prepares our `data` for insertion. We first convert our `Items` to `dicts`. We then encode them in the JSON format using `json.dumps()`. `ensure_ascii=False` makes the output more compact by not escaping non-ASCII characters. We then encode these JSON strings to UTF-8, the default encoding according to the JSON standard.

The last line uses the `post()` method of `treq` to perform a POST request that inserts our documents in ElasticSearch. `es_url`, such as `http://es:9200/properties/property` is stored in our `settings.py` file (the `ES_PIPELINE_URL` setting), and it provides essential information, such as the IP and port of our ES server (`es:9200`), the collection name (`properties`), and the object type (`property`) that we want to write to.

In order to enable the pipeline, we have to add it on an `ITEM_PIPELINES` setting inside `settings.py` and initialize our `ES_PIPELINE_URL` setting:

```
ITEM_PIPELINES = {
    'properties.pipelines.tidyup.TidyUp': 100,
    'properties.pipelines.es.EsWriter': 800,
}
ES_PIPELINE_URL = 'http://es:9200/properties/property'
```

After doing so, we can go to the appropriate directory:

```
$ pwd
/root/book/ch09/properties
$ ls
properties   scrapy.cfg
```

Then we can run our spider:

```
$ scrapy crawl easy -s CLOSESPIDER_ITEMCOUNT=90
...
INFO: Enabled item pipelines: EsWriter...
INFO: Closing spider (closespider_itemcount)...
   'item_scraped_count': 106,
```

If we now visit `http://localhost:9200/properties/property/_search`, we will be able to see the number of inserted items in the `hits/total` field of the response as well as the first 10 results. We can also add a `?size=100` parameter to get more results. By adding the `q=` argument in the search URL, we can search for specific keywords everywhere or just in certain fields. More relevant results will appear first. For example, `http://localhost:9200/properties/property/_search?q=title:london` gives us properties with "London" in their title. For more complex queries, one can consult ES's documentation at `https://www.elastic.co/guide/en/elasticsearch/reference/current/query-dsl-query-string-query.html`.

ES needed no configuration because it auto-detects the schema (types of fields) from the first property that we provide it. By visiting `http://localhost:9200/properties/`, one is able to see the mappings that it has auto-detected.

Let's have a quick look at performance and rerun a `scrapy crawl easy -s CLOSESPIDER_ITEMCOUNT=1000` as we did at the end of the last chapter. The average latency jumped from 0.78 seconds to 0.81 seconds due to the average time in pipelines increasing from 0.12 seconds to 0.15 seconds. The throughput remains the same ~25 items per second.

> Is it a great idea to use pipelines to insert Items in our datebases? The answer is no. Usually, databases provide orders of magnitude more efficient ways to bulk insert entries, and we should definitely use them instead. This would mean bulking Items and batch inserting them or performing inserts as a post-processing step at the end of a crawl. We will see such approaches in our last chapter. Still, many people use item pipelines to insert to databases and using Twisted APIs instead of generic/blocking ones is the right way to implement this approach.

A pipeline that geocodes using the Google Geocoding API

We have area names for our properties, and we would like to geocode them, that is, find their respective coordinates (latitude, longitude). We can use these coordinates to put properties on maps or order search results according to their distance from a location. Building such functionality requires complex databases, sophisticated text matching, and complex spatial computations. Using the Google Geocoding API, we can avoid developing any of these. Let's try this by opening it in a browser or using `curl` to retrieve data for the following URL:

```
$ curl "https://maps.googleapis.com/maps/api/geocode/json?sensor=false&address=london"
{
    "results" : [
        ...
        "formatted_address" : "London, UK",
        "geometry" : {
            ...
            "location" : {
                "lat" : 51.5073509,
                "lng" : -0.1277583
```

```
            },
            "location_type" : "APPROXIMATE",
            ...
    ],
    "status" : "OK"
}
```

We can see a JSON object, and if we search for "location", we will quickly find the coordinates of what Google considers the center of London. If we keep searching, we will see that there are other locations in the same document. The first one is the most relevant. As a result, results[0].geometry.location, if it exists, has the information we need.

The Google Geocoding API is accessible using the same techniques as before (treq). With just a few lines, we can find the location of an address (look at geo.py in the pipelines directory) as follows:

```
@defer.inlineCallbacks
def geocode(self, address):
    endpoint = 'http://web:9312/maps/api/geocode/json'

    parms = [('address', address), ('sensor', 'false')]
    response = yield treq.get(endpoint, params=parms)
    content = yield response.json()

    geo = content['results'][0]["geometry"]["location"]
    defer.returnValue({"lat": geo["lat"], "lon": geo["lng"]})
```

This function forms a URL that is similar to the one we used before, but we now point to a fake implementation that makes execution faster, less intrusive, available offline, and more predictable. You can use endpoint = 'https://maps.googleapis.com/maps/api/geocode/json' to hit Google's servers, but please keep in mind that they have strict limits on the requests they allow. The address and the sensor values are URL-encoded automatically using the params argument of treq's get() method. treq.get() returns a deferred, and we yield it in order to resume when a response is available. A second yield, now on response.json(), is required for us to wait until response's body is completely loaded and parsed into Python objects. At this point, we find the location information of the first result, format it as a dict, and return it using defer.returnValue() - the appropriate way to return values from methods that use inlineCallbacks. If anything goes wrong, the method throws exceptions that Scrapy reports to us.

By using geocode(), process_item() becomes a single line as follows:

```
item["location"] = yield self.geocode(item["address"][0])
```

Let's enable this pipeline by adding it to our settings' ITEM_PIPELINES with a priority number that is smaller than ES's so that ES gets our location values:

```
ITEM_PIPELINES = {
    ...
    'properties.pipelines.geo.GeoPipeline': 400,
```

Let's run a quick crawl with debug data enabled:

```
$ scrapy crawl easy -s CLOSESPIDER_ITEMCOUNT=90 -L DEBUG
...
{'address': [u'Greenwich, London'],
...
 'image_urls': [u'http://web:9312/images/i06.jpg'],
 'location': {'lat': 51.482577, 'lon': -0.007659},
 'price': [1030.0],
...
```

We can now see the location field set for our Items. This is great! If we temporarily run it using the real Google API's URL though, we will soon get exceptions like this:

```
File "pipelines/geo.py" in geocode (content['status'], address))
Exception: Unexpected status="OVER_QUERY_LIMIT" for
address="*London"
```

This is a check that we've put in place in the full code to ensure that the status field of the Geocoding API's response has the OK value. Unless that's true, the data that we get back won't have the format we expect and can't be safely used. In this case, we get the OVER_QUERY_LIMIT status, which clearly indicates that we did something wrong. This is an important problem that we will likely face in many cases. With Scrapy's high performance engine, being able to cache and throttle requests to resources becomes a necessity.

We can visit the Geocoder API's documentation to read about its limits; "*Users of the free API: 2500 requests per 24 hour period, 5 requests per second*". Even if we use the paid version of the Google Geocoding API, it's also throttled at 10 requests per second, which means that this discussion is still relevant.

> The implementations that follow may look complex, but they have to be judged in context. Creating such components in a typical multithreaded environment would require thread pools and synchronization that leads to quite complex code.

Here is a simple and good enough implementation of a throttling engine using Twisted's techniques:

```python
class Throttler(object):
    def __init__(self, rate):
        self.queue = []
        self.looping_call = task.LoopingCall(self._allow_one)
        self.looping_call.start(1. / float(rate))

    def stop(self):
        self.looping_call.stop()

    def throttle(self):
        d = defer.Deferred()
        self.queue.append(d)
        return d

    def _allow_one(self):
        if self.queue:
            self.queue.pop(0).callback(None)
```

This allows us to enqueue Deferreds in a list and fire them one by one each time that `_allow_one()` gets called; `_allow_one()` checks whether the queue is empty and if it's not, it calls the `callback()` of the oldest deferred (FIFO). We call `_allow_one()` periodically using Twisted's `task.LoopingCall()` API. It's easy to use `Throttler`. We initialize it in our pipeline's `__init__` and clean it up when our spider stops:

```python
class GeoPipeline(object):
    def __init__(self, stats):
        self.throttler = Throttler(5)  # 5 Requests per second

    def close_spider(self, spider):
        self.throttler.stop()
```

Just before we use the resource that we want to throttle (in our case calling `geocode()` in `process_item()`), we `yield` throttler's `throttle()` method:

```python
yield self.throttler.throttle()
item["location"] = yield self.geocode(item["address"][0])
```

On the first `yield`, the code will pause and will resume after sufficient time elapses. For example, if at some point there are 11 deferreds queued, and we have a rate limit of five requests per second, our code will resume after the queue empties in about $11/5 = 2.2$ seconds.

Using `Throttler`, we no longer get errors but our spider is dead slow. We observe that our demo properties have just a few distinct locations. This is a great opportunity for caching. We could use a simple Python `dict` to do this, but we would get race conditions, which cause spurious API calls. Here is a cache that doesn't have this problem and demonstrates some interesting features of Python and Twisted:

```
class DeferredCache(object):
    def __init__(self, key_not_found_callback):
        self.records = {}
        self.deferreds_waiting = {}
        self.key_not_found_callback = key_not_found_callback

    @defer.inlineCallbacks
    def find(self, key):
        rv = defer.Deferred()

        if key in self.deferreds_waiting:
            self.deferreds_waiting[key].append(rv)
        else:
            self.deferreds_waiting[key] = [rv]

            if not key in self.records:
                try:
                    value = yield self.key_not_found_callback(key)
                    self.records[key] = lambda d: d.callback(value)
                except Exception as e:
                    self.records[key] = lambda d: d.errback(e)

            action = self.records[key]
            for d in self.deferreds_waiting.pop(key):
                reactor.callFromThread(action, d)

        value = yield rv
        defer.returnValue(value)
```

This cache looks a bit different to what one would typically expect. It consists of two components:

- `self.deferreds_waiting`: This is a queue of deferreds that wait for a value for a given key

- `self.records`: This is a `dict` with already seen key-action pairs

If we look at the middle of the find() implementation, we observe that if we don't find a key in self.records, we call a predefined callback function to retrieve the missing value (yield self.key_not_found_callback(key)). This callback function may throw an exception. How do we store values or exceptions in a compact way in Python? Since Python is a functional language, we store little functions (lambdas) that call either deferred's callback or errback in self.records depending on whether there was an exception or not. The value or the exception gets attached to the lambda function while defining it. This attachment of variables to functions is called closure and is one of the most distinctive and powerful features of most functional programming languages.

 It's a bit unusual to cache exceptions, but this means that if you look up a key for first time and key_not_found_callback(key) throws an exception, the same exception will be rethrown in any subsequent lookup for the same key without performing extra calls.

The rest of the find() implementation provides us with a mechanism that helps us avoid race conditions. If the lookup for a key is already in process, there will be a record in the self.deferreds_waiting dict. In this case, we don't make another call to key_not_found_callback(), but we just add ourselves to the list of deferreds waiting for that key. When key_not_found_callback() returns and the value for this key becomes available, we fire every deferred that is waiting for this key. We could directly perform action(d) instead of using reactor.callFromThread(), but then we would have to handle any exceptions that are thrown downstream, and we would create unnecessary long deferred chains.

It's very easy to use this cache. We initialize it in __init__() and set the callback function as one that performs the API call. In process_item(), we look up using the cache as follows:

```python
def __init__(self, stats):
    self.cache = DeferredCache(self.cache_key_not_found_callback)

@defer.inlineCallbacks
def cache_key_not_found_callback(self, address):
    yield self.throttler.enqueue()
    value = yield self.geocode(address)
    defer.returnValue(value)

@defer.inlineCallbacks
def process_item(self, item, spider):
    item["location"] = yield self.cache.find(item["address"][0])
    defer.returnValue(item)
```

The code in Git contains some more error handling code, retries calls in case of failure due to throttling (a simple `while` loop), and also contains code that updates spider's statistics.

 The full code for this example is in `ch09/properties/properties/pipelines/geo2.py`.

In order to enable this pipeline, we disable (comment out) our previous implementation and add this to `ITEM_PIPELINES` in `settings.py` as follows:

```
ITEM_PIPELINES = {
    'properties.pipelines.tidyup.TidyUp': 100,
    'properties.pipelines.es.EsWriter': 800,
    # DISABLE 'properties.pipelines.geo.GeoPipeline': 400,
    'properties.pipelines.geo2.GeoPipeline': 400,
}
```

We can then run the spider with the following code:

```
$ scrapy crawl easy -s CLOSESPIDER_ITEMCOUNT=1000
...
Scraped... 15.8 items/s, avg latency: 1.74 s and avg time in pipelines:
0.94 s
Scraped... 32.2 items/s, avg latency: 1.76 s and avg time in pipelines:
0.97 s
Scraped... 25.6 items/s, avg latency: 0.76 s and avg time in pipelines:
0.14 s
...
: Dumping Scrapy stats:...
   'geo_pipeline/misses': 35,
   'item_scraped_count': 1019,
```

We will observe that the latency of crawling starts high while populating the cache, but then, it reverts to its previous values. Statistics also indicate 35 misses, which is the exact number of different locations that are used in the demo dataset. Obviously, there were *1019 - 35= 984* hits in the case above. If we use the real Google API and increase the allowed number of API requests per second slightly, for example from 5 to 10 by changing `Throttler(5)` to `Throttler(10)`, we will get retries recorded in the `geo_pipeline/retries` stat. If there are any errors, for example, if a location can't be found using the API, an exception will be thrown, and this is captured in the `geo_pipeline/errors` stat. If the location somehow (we will see how in later sections) is already set, it will be indicated in the `geo_pipeline/already_set` stat. Finally, if we check ES for properties by navigating to `http://localhost:9200/properties/property/_search`, we will see entries with location values, such as `{..."location": {"lat": 51.5269736, "lon": -0.0667204}...}`, as expected (make sure you don't see old values by clearing the collection before your run).

Enabling geoindexing on Elasticsearch

Now that we have locations, we can, for example, sort the results by distance. Here is an HTTP POST request (done using `curl`) that returns properties that have "Angel" in their title and are sorted by their distance from the point {51.54, -0.19}:

```
$ curl http://es:9200/properties/property/_search -d '{
    "query" : {"term" : { "title" : "angel" } },
    "sort": [{"_geo_distance": {
        "location":       {"lat":  51.54, "lon": -0.19},
        "order":          "asc",
        "unit":           "km",
        "distance_type": "plane"
}}]}'
```

The only problem is that if we try to run it, we will see it failing with a `"failed to find mapper for [location] for geo distance based sort"` error message. This indicates that our location field doesn't have the proper format for spatial operations. In order to set the proper type, we will have to manually override the defaults. First, we save the autodetected mapping in a file as a starting point:

```
$ curl 'http://es:9200/properties/_mapping/property' > property.txt
```

Then we edit `property.txt` as follows:

```
"location":{"properties":{"lat":{"type":"double"},"lon":{"type":"d
ouble"}}}
```

We replace this line of code with the following one:

```
"location": {"type": "geo_point"}
```

We also delete `{"properties":{"mappings":` and two `}}` at the end of the file. We are then done with the file. We can now delete the old type and create a new one with our explicit schema as follows:

```
$ curl -XDELETE 'http://es:9200/properties'
```

```
$ curl -XPUT 'http://es:9200/properties'
```

```
$ curl -XPUT 'http://es:9200/properties/_mapping/property' --data
@property.txt
```

We can now rerun a quick crawl, and we will be able to run the `curl` command that we saw earlier in this section and get results sorted by distance. Our search returns JSONs with properties with an extra `sort` field with its distance from the search point in km.

Interfacing databases with standard Python clients

There are many important databases, including MySQL, PostgreSQL, Oracle, Microsoft SQL Server, and SQLite, that adhere to the Python Database API Specification 2.0. Their drivers are often complex and very well tested, and it would be a big waste if they had to be reimplemented for Twisted. One can use these database clients in Twisted applications, such as Scrapy using the `twisted.enterprise.adbapi` library. We will use MySQL as an example to demonstrate its usage, but the same principles apply to any other compliant database.

A pipeline that writes to MySQL

MySQL is a great and very popular database. We will write a pipeline that writes items to it. We already have a MySQL instance running on our virtual environment. We will need to perform some basic administration using the MySQL command-line tool, which is also preinstalled on our dev machine, as follows:

```
$ mysql -h mysql -uroot -ppass
```

We will get a MySQL prompt indicated by `mysql>`, and we can now create a simple database table with a few fields, as follows:

```
mysql> create database properties;
mysql> use properties
mysql> CREATE TABLE properties (
  url varchar(100) NOT NULL,
  title varchar(30),
  price DOUBLE,
  description varchar(30),
  PRIMARY KEY (url)
);
mysql> SELECT * FROM properties LIMIT 10;
Empty set (0.00 sec)
```

Great, now that we have a MySQL database and a table named `properties` with a few fields, we are ready to create our pipeline. Keep the MySQL console open as we will get back to it in a bit to check whether the values were inserted. In case we need to exit it, we just type `exit`.

 In the course of this section, we are going to insert properties in the MySQL database. If you need to erase them, use the following command:

```
mysql> DELETE FROM properties;
```

We will use the MySQL client for Python. We will also install a little utility module that is named `dj-database-url` to help us parse connection URLs (it just saves us from having distinct settings for IP, port, password, and so on.) We can install these two using `pip install dj-database-url MySQL-python`, but we have them already installed in our dev environment. Our MySQL pipeline is very simple, as follows:

```python
from twisted.enterprise import adbapi
...
class MysqlWriter(object):
    ...
    def __init__(self, mysql_url):
        conn_kwargs = MysqlWriter.parse_mysql_url(mysql_url)
        self.dbpool = adbapi.ConnectionPool('MySQLdb',
                                            charset='utf8',
                                            use_unicode=True,
                                            connect_timeout=5,
                                            **conn_kwargs)

    def close_spider(self, spider):
        self.dbpool.close()

    @defer.inlineCallbacks
    def process_item(self, item, spider):
        try:
            yield self.dbpool.runInteraction(self.do_replace, item)
        except:
            print traceback.format_exc()

        defer.returnValue(item)

    @staticmethod
    def do_replace(tx, item):
        sql = """REPLACE INTO properties (url, title, price,
```

```
description) VALUES (%s,%s,%s,%s)"""

args = (
    item["url"][0][:100],
    item["title"][0][:30],
    item["price"][0],
    item["description"][0].replace("\r\n", " ")[:30]
)

tx.execute(sql, args)
```

 The full code for this example is in ch09/properties/
properties/pipelines/mysql.py.

Essentially, most of it is boilerplate spider code. The code that we have omitted for brevity parses a URL in the format mysql://user:pass@ip/database that is contained in the MYSQL_PIPELINE_URL setting to individual arguments. In our spider's __init__(), we pass them to adbapi.ConnectionPool(), which uses the infrastructure of adbapi to initialize a MySQL connection pool. The first argument is the name of the module that we want to import. In our MySQL case, this is MySQLdb. We set a few extra arguments for the MySQL client to properly handle Unicode and timeouts. All these arguments go to the underlying MySQLdb.connect() function every time adbapi needs to open new connections. On spider close, we call the close() method for that pool.

Our process_item() method essentially wraps dbpool.runInteraction(). This method queues a callback method that will be called at some later point when a Transaction object from one of the connections in the connection pool becomes available. The Transaction object has an API that is similar to a DB-API cursor. In our case, the callback method is do_replace(), which is defined a few lines later. @staticmethod means that the method refers to the class and not a specific class instance, thus, we can omit the usual self argument. It's good practice to make methods static if they don't use any members, but even if you forget it, it's okay. This method prepares a SQL string, a few arguments, and calls the execute() method of Transaction to perform the insertion. Our SQL uses REPLACE INTO instead of the more common INSERT INTO to replace existing entries with the same primary key if they already exist. This is convenient in our case. If we wanted to use SQL that returns data, such as the SELECT statements, we would use dbpool.runQuery(), and we may want to change the default cursor that is used by setting the cursorclass argument of adbapi.ConnectionPool() to, for example, cursorclass=MySQLdb.cursors.DictCursor as it's more convenient for data retrieval.

In order to use this pipeline, we have to add it in our ITEM_PIPELINES dict in settings.py, as well as set the MYSQL_PIPELINE_URL appropriately:

```
ITEM_PIPELINES = { ...
    'properties.pipelines.mysql.MysqlWriter': 700,
...
MYSQL_PIPELINE_URL = 'mysql://root:pass@mysql/properties'
```

Execute the following command:

```
scrapy crawl easy -s CLOSESPIDER_ITEMCOUNT=1000
```

After running this command, we can go back to the MySQL prompt and see the records on the database as follows:

```
mysql> SELECT COUNT(*) FROM properties;
+----------+
|     1006 |
+----------+
mysql> SELECT * FROM properties LIMIT 4;
+-----------------+--------------------------+--------+-------------+
| url             | title                    | price  | description |
+-----------------+--------------------------+--------+-------------+
| http://...0.html | Set Unique Family Well   | 334.39 | website c   |
| http://...1.html | Belsize Marylebone Shopp | 388.03 | features    |
| http://...2.html | Bathroom Fully Jubilee S | 365.85 | vibrant own |
| http://...3.html | Residential Brentford Ot | 238.71 | go court    |
+-----------------+--------------------------+--------+-------------+
4 rows in set (0.00 sec)
```

The performance, both latency and throughput, remains exactly the same as before. This is quite impressive.

Interfacing services using Twisted-specific clients

Until now, we saw how to use REST-like APIs using treq. Scrapy can interface with many other services using Twisted-specific clients. For example, if we want to interface MongoDB, and we search for "MongoDB Python", we will get PyMongo, which is blocking/synchronous and shouldn't be used with Twisted unless we use threads as described in the pipeline that handle blocking operations in a later section. If we search for "MongoDB Twisted Python", we get txmongo, which is perfectly fine to use with Twisted and Scrapy. Usually, the communities behind Twisted clients are smaller, but this is still a better option than writing our own client. We will use such a Twisted-specific client to interface with the Redis key-value store.

A pipeline that reads/writes to Redis

The Google Geocoding API limit is per-IP. One may have access to multiple IPs (for example, many servers) and would like to avoid making duplicate requests for addresses that another machine has already geocoded. This also applies for the addresses that one has seen recently in previous runs. We wouldn't like to waste our precious quotas.

 Talk to the API vendor to ensure that this is okay with their policies. You may have to, for example, discard cached records every few minutes/hours or caching may not be allowed at all.

We can use Redis key-value cache as, essentially, a distributed dict. We already run a Redis instance in our vagrant environment, and we should be able to connect to it and perform basic operations using redis-cli from dev:

```
$ redis-cli -h redis
redis:6379> info keyspace
# Keyspace
redis:6379> set key value
OK
redis:6379> info keyspace
# Keyspace
db0:keys=1,expires=0,avg_ttl=0
redis:6379> FLUSHALL
```

```
OK
redis:6379> info keyspace
# Keyspace
redis:6379> exit
```

By Googling "Redis Twisted", we find the `txredisapi` library. What makes it
fundamentally different is that it isn't just a wrapper around synchronous Python
libraries, but this is a proper Twisted library that connects to Redis using `reactor.
connectTCP()`, implements Twisted protocols, and so on. We use it in a similar
manner to other libraries, but it is bound to be slightly more efficient when used
in a Twisted application. We can install it along with a utility library, `dj_redis_
url`, which parses Redis configuration URLs, by using `pip` (`sudo pip install
txredisapi dj_redis_url`), and as usual, it's preinstalled in our dev.

We initialize our `RedisCache` pipeline as follows:

```
from txredisapi import lazyConnectionPool

class RedisCache(object):
...
    def __init__(self, crawler, redis_url, redis_nm):
        self.redis_url = redis_url
        self.redis_nm = redis_nm

        args = RedisCache.parse_redis_url(redis_url)
        self.connection = lazyConnectionPool(connectTimeout=5,
                                             replyTimeout=5,
                                             **args)

        crawler.signals.connect(
                self.item_scraped,signal=signals.item_scraped)
```

This pipeline is quite simple. In order to connect with a Redis server, we need the
host, port, and so on, which we all store in a URL format. We parse the format using
our `parse_redis_url()` method (omitted for brevity). It's also very common to use
a namespace that prefixes our keys, which, in our case, we store in `redis_nm`. We
then use `lazyConnectionPool()` of `txredisapi` to open a connection to the server.

The last line has an interesting function. What we're aiming to do is to wrap the geo-
pipeline with this pipeline. If we don't have a value in Redis, we won't set a value,
and our geo-pipeline will use the API to geocode the address as before. After it does
so, we have to have a way to cache these key-value pairs in Redis, and we do this
by connecting to the `signals.item_scraped` signal. The callback we define (our
`item_scraped()` method, which we will see in a bit) will be called at the very end, at
which point the location will be set.

The full code for this example is in `ch09/properties/`
`properties/pipelines/redis.py`.

We keep this cache simple by looking up and recording addresses and locations for every `Item`. This makes sense for Redis because it very often runs on the same server, which makes it very fast. If that's not the case one may want to add a `dict`-based cache that is similar to the one that we have in our geo-pipeline. This is how we process incoming Items:

```
@defer.inlineCallbacks
def process_item(self, item, spider):
    address = item["address"][0]
    key = self.redis_nm + ":" + address
    value = yield self.connection.get(key)
    if value:
        item["location"] = json.loads(value)
    defer.returnValue(item)
```

This is nothing more than one would expect. We get the address, prefix it, and look it up in Redis using `get()` of `txredisapi connection`. We store JSON-encoded objects as values in Redis. If a value is set, we use JSON to decode it and set it as a location.

When an `Item` reaches the end of all our pipelines, we recapture it in order to store to Redis location values. Here is how we do this:

```
from txredisapi import ConnectionError

def item_scraped(self, item, spider):
    try:
        location = item["location"]
        value = json.dumps(location, ensure_ascii=False)
    except KeyError:
        return

    address = item["address"][0]
    key = self.redis_nm + ":" + address
    quiet = lambda failure: failure.trap(ConnectionError)
    return self.connection.set(key, value).addErrback(quiet)
```

There are no big surprises here either. If we find a location, we get the address, prefix it and use them as keys and values for the `txredisapi` connection's `set()` methods. You will notice that this function doesn't use `@defer.inlineCallbacks` because it isn't supported while handling `signals.item_scraped`. This means that we can't use our very convenient `yield` for `connection.set()`, but what we can do is return a deferred that Scrapy will use to chain any further signal listeners. In any case, if a connection to Redis can't be made to `connection.set()`, it will throw an exception. We can ignore this exception quietly by adding a custom error handler to the deferred that `connection.set()` returns. In this error handler, we take the failures that are passed as arguments, and we tell them to `trap()` any `ConnectionError`. This is a nice feature of Twisted's `Deferred` API. By using `trap()` on the expected exceptions, we can quietly ignore them in a compact form.

To enable this pipeline, all we have to do is add it to our `ITEM_PIPELINES` settings and provide a `REDIS_PIPELINE_URL` inside `settings.py`. It is important to give this a priority value that sets it before the geo-pipeline otherwise it will be too late to be useful:

```
ITEM_PIPELINES = { ...
    'properties.pipelines.redis.RedisCache': 300,
    'properties.pipelines.geo.GeoPipeline': 400,
...
REDIS_PIPELINE_URL = 'redis://redis:6379'
```

We can run this spider as usual. The first run will be similar to before, but any subsequent run will be as follows:

```
$ scrapy crawl easy -s CLOSESPIDER_ITEMCOUNT=100
...
INFO: Enabled item pipelines: TidyUp, RedisCache, GeoPipeline,
MysqlWriter, EsWriter
...
Scraped... 0.0 items/s, avg latency: 0.00 s, time in pipelines: 0.00 s
Scraped... 21.2 items/s, avg latency: 0.78 s, time in pipelines: 0.15 s
Scraped... 24.2 items/s, avg latency: 0.82 s, time in pipelines: 0.16 s
...
INFO: Dumping Scrapy stats: {...
   'geo_pipeline/already_set': 106,
   'item_scraped_count': 106,
```

We can see that both the `GeoPipeline` and the `RedisCache` are enabled and that RedisCache comes first. Also notice in the stats `geo_pipeline/already_set:` `106`. These are items that GeoPipeline finds prepopulated from our Redis cache, and in all these cases, it won't make a Google API call. If the Redis cache is empty, you will see a few keys being handled using the Google API as expected. In terms of performance, what we observe is that the start-behavior that was induced by GeoPipeline is now gone. Indeed, as we now use the cache, we bypass the five requests per second API limit. If we use Redis, we should consider using expiring keys to make our system refresh its cached data periodically.

Interfacing CPU-intensive, blocking, or legacy functionality

This final section talks about accessing the most non-Twisted-like workloads. Despite the tremendous benefits of having efficient asynchronous code, it's neither practical nor realistic to assume that every library will be rewritten for Twisted and Scrapy. Using Twisted's thread pools and the `reactor.spawnProcess()` method, we can use any Python library and binaries that are written in any language.

A pipeline that performs CPU-intensive or blocking operations

As we highlighted in *Chapter 8, Programming Scrapy,* the reactor is ideal for short, nonblocking tasks. What can we do if we have to do something more complex or something that involves blocking? Twisted provides thread pools that can be used to execute slow operations in some thread other than the main (Twisted's reactor) using the `reactor.callInThread()` API call. This means that the reactor will keep running its processing and reacting to events while the computation takes place. Please keep in mind that processing that is happening in the thread pool isn't thread safe. This means that you have all the traditional synchronization problems of multithreaded programming when you use global state. Let's start with a simple version of this pipeline, and we will build towards the complete code:

```
class UsingBlocking(object):
    @defer.inlineCallbacks
    def process_item(self, item, spider):
        price = item["price"][0]

        out = defer.Deferred()
        reactor.callInThread(self._do_calculation, price, out)
```

```
        item["price"][0] = yield out

        defer.returnValue(item)

    def _do_calculation(self, price, out):
        new_price = price + 1
        time.sleep(0.10)
        reactor.callFromThread(out.callback, new_price)
```

In the preceding pipeline, we see the basic primitives in action. For every `Item`, we extract the price, and we want to process it using the `_do_calucation()` method. This method uses `time.sleep()`, a blocking operation. We will let it run in another thread using the `reactor.callInThread()` call. This takes the function to call as arguments and any number of arguments that pass to our function. Obviously, we pass the `price` but we also create and pass a `Deferred` that is named `out`. When our `_do_calucation()` completes its calculations, we will use the `out` callback to return the value. In the next step, we yield this `Deferred` and set the new value for the price, and we finally return the `Item`.

Inside `_do_calucation()`, we notice a trivial calculation—an increase of the price by one—and then a sleep of 100ms. That's a lot of time, and if called in the reactor thread, it would prevent us from being able to process more than 10 pages per second. By running it in another thread, we don't have this problem. Tasks will queue up in the thread pool waiting for a thread to become available and as soon as this happens, that thread will sleep for 100ms. The final step is to fire the `out` callback. Normally, we could do this using `out.callback(new_price)`, but since we are now in another thread, it's not safe to do so. If we were doing so, the code of `Deferred` and, consequently, Scrapy's functionality would be called from another thread, which would sooner or later result in corrupted data. Instead of doing this, we use `reactor.callFromThread()`, which also takes a function as argument and any number of extra arguments to be passed to our function. This function will be queued and called from the reactor thread, which in turn will unblock `process_item()` objects `yield` and resume Scrapy's operation for this `Item`.

What happens if we have global state, for example counters, moving averages, and so on, that we need to use in our `_do_calucation()`? Let's, for example, add two variables, `beta` and `delta`, as follows:

```
    class UsingBlocking(object):
        def __init__(self):
            self.beta, self.delta = 0, 0
        ...
        def _do_calculation(self, price, out):
            self.beta += 1
            time.sleep(0.001)
```

```
        self.delta += 1
        new_price = price + self.beta - self.delta + 1
        assert abs(new_price-price-1) < 0.01

        time.sleep(0.10)...
```

The preceding code is wrong and gives us assertion errors. That's because if a thread switch happens between `self.beta` and `self.delta`, and another thread resumes calculating the price using these `beta`/`delta` values, it will find them in an inconsistent state (`beta` being larger than `delta`), thus, calculate erroneous results. The short sleep makes this more likely, but even without it, the race condition would soon demonstrate itself. To prevent this from happening, we have to use a lock, for example, Python's `threading.RLock()` recursive lock. Using it, we ensure that no two threads will execute the critical section it protects at the same time:

```
    class UsingBlocking(object):
        def __init__(self):
            ...
            self.lock = threading.RLock()
        ...
        def _do_calculation(self, price, out):
            with self.lock:
                self.beta += 1
                ...
                new_price = price + self.beta - self.delta + 1

            assert abs(new_price-price-1) < 0.01 ...
```

The preceding code is now correct. Please note that we don't need to protect the entire code but just enough to cover the use of global state.

> The full code for this example is in `ch09/properties/properties/pipelines/computation.py`.

To use this pipeline, we just have to add it to the `ITEM_PIPELINES` setting inside `settings.py` as follows:

```
    ITEM_PIPELINES = { ...
        'properties.pipelines.computation.UsingBlocking': 500,
```

We can run the spider as usual. The pipeline latency jumps significantly by 100 ms, as expected, but we will surprisingly find that throughput remains exactly the same—about 25 items per second.

A pipeline that uses binaries or scripts

The most agnostic interface one can have to a piece of legacy functionality is that of a standalone executable or script. It may take a few seconds to start (for example, loading data from databases), but after that, it will likely be able to process many values with a small latency. Even in this case, Twisted has us covered. We can use the `reactor.spawnProcess()` API and the relevant `protocol.ProcessProtocol` to run executables of any kind. Let's take a look at an example. Our sample script will be as follows:

```bash
#!/bin/bash
trap "" SIGINT
sleep 3


while read line
do
    # 4 per second
    sleep 0.25
    awk "BEGIN {print 1.20 * $line}"
done
```

This is a simple bash script. As soon as it starts, it disables *Ctrl + C*. This is to overcome a peculiarity of the system that propagates *Ctrl + C* to subprocesses and terminates them prematurely causing Scrapy itself to not terminate while waiting indefinitely for a result from these processes. After disabling *Ctrl + C*, it sleeps for three seconds to emulate boot time. Then it reads lines from the input, waits 250ms, and then returns the resulting price, which is the original that is multiplied by 1.20 as calculated by the `awk` Linux command. The maximum throughput that this script could have is $1/250ms = 4$ Items per second. Let's test it with a short session as follows:

```
$ properties/pipelines/legacy.sh
12 <- If you type this quickly you will wait ~3 seconds to get results
14.40
13 <- For further numbers you will notice just a slight delay
15.60
```

As *Ctrl + C* has been deactivated, we have to terminate the session with *Ctrl + D*. Great! So, how do we use this script from Scrapy? Again, we start with a slightly simplified version:

```python
class CommandSlot(protocol.ProcessProtocol):
    def __init__(self, args):
```

```
        self._queue = []
        reactor.spawnProcess(self, args[0], args)

    def legacy_calculate(self, price):
        d = defer.Deferred()
        self._queue.append(d)
        self.transport.write("%f\n" % price)
        return d

    # Overriding from protocol.ProcessProtocol
    def outReceived(self, data):
        """Called when new output is received"""
        self._queue.pop(0).callback(float(data))

class Pricing(object):
    def __init__(self):
        self.slot = CommandSlot(['properties/pipelines/legacy.sh'])

    @defer.inlineCallbacks
    def process_item(self, item, spider):
        item["price"][0] = yield self.slot.legacy_calculate(item["price"][0])
        defer.returnValue(item)
```

We find the definitions of a `ProcessProtocol` named `CommandSlot` and our `Pricing` spider here. Inside `__init__()`, we create the new `CommandSlot`, which in its constructor initializes an empty queue and starts a new process using `reactor.spawnProcess()`. This call takes as its first argument a `ProcessProtocol` that is used to send and receive data from the process. In this case, it's `self` because `spawnProcess()` is called from within the `protocol` class. The second argument is the name of the executable. The third argument, `args`, keeps all the command-line arguments for this binary as a sequence of strings.

Inside pipeline's `process_item()`, we essentially delegate all the work in the `legacy_calculate()` method of `CommandSlot`, which returns a `Deferred` that we yield. `legacy_calculate()` creates a `Deferred`, enqueues it, and writes the price to the process using `transport.write()`. `transport` is provided by `ProcessProtocol` in order to allow us to communicate with the process. Whenever we receive data from the process, `outReceived()` gets called. By enqueuing `Deferred` and since processing from our shell script happens in order, we can just pop the oldest `Deferred` from the queue and fire it with the received value. That's all. We can enable this pipeline by adding it to `ITEM_PIPELINES` and running it as usual:

```
ITEM_PIPELINES = {...
    'properties.pipelines.legacy.Pricing': 600,
```

If we perform a run, the one thing that we will observe is that the performance is horrible. As we would expect, our process becomes a bottleneck and limits the throughput to four `Items` per second. To increase it, all we need to do is modify the pipeline slightly to allow multiple such processes to run in parallel, as follows:

```
class Pricing(object):
    def __init__(self):
        self.concurrency = 16
        args = ['properties/pipelines/legacy.sh']
        self.slots = [CommandSlot(args)
                        for i in xrange(self.concurrency)]
        self.rr = 0

    @defer.inlineCallbacks
    def process_item(self, item, spider):
        slot = self.slots[self.rr]
        self.rr = (self.rr + 1) % self.concurrency
        item["price"][0] = yield
                        slot.legacy_calculate(item["price"][0])
        defer.returnValue(item)
```

This is nothing more than starting 16 instances and sending prices in each of them in a round-robin fashion. This pipeline now provides a maximum throughput of *16*4 = 64* items per second. We can confirm it with a quick crawl as follows:

```
$ scrapy crawl easy -s CLOSESPIDER_ITEMCOUNT=1000
...
Scraped... 0.0 items/s, avg latency: 0.00 s and avg time in pipelines:
0.00 s
Scraped... 21.0 items/s, avg latency: 2.20 s and avg time in pipelines:
1.48 s
Scraped... 24.2 items/s, avg latency: 1.16 s and avg time in pipelines:
0.52 s
```

The latency, as expected, increased by 250 ms, but the throughput is still ~25 items/s.

Please keep in mind that the preceding method uses `transport.write()` to queue all the prices in this shell script's input. This may or may not be okay for your application, especially if it uses way more data than just a few numbers. The full code on Git enqueues both values and callbacks, and it doesn't send a new value to the script unless the result for the previous one has been received. You may find this way friendlier to your legacy applications, but it adds some complexity.

Summary

You just studied quite a few sophisticated Scrapy pipelines. By now, you have seen everything you may need in terms of Twisted programming, and you know how to implement complex functionality including processing, and storing Items using Item Processing Pipelines. We saw how performance changes by adding more pipeline stages in terms of latency and throughput. Usually, latency and throughput are considered inversely proportional, but this is under the assumption of constant concurrency (for example, a limited number of threads). In our case, we started with a concurrency of $N = S \cdot T = 25 \cdot 0.77 \cong 19$, and after adding pipeline stages, we ended up $N = 25 \cdot 3.33 \cong 83$ with without facing any performance problems. That's the power of Twisted programming! It's now time to move on to *Chapter 10, Understanding Scrapy's Performance,* to make perfect sense of Scrapy's performance.

10
Understanding Scrapy's Performance

Generally, it's easy to get performance wrong. With Scrapy, it's not just easy—it's almost certain because there are quite a few counterintuitive behaviors. Unless you have a good understanding of Scrapy's internals, you will find yourself working hard, optimizing performance while getting zero gains. That is part of the complexity of working with high-performance, low-latency, and highly-concurrent environments. Amdahl's law still holds true while optimizing bottleneck performance, but unless you identify the real bottleneck, optimizations on any other part of the system will not increase the number of items you scrape per second (throughput). More intuition can be gained by reading the classic *The Goal* by *Dr. Goldratt*, a business book that explains, with some excellent metaphors, the idea of the bottleneck, latency, and throughput. The same concepts hold identically true to software too. This chapter will help you identify the bottleneck on your Scrapy configuration and will help you avoid obvious mistakes.

Please keep in mind that this is a quite advanced chapter and some mathematics are involved. The calculations are simple and accompanied with diagrams and plots that demonstrate the same concepts. If you don't like math, just ignore the formulas and you will still gain a significant insight into how Scrapy's performance works.

Scrapy's engine – an intuitive approach

Parallel systems look a lot like piping systems. In computer science, we use the queue symbol to represent queues and processing elements (*Figure 1.* on the left). A fundamental law for queue systems is Little's law, which asserts that the number of elements in the queuing system (*N*) in equilibrium is equal to the throughput of the system (*T*) multiplied by the total queuing/service time (*S*); $N = T \cdot S$. The other two forms, $T = N / S$ and $S = N / T$, are also useful for calculations.

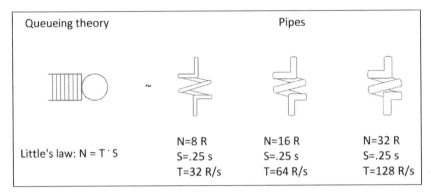

Figure 1. Little's law, queuing systems, and pipes

There's a similar law for the geometry of a pipe (*Figure 1.* on the right). The volume of a pipe (*V*) equals the length of the pipe *L* multiplied by cross-sectional area (A); $V = L \cdot A$.

If we imagine length representing service time ($L \sim S$), volume representing elements in the processing system ($V \sim N$), and across-sectional area representing throughput ($A \sim N$), then Little's law and the volume formula are the same thing.

Does this analogy make sense? The answer is almost. If we imagine units of work as small drops of liquid moving with constant speed inside the pipe, then $L \sim S$ absolutely makes sense because the longer the pipe, the more time a drop will spend in it. $V \sim N$ also makes sense because the larger the pipe, the more drops it will be able to fit in it. Annoyingly, we can also squeeze more drops in a pipe by applying more pressure. $A \sim T$ is where the analogy falls over. In pipes, the real throughput, that is, the number of drops that goes in/out of it per second, is called "volumetric flow rate" and unless special conditions are met (orifices), it is proportional to A^2 instead of A. This is because a wider pipe doesn't mean just more liquid out, but also liquid moving faster because there's more space between the walls of the pipe. For the purposes of this chapter though, we can ignore these geeky details and live in a fantasy world where pressure and speed are constant and throughput is directly proportional to the cross-sectional area.

Little's law is very similar to the simple volume formula, and this is what makes this "pipe model" so intuitive and powerful. Let's examine the examples of *Figure 1* (on the right) in a bit more detail. Let's assume that the pipe system represents the downloader of Scrapy. The first one—a very "thin" downloader—may have a total volume/concurrency level (N) = 8 concurrent requests. The length/latency (S) could be something, such as S = 250 ms, for a fast website. Given N and S, we can now calculate the volume/throughput of the processing element T = N/S = 8/0.25 = 32 requests per second.

You will note that latency is mostly out of our control because it depends on the performance of the remote server and our network's latencies. What we can easily control is the level of concurrency (N) on the downloader by increasing it from 8 to 16 or 32 parallel requests, as we see in the second and third pipe on *Figure 1*. With constant length (outside our control), we can only increase volume by increasing the cross-section , that is, increasing throughput! In Little's law terms, with 16 Requests in parallel, we have T = N/S = 16/0.25 = 64 requests per second, and with 32 requests in parallel, we get T = N/S = 32/0.25 = 128 requests per second. Excellent! It seems like we can make a system infinitely fast by increasing concurrency. Before we rush to such conclusions though, we should also consider the effects of cascading queuing systems.

Cascading queuing systems

When you connect several pipes with different cross-sectional areas/throughputs one after the other, intuitively one can understand that the flow of the overall system will be limited by the flow of the narrowest (smallest throughput: T) pipe (see *Figure 2*).

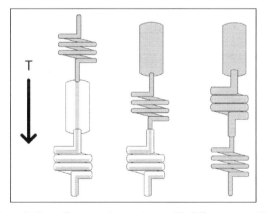

Figure 2. Cascading queuing systems with different capacities

You can also observe that the placement of the narrowest pipe — the bottleneck — defines how "full" other pipes are. If you think about fullness relating it with the memory requirements for your system, you realize that the placement of the bottleneck is very important. It's better to have a configuration that keeps full pipes where one unit of work costs us little. In Scrapy, a unit of work (crawling a page) consists mostly of a URL (a few bytes) before the downloader and the URL plus the server's response (way larger) after it.

> This is why it's wise in a Scrapy system to place the bottleneck in the downloader.

Identifying the bottleneck

A very important benefit of our piping system metaphor is that it makes the process of identifying the bottleneck visually intuitive. If you look at *Figure 2*, you will notice that everything before "the bottleneck" is full while everything after it isn't.

The good news is that, in most systems, we can monitor how full a queuing system is using the system's metrics relatively easily. By careful inspection of Scrapy's queues, we can understand where the bottleneck is, and if it's not in the downloader, we can adjust the settings in order to make it so. Any improvement that doesn't improve the bottleneck will give no throughput benefit. The only thing one can achieve by hacking other parts of the system is to make things worse, likely moving the bottleneck somewhere else. This feels a bit like tail chasing, and it can take for ages and make you feel despair. You have to follow a systematic approach, identify the bottleneck, and "know where to hit with a hammer" before you hack any code or configuration. As you will see in many cases, including most examples of this book, the bottleneck is not where one would expect it to be.

Scrapy's performance model

Let's return to Scrapy and see its performance model in detail (see *Figure 3*).

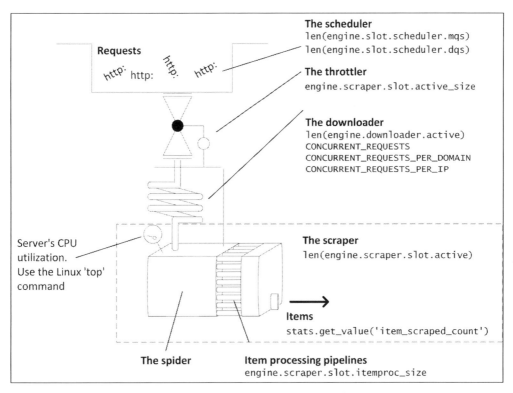

Figure 3. Scrapy's performance model

Scrapy consists of the following:

- **The scheduler**: This is where multiple Request get queued until the downloader is ready to process them. They consist mostly of just URLs and, thus, are quite compact, which means that having many of them doesn't hurt that much and allows us to keep the downloader fully utilized in case of irregular flow of incoming Request.

- **The throttler**: This is a safety valve that feeds back from the scraper (the large tank) and if the aggregated size of Response in progress is larger than 5 MB it stops the flow of further Request into the downloader. This can cause unexpected performance fluctuations.

- **The downloader**: This is the most important component of Scrapy in terms of performance. It poses a complex limit on the number of `Request` it can perform in parallel. Its delay (the length of the pipe) is equal to the time it takes the remote server to respond, plus any network/operating system and Python/Twisted delays. We can adjust the number of parallel `Requests`, but we, typically, have little control over delays. The capacity of the downloader is limited by the `CONCURRENT_REQUESTS*` settings, as we shall soon see.

- **The Spider**: This is the part of the scraper that turns `Response` to `Item` and a further `Request`. We write these, and typically they aren't a performance bottleneck as long as we follow the rules.

- **Item pipelines**: This is the second part of the scraper that we write. Our spiders might generate hundreds of `Items` per `Request`, and only `CONCURRENT_ITEMS` will be processed in parallel at a time. This is important because if, for example, you're doing database accesses in your pipelines, you might unintentionally flood your database and the default (100) seems dangerously high.

Both spiders and pipelines should have asynchronous code and may induce as much latency as necessary but still shouldn't be the bottleneck. Rarely, our spiders/pipelines do heavy processing. If this is the case, then our server's CPU might become the bottleneck.

Getting component utilization using telnet

In order to understand how `Requests`/`Items` flow though the pipes, we aren't really able to measure the flows (although this would be a cool feature). Instead, we can easily measure how much liquid, that is, `Requests`/`Responses`/`Items`, exists in each of Scrapy's processing stages.

Scrapy runs the telnet service via which we can get performance information. We can connect to it by using the telnet command on port `6023`. We then get a Python prompt inside Scrapy. Be careful, if you do something blocking there, such as `time.sleep()`, it will halt the crawler's functionality. Several interesting metrics get printed by the built-in `est()` function. Some of them are either very specialized or can be deduced from a few core metrics. I will only show you the latter in the rest of the chapter. Let's explore them with an example run. While we run a crawl, we open a second terminal on our dev machine, telnet on port `6023`, and run `est()`.

The code from this chapter is in the ch10 directory. This example in particular is in the ch10/speed directory.

On the first terminal, we run the following code:

```
$ pwd
/root/book/ch10/speed
$ ls
scrapy.cfg  speed

$ scrapy crawl speed -s SPEED_PIPELINE_ASYNC_DELAY=1
INFO: Scrapy 1.0.3 started (bot: speed)
...
```

Don't worry about what this scrapy crawl speed and its arguments mean for now. We will explain all of them in the rest of the chapter. On the second terminal, run the following:

```
$ telnet localhost 6023
>>> est()
...
len(engine.downloader.active)                    : 16
...
len(engine.slot.scheduler.mqs)                   : 4475
...
len(engine.scraper.slot.active)                  : 115
engine.scraper.slot.active_size                  : 117760
engine.scraper.slot.itemproc_size                : 105
```

Then press *Ctrl* + *D* on the second terminal to exit telnet and get back to the first terminal, and press *Ctrl* + *C* to stop the crawl.

 We ignore dqs for now. If you have enabled persistence support by setting the JOBDIR setting, you will also get non-zero dqs (len(engine.slot.scheduler.dqs)), which you should add to the size of mqs to follow the rest of analysis.

Let's see what these core metrics mean in this example. `mqs` indicates that there are quite a few (4,475 requests) waiting on our scheduler. That's okay. `len(engine.downloader.active)` indicates that, right now, there are 16 requests actively being downloaded by the downloader. This is equal to what we've set for CONCURRENT_REQUESTS on the settings of this spider so that's excellent. `len(engine.scraper.slot.active)` tells us that there are 115 Responses actively being processed in the scraper. The total size of those Responses is 115 kb told to us by `(engine.scraper.slot.active_size)`. Out of those Responses, 105 Items are currently in process by our pipelines, `(engine.scraper.slot.itemproc_size)`, which means that the rest of them (10) are in progress in our spider. Overall—we see that the bottleneck seems to be the downloader as, before that, we have a huge queue of work (`mqs`) and the downloader is fully utilized; after that, we have a high but more or less stable amount of work (you can confirm this by performing `est()` a few times).

Another interesting source of information is the `stats` object—the one that typically gets printed at the end of a crawl. We can access it at any point as a `dict` from telnet via `stats.get_stats()` and print it nicely using the `p()` function:

```
$ p(stats.get_stats())
{'downloader/request_bytes': 558330,
...
 'item_scraped_count': 2485,
...}
```

The most interesting metric for us right now is `item_scraped_count`, which is accessible directly through `stats.get_value('item_scraped_count')`. This tells us how many items have been scraped up to now and should be increasing with a rate that is the throughput of the system (Items/second).

Our benchmark system

For *Chapter 10, Understanding Scrapy's Performance,* I wrote a simple benchmark system that allows us to evaluate performance under different scenarios. The code is somewhat cumbersome, and you can find it in `speed/spiders/speed.py`, but we won't go into it in depth there.

The system consists of the following:

- The handlers of the `http://localhost:9312/benchmark/...` directories on our web server. We can control the structure (See *Figure 4*) of the fake website as well as how quickly pages load by adjusting URL arguments/Scrapy settings. Don't worry about the details—we will see many examples soon. For now, you can notice the differences between `http://localhost:9312/benchmark/index?p=1` and `http://localhost:9312/benchmark/id:3/rr:5/index?p=1`. The first one loads within half a second and has single-item detail pages, while the second takes five seconds to load and has three items per detail page. We can also add some hidden garbage data in pages to make them a bit heavier. For example, check out `http://localhost:9312/benchmark/ds:100/detail?id0=0`. By default (see `speed/settings.py`), pages render in SPEED_T_RESPONSE = 0.125 seconds and the fake website has SPEED_TOTAL_ITEMS = 5000 Items.

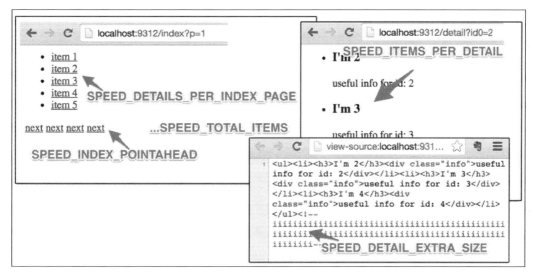

Figure 4. Our benchmarking server creates a fake website with adjustable structure

- A spider, `SpeedSpider`, fakes a few ways of retrieving `start_requests()` controlled by the SPEED_START_REQUESTS_STYLE setting, and provides a trivial `parse_item()` method. By default, we feed all starting URLs directly to Scrapy's scheduler using the `crawler.engine.crawl()` method.

- A pipeline, DummyPipeline, that fakes some processing. It has four different types of delays that this processing might induce. Blocking/computing/synchronous delay (SPEED_PIPELINE_BLOCKING_DELAY — this is bad), asynchronous delay (SPEED_PIPELINE_ASYNC_DELAY — this is okay), remote API call using the treq library (SPEED_PIPELINE_API_VIA_TREQ — this is okay), and a remote API call using Scrapy's crawler.engine.download() (SPEED_PIPELINE_API_VIA_DOWNLOADER — this is not that okay). By default, the pipeline doesn't add any delays.

- A set of high performance settings in settings.py. Everything that could even slightly slow down the system has been disabled. We also disable the per-domain request limit because we hit our local server only.

- A little metrics capture extension that is similar to the one from *Chapter 8, Programming Scrapy*. This periodically prints core metrics.

We've already used the system in the previous example, but let's rerun a simulation while also using Linux's time utility to measure the total execution time. We will see the core metrics being printed as follows:

```
$ time scrapy crawl speed
...
INFO:   s/edule  d/load  scrape  p/line    done      mem
INFO:        0       0       0       0       0         0
INFO:     4938      14      16       0      32     16384
INFO:     4831      16       6       0     147      6144
...
INFO:      119      16      16       0    4849     16384
INFO:        2      16      12       0    4970     12288
...
real   0m46.561s
```

Column	Metric
s/edule	len(engine.slot.scheduler.mqs)
d/load	len(engine.downloader.active)
scrape	len(engine.scraper.slot.active)
p/line	engine.scraper.slot.itemproc_size
done	stats.get_value('item_scraped_count')
mem	engine.scraper.slot.active_size

This level of transparency is remarkable. I've shortened the column names a bit, but they should still make sense. We start with 5,000 URLs in the scheduler and end up with 5,000 items in the done column. The downloader is the fully utilized bottleneck having 16 active `Requests` consistently with the settings. The scraper, mainly a spider because pipelines are empty as we see in the p/line column, is somewhat utilized but not fully as is typically the case past the bottleneck. It takes us 46 seconds to scrape 5,000 `Items` with $N=16$ parallel requests, which means that the average time per request is $46 \cdot 16/5000 = 147ms$ instead of our expected $125ms$, which is okay.

The standard performance model

The standard performance model holds true when Scrapy is functioning properly and the downloader is the performance bottleneck. In this case, you will see some requests in the scheduler, and the maximum number of concurrent requests in the downloader. The scraper (spider and pipelines) will be lightly loaded and the number of `Responses` in progress will not be constantly increasing.

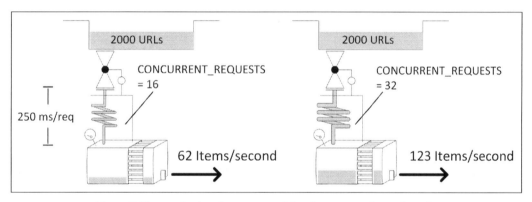

Figure 5. The standard performance model and some experimental results

There are three main settings that control the downloader's capacity: CONCURRENT_ REQUESTS, CONCURRENT_REQUESTS_PER_DOMAIN, and CONCURRENT_REQUESTS_PER_ IP. The first one gives coarse control. No matter what, there won't be more than CONCURRENT_REQUESTS active at a given time. On the other hand, if you target a single domain or relatively few domains, the CONCURRENT_REQUESTS_PER_DOMAIN might limit further the number of active requests. If you set CONCURRENT_REQUESTS_ PER_IP, CONCURRENT_REQUESTS_PER_DOMAIN will get ignored, and the effective limit will be the number of requests per single (target) IP. In the case of targeting some shared hosting sites, for example, many domains may point to a single server and this helps you not hit that server excessively.

To keep our performance exploration simple for now, we disable the per-IP limit by leaving CONCURRENT_REQUESTS_PER_IP to the default value (0) and setting CONCURRENT_REQUESTS_PER_DOMAIN to a very large number (1000000). This combination effectively disables those limits and the downloader's concurrency is controlled entirely by CONCURRENT_REQUESTS.

We expect the throughput of our system to depend on the average time that it takes to download a page, which includes the remote server's component and our system's (Linux, Twisted/Python) latencies $t_{download} = t_{response} + t_{overhead}$. It's also good to account for some startup and shutdown time. This includes the lag between the time you get a Response and the time its Items get out on the other end of your pipeline, as well as the time until you get your first responses and some inferior performance while caches are cold.

Overall, if you need to complete a job of N Requests and our Spider is properly tuned, you should be able to complete it in:

$$t_{job} = \frac{N \cdot \left(t_{response} + t_{overhead} \right)}{\text{CONCURRENT\_REQUESTS}} + t_{start/stop}$$

It is somewhat relieving that we don't have control over most of these parameters. We might be able to control $t_{overhead}$ slightly using a more powerful server and similarly $t_{start/stop}$ (which is hardly ever worth the effort because we pay that cost only once per run). Apart from slight improvements for a given workload of N requests, all we can seriously tune is the number of CONCURRENT_REQUESTS, which quite often depends on how hard we are allowed to hit remote servers. If we are okay to set it to a very large number, at some point we will saturate either our server's CPU capacity or the remote's ability to respond in a timely manner, that is, $t_{response}$ will skyrocket because the target website(s) will be throttling us, ban us, or we just got their servers down.

Let's run an experiment to check our theory. We will crawl 2,000 items with $t_{response} \in \{0.125s, 0.25s, 0.5s\}$ and CONCURRENT_REQUESTS $\in \{8, 16, 32, 64\}$ as follows:

```
$ for delay in 0.125 0.25 0.50; do for concurrent in 8 16 32 64; do
    time scrapy crawl speed -s SPEED_TOTAL_ITEMS=2000 \
    -s CONCURRENT_REQUESTS=$concurrent -s SPEED_T_RESPONSE=$delay
  done; done
```

On my laptop, I get the following times (in seconds) for completing 2,000 requests:

CONCURRENT_REQUESTS	125 ms/req	250 ms/req	500 ms/req
8	36.1	67.3	129.7
16	19.4	35.3	66.1
32	11.1	19.3	34.7
64	7.4	11.1	19.0

Warning: geeky calculations ahead! Feel free to skim through this paragraph. We can see some of those results in *Figure 5*. By reordering the last equation, we can bring it to the simple form $y = t_{overhead} \cdot x + t_{start/stop}$ where $x = N / CONCURRENT\_REQUESTS$ and $y = t_{job} \cdot x + t_{response}$. Using the least squares (LINEST Excel function) and the preceding data, we calculate $t_{overhead}$ = 6 ms and $t_{start/stop}$ = 3.1s. $t_{overhead}$ turns out to be a negligible number but start time is significant and favors long runs with thousands of URLs. As a result, a very useful formula that we are going to use to approximate the throughput of the system in Requests/second is the following:

$$T = \frac{N}{t_{job} - t_{start/stop}}$$

By running a long job of N Requests, we can measure the t_{job} aggregated time and then it's straightforward to calculate T.

Solving performance problems

Now that we have a thorough understanding of what the expected performance of our system should be, let's take a look at what we should do in case we don't get the performance we want. We will present different problematic cases by exploring symptoms, performing example crawls that reproduce them, discussing the root cause, and finally providing actions that fix them. The order the cases are presented in is from higher-level system issues to lower-level Scrapy technical details. This means that more common cases may appear after less common ones. Please read the entire chapter before you start exploring your performance issues.

Case #1 – saturated CPU

Symptoms: At some point you will be increasing the level of concurrency, but you will be getting no performance gains. When you reduce the level of concurrency, everything works as expected. Your downloader is well utilized, but it seems like the average time per request is exploding. You find out how loaded the CPU is using the top command in Unix/Linux, ps on Power Shell, or the Task Manager on Windows, and it seems quite high.

Example: Let's assume that you run the following command:

```
$ for concurrent in 25 50 100 150 200; do
    time scrapy crawl speed -s SPEED_TOTAL_ITEMS=5000 \
    -s CONCURRENT_REQUESTS=$concurrent
  done
```

You get the time it takes to scrape 5,000 URLs. The Expected column is calculated based on the previously derived formula, and the CPU load is observed with top (you can run this command on a second terminal to dev):

CONCURRENT_REQUESTS	Expected (sec)	Actual (sec)	% of expected	CPU load
25	29.3	30.34	97%	52%
50	16.2	18.7	87%	78%
100	9.7	14.1	69%	92%
150	7.5	13.9	54%	100%
200	6.4	14.2	45%	100%

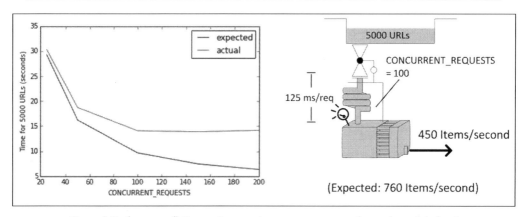

Figure 6. Performance flattens out as you increase concurrency beyond a certain level

In our experiment, we hardly perform any processing and that's why we can get that high concurrencies. In a more sophisticated system, you will most likely see this behavior earlier.

Discussion: Scrapy heavily uses a single thread and as you reach high levels of concurrency, the CPU might become the bottleneck. The recommended level of CPU Scrapy should be using, assuming that you don't use any thread pools, is around 80-90%. Please keep in mind that you can have similar problems with other system resources, such as network bandwidth, memory, or disk throughput, but all these are less likely and fall into the general system administration realm, so we won't address them any further here.

Solution: I will assume that your code is, in general, efficient. You can get aggregated concurrency larger than CONCURRENT_REQUESTS by running many Scrapy crawlers on the same server. This will help you utilize more of the available cores especially if other services or other threads from your pipelines don't use them. If you need even more concurrency, you can use multiple servers (see *Chapter 11, Distributed Crawling with Scrapyd and Real-Time Analytics*), in which case you will likely have more memory, network bandwidth, and hard disk throughput available as well. Always double-check that CPU usage is your primary constraint.

Case #2 – blocking code

Symptoms: The behavior that you're observing doesn't make any sense. The system is very slow compared to what you expect and curiously the speed doesn't significantly change when you change CONCURRENT_REQUESTS. The downloader looks almost empty (way less than CONCURRENT_REQUESTS) and the scraper has quite a few Responses.

Example: You can use two benchmark settings, SPEED_SPIDER_BLOCKING_DELAY and SPEED_PIPELINE_BLOCKING_DELAY (they have identical effects), to enable a 100-ms blocking delay per Response. We would expect 100 URLs to take 2-3 seconds at the given concurrency levels, but we consistently get ~13 seconds irrespective of the value of CONCURRENT_REQUESTS:

```
for concurrent in 16 32 64; do
  time scrapy crawl speed -s SPEED_TOTAL_ITEMS=100 \
  -s CONCURRENT_REQUESTS=$concurrent -s SPEED_SPIDER_BLOCKING_DELAY=0.1
done
```

CONCURRENT_REQUESTS	Total time (sec)
16	13.9
32	13.2
64	12.9

Discussion: Any trace of blocking code instantly nullifies Scrapy's concurrency and essentially sets CONCURRENT_REQUESTS = 1. Indeed the simple formula; 100 URLs · 100 ms (blocking delay) = 10 seconds + $t_{start/stop}$, fully explains the delays that we see.

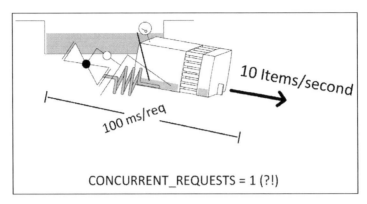

Figure 7. Blocking code invalidates concurrency in unpredictable ways

No matter whether the blocking code is in one of your pipelines or your spider, you will see scraper being fully utilized and everything before and after it being empty. This seems to go against the pipeline physics that we talked about before, but we don't have a parallel system any more, so pipeline rules don't apply. It's so easy to make this mistake (for example, using blocking APIs) that you will certainly get this wrong at some point. You will note that a similar discussion applies to computationally complex code. You should be using multiple threads for such code, as we've seen in *Chapter 9*, *Pipeline Recipes*, or performing it in batch outside Scrapy, an example of which we will see in *Chapter 11*, *Distributed Crawling with Scrapyd and Real-Time Analytics*.

Solution: I will assume that you inherited the code base, and you have no intuition on where the blocking code is. If the system can be functional without any pipelines, then disable your pipelines and check whether the odd behavior persists. If yes, then your blocking code is in your spider. If not, then enable pipelines one-by-one and see when the problem starts. If the system can't be functional without everything running, then add some log messages on each pipeline stage (or interleave dummy pipelines that print timestamps) in between your functional ones. By checking the logs, you will easily detect where your system spends most of its time. If you want a more long-term/reusable solution, you can trace your Requests using dummy pipelines that add timestamps at each stage to the meta fields of Request. At the end, hook to the item_scraped signal and log the timestamps. As soon as you find your blocking code, convert it to Twisted/asynchronous or use Twisted's thread pools. To see the effects of this conversion, rerun the previous example while replacing SPEED_PIPELINE_BLOCKING_DELAY with SPEED_PIPELINE_ASYNC_DELAY. The change in performance is stunning.

Case #3 – "garbage" on the downloader

Symptoms: You get way less than the expected throughput. The downloader sometimes looks like it has more `Request`s than `CONCURRENT_REQUESTS`.

Example: We simulate downloading 1,000 pages with a 0.25 sec response time. With the default concurrency of 16, this should take about ~ 19 sec according to our formulas. We use a pipeline that uses `crawler.engine.download()` to make an extra HTTP request to a fake API that responds within one second. You can try it on `http://localhost:9312/benchmark/ar:1/api?text=hello`. Let's run a crawl:

```
$ time scrapy crawl speed -s SPEED_TOTAL_ITEMS=1000 -s SPEED_T_
RESPONSE=0.25 -s SPEED_API_T_RESPONSE=1 -s SPEED_PIPELINE_API_VIA_
DOWNLOADER=1

...

s/edule   d/load   scrape   p/line     done       mem
    968       32       32       32        0      32768
    952       16        0        0       32          0
    936       32       32       32       32      32768

...

real 0m55.151s
```

This is really weird. Not only did our job take three times more time than expected, but we also have more than the 16 active requests that `CONCURRENT_REQUESTS` defines in the downloader (`d/load`). The downloader is clearly the bottleneck because it seems to work over capacity! Let's rerun the crawl, and on another console, open a telnet connection to Scrapy. We can then check which `Request`s are active on the downloader:

```
$ telnet localhost 6023
```

```
>>> engine.downloader.active
```

```
set([<POST http://web:9312/ar:1/ti:1000/rr:0.25/benchmark/api>,  ... ])
```

It looks like it does mostly API `Request`s instead of downloading regular pages.

Discussion: You would expect that nobody uses `crawler.cngine.download()` as it looks a bit complex to use, but it is used twice in Scrapy's code base for the `robots.txt` middleware and the media pipeline. As a result, it's reasonably suggested as a solution when people need to consume web APIs. Using this is way better than using blocking APIs such as the popular `requests` Python package that we saw in the previous section. It's also slightly simpler to use than understanding Twisted programming and using `treq`. Now that this book exists though, this isn't an excuse anymore. Puns aside, this mistake is quite hard to debug, so proactively take a look at the active requests on your downloader while investigating performance. If you find API or media URLs that aren't directly targeted by your crawl, it means that some of your pipelines use `crawler.engine.download()` to perform HTTP requests. Our CONCURRENT_REQUESTS limit doesn't apply for these `Request`, which means that we will likely see the downloader loaded with more than CONCURRENT_REQUESTS, which seems paradoxical at first sight. Unless the number of spurious `Request`s falls below CONCURRENT_REQUESTS, no new normal page `Request`s will be fetched from the scheduler.

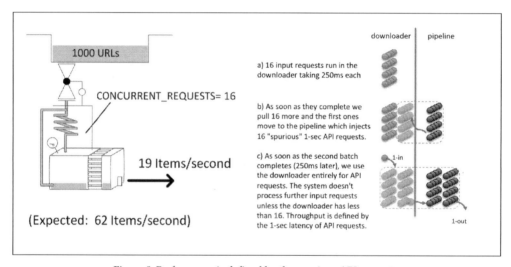

Figure 8. Performance is defined by the spurious API requests

As a result, it's not a coincidence that the throughput that we get from the system corresponds to what we would get if our original `Request` lasted 1 sec (the API latency) instead of 0.25 sec (the page download latency). This case is especially confusing because unless API calls are slower than our page requests, we won't notice any performance degradation.

Solution: We can solve this problem using `treq` instead of `crawler.engine.download()`. You will note that this will skyrocket the scraper's performance, which might be bad news for your API infrastructure. I would start with a low number of CONCURRENT_REQUESTS and increase gradually to make sure I don't overload the API servers.

Here's an example of the same run as before but using `treq`:

```
$ time scrapy crawl speed -s SPEED_TOTAL_ITEMS=1000 -s SPEED_T_
RESPONSE=0.25 -s SPEED_API_T_RESPONSE=1 -s SPEED_PIPELINE_API_VIA_TREQ=1
...
s/edule  d/load  scrape  p/line    done      mem
    936      16      48      32       0     49152
    887      16      65      64      32     66560
    823      16      65      52      96     66560
...
real 0m19.922s
```

You will observe one very interesting thing. The pipeline (`p/line`) seems to have many more items than the downloader (`d/load`). That's perfectly fine and it's interesting to understand why.

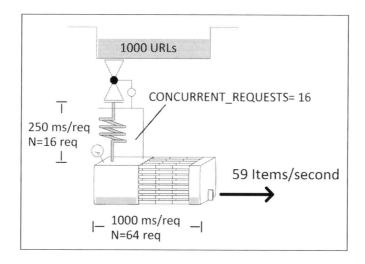

Figure 9. It's perfectly fine to have long pipelines (check "industrial heat exchanger" in Google images).

The downloader is fully loaded with 16 `Request`s as expected. This means that the throughput of the system is $T = N/S = 16/0.25 = 64$ `Request`s per second. We can confirm this by noticing the increase on the `done` column. A `Request` will spend 0.25 sec inside the downloader, but it will spend 1 sec inside the pipeline because of the slow API request. This means that in the pipeline (`p/line`), we expect to see on average $N = T \cdot S = 64 \cdot 1 = 64$ `Items`. That's perfectly fine. Does it mean that the pipeline is now the bottleneck? No because we have no limit on the number of `Response`s that we can process simultaneously on our pipelines. As long as the number doesn't increase indefinitely, we are fine. More on this in the next section.

Case #4 – overflow due to many or large responses

Symptoms: The downloader works almost at full capacity and after a while it turns off. This pattern repeats itself. The memory usage of your scraper is high.

Example: Here, we have exactly the same setup as before (using `treq`), but the responses are somewhat heavy having about 120 kB of HTML. As you can see, this takes 31 seconds to complete instead of about 20:

```
$ time scrapy crawl speed -s SPEED_TOTAL_ITEMS=1000 -s SPEED_T_
RESPONSE=0.25 -s SPEED_API_T_RESPONSE=1 -s SPEED_PIPELINE_API_VIA_TREQ=1
-s SPEED_DETAIL_EXTRA_SIZE=120000
```

s/edule	d/load	scrape	p/line	done	mem
952	16	32	32	0	3842818
917	16	35	35	32	4203080
876	16	41	41	67	4923608
840	4	48	43	108	5764224
805	3	46	27	149	5524048

```
...

real    0m30.611s
```

Discussion: We may naively try to interpret this latency as "it takes more time to create, transfer, or process pages", but that's not what's happening here. There exists a hardcoded (at the time of writing) limit for the total size of `Responses` of `max_active_size = 5000000`. Each `Response` is assumed to have a size equal to the size of its body and at least 1 kB.

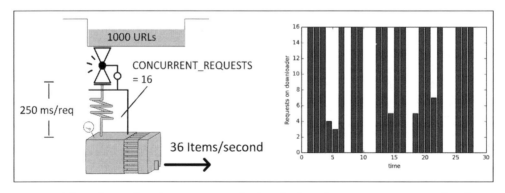

Figure 10. Irregular number of `Requests` on the downloader indicates `Response` size throttling

One important detail here is that this limit is maybe the most subtle and essential mechanism that Scrapy has to protect itself against slow spiders or pipelines. If the throughput of any of your pipelines is slower than the throughput of the downloader, this will eventually happen. It's easy to hit this limit even with small Responses when we have large pipeline processing time. Here's one such extreme example of very long pipeline where the problems start after 80 seconds:

```
$ time scrapy crawl speed -s SPEED_TOTAL_ITEMS=10000 -s SPEED_T_
RESPONSE=0.25 -s SPEED_PIPELINE_ASYNC_DELAY=85
```

Solution: There isn't much you can do for this problem with the existing infrastructure. It would be nice to be able to clear the body of Response as soon as you don't need it anymore—likely after your spider, but doing so won't reset Scraper's counters at the time of writing. All you can really do is try to reduce your pipeline's processing time effectively reducing the number of Responses in progress in the Scraper. You can achieve this with traditional optimization: checking whether APIs or databases you potentially interact with can support your scraper's throughput, profiling the scraper, moving functionality from your pipelines to batch/postprocessing systems, and potentially using more powerful servers or distributed crawling.

Case #5 – overflow due to limited/excessive item concurrency

Symptoms: Your spider creates multiple Items per Response. You get lower than expected throughput and likely the same on/off pattern as in the previous case.

Example: Here, we have a slightly unusual setup where we have 1,000 requests that return pages with 100 items each. The response time is 0.25 sec and there's a 3 sec item pipeline processing time. We perform several runs with values of CONCURRENT_ITEMS ranging from 10 to 150:

```
for concurrent_items in 10 20 50 100 150; do
time scrapy crawl speed -s SPEED_TOTAL_ITEMS=100000 -s  \
SPEED_T_RESPONSE=0.25 -s SPEED_ITEMS_PER_DETAIL=100 -s  \
SPEED_PIPELINE_ASYNC_DELAY=3 -s \
CONCURRENT_ITEMS=$concurrent_items
done
...
```

s/edule	d/load	scrape	p/line	done	mem
952	16	32	180	0	243714

| 920 | 16 | 64 | 640 | 0 | 487426 |
| 888 | 16 | 96 | 960 | 0 | 731138 |

. . .

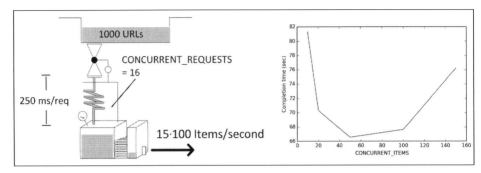

Figure 11. Crawl time as a function of CONCURRENT_ITEMS

Discussion: It's worth noting again that this only applies to cases where your spider generates many Items per Response. Unless this is the case, you can set CONCURRENT_ITEMS = 1 and forget about it. It's also worth noting that this is quite a synthetic example since the throughputs are quite large in the order of 1,300 Items per second. We get such high throughput due to low and stable latencies, almost no real processing, and the very low size of Responses. These conditions aren't common.

The first thing that we notice is that, while up to now the scrape and p/line columns used to show the same number, now p/line shows CONCURRENT_ITEMS · scrape. This is expected because scrape shows Reponses while p/line shows Items.

The second interesting thing is the bathtub performance function of *Figure 11*. The plot makes it look a bit more dramatic than it really is because the vertical axis is scaled. On the left side, we have very high latency because we hit the memory limits we mentioned on the previous section. On the right side, we have too much concurrency, and we use too much CPU. Getting the optimum exactly right isn't that important because it can easily shift left or right.

Solution: It's very easy to detect both problematic symptoms of this case. If you get very high CPU usage, it's good to reduce the number of CONCURRENT_ITEMS. If you hit the 5 MB Response limit, then your pipeline can't follow your downloader's throughput and increasing CONCURRENT_ITEMS might be able to quickly fix this. If it doesn't make any difference, then follow the advice in the previous section and ask yourself twice if the rest of the system is able to support your Scraper's throughput.

Case #6 – the downloader doesn't have enough to do

Symptoms: You increase CONCURRENT_REQUESTS, but the downloader can't keep up and is underutilized. The scheduler is empty.

Example: First of all, let's run an example without the problem. We will switch to a 1 sec response time because this simplifies calculations making downloader throughput $T = N/S = N/1 =$ CONCURRENT_REQUESTS. Let's assume that we run the following:

```
$ time scrapy crawl speed -s SPEED_TOTAL_ITEMS=500 \
-s SPEED_T_RESPONSE=1 -s CONCURRENT_REQUESTS=64
s/edule  d/load  scrape  p/line    done      mem
    436      64       0       0        0         0
...
real  0m10.99s
```

We get a fully utilized downloader (64 requests) and overall time of 11 seconds, which matches our model for 500 URLs at 64 requests/second $\left(S = N / T + t_{start/stop} = 500 / 64 + 3.1 = 10.91 \text{ sec} \right)$.

Now, let's do the same crawl, but instead of providing the URLs from a list, as we do by default on all those examples, let's use index pages to extract URLs using SPEED_START_REQUESTS_STYLE=UseIndex. This is exactly the mode that we've used in every other chapter of this book. Each index page by default gives us 20 URLs:

```
$ time scrapy crawl speed -s SPEED_TOTAL_ITEMS=500 \
-s SPEED_T_RESPONSE=1 -s CONCURRENT_REQUESTS=64 \
-s SPEED_START_REQUESTS_STYLE=UseIndex
s/edule  d/load  scrape  p/line    done      mem
     0       1       0       0        0         0
     0      21       0       0        0         0
     0      21       0       0       20         0
...
real 0m32.24s
```

Clearly this doesn't look anything like the previous case. Somehow, the downloader runs in less than the maximum capacity and the throughput is $T = N / S - t_{start/stop} = 500 / \left(32.2 - 3.1 \right) = 17$ requests/second.

Discussion: A quick look at the `d/load` column will convince us that the downloader is underutilized. This is because we don't have enough URLs to feed it. Our scraping process generates URLs slower than its maximum consuming capacity. In this case, 20 URLs + 1 for the next index page get generated from each index page. The throughput couldn't by any means be more than 20 Requests per second because we don't get source URLs fast enough. This problem is too subtle and easy to overlook.

Solution: If each index page has more than one next page link, we can utilize them to accelerate our URL generation. If we can find pages that show more results (for example, 50) per index page even better. We can observe the behavior by running a few simulations:

```
$ for details in 10 20 30 40; do for nxtlinks in 1 2 3 4; do
time scrapy crawl speed -s SPEED_TOTAL_ITEMS=500 -s SPEED_T_RESPONSE=1 \
-s CONCURRENT_REQUESTS=64 -s SPEED_START_REQUESTS_STYLE=UseIndex \
-s SPEED_DETAILS_PER_INDEX_PAGE=$details \
-s SPEED_INDEX_POINTAHEAD=$nxtlinks
done; done
```

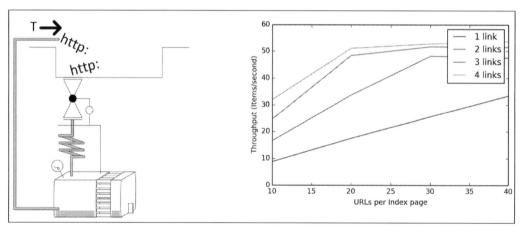

Figure 12. Throughput as a function of details and next page links per index page

In *Figure 12*, we can see how throughput scales with these two parameters. We observe linear behavior, both in terms of next page links, as well as pages until we reach the system's limits. You can experiment by reordering the crawler's `Rules`. If you are using LIFO (default) order, you might see a small improvement if you dispatch your index page requests first by putting the `Rule` that extracts them last in your list. You can also try to set a higher priority to the `Requests` that hit the index. Both techniques don't give impressive improvements, but you can try them by setting `SPEED_INDEX_RULE_LAST=1` and `SPEED_INDEX_HIGHER_PRIORITY=1`, respectively. Please keep in mind that both these solutions will tend to download the entire index first (due to high priority), thus, generating lots of URLs in the scheduler, which will increase memory requirements. They will also give very few results until they finish with the index. For small indices this might be okay, but for larger indices, this is certainly undesirable.

An easier and more powerful technique is to shard the index. This requires you to use more than one initial index URLs that have maximum distance between them. For example, if the index has 100 pages, you may choose page 1 and 51 as the starting ones. The crawler is then able to use the next links to traverse the index effectively in twice the speed. A similar thing can be done if you can find a way to traverse the index, for example based on the brand of the products or any other property that is provided to you, and can split the index in roughly equal segments. You can simulate this using the `-s SPEED_INDEX_SHARDS` setting:

```
$ for details in 10 20 30 40; do for shards in 1 2 3 4; do
time scrapy crawl speed -s SPEED_TOTAL_ITEMS=500 -s SPEED_T_RESPONSE=1 \
-s CONCURRENT_REQUESTS=64 -s SPEED_START_REQUESTS_STYLE=UseIndex \
-s SPEED_DETAILS_PER_INDEX_PAGE=$details -s SPEED_INDEX_SHARDS=$shards
done; done
```

The results are better than the previous technique, and I would recommend this method if it works for you because it's way simpler and cleaner.

Troubleshooting flow

To summarize, Scrapy is designed to have the downloader as a bottleneck. Start with a low value of `CONCURRENT_REQUESTS` and increase until just before you hit one of the following limits:

* CPU usage > 80-90%
* Source website latency increasing excessively
* Memory limit of 5 Mb of `Responses` in your scraper

At the same time also perform the following:

- Keep at least a few `Requests` at all times in the scheduler's queues (mqs/dqs) to prevent the downloader's URL starvation
- Never use any blocking code or CPU-intensive code

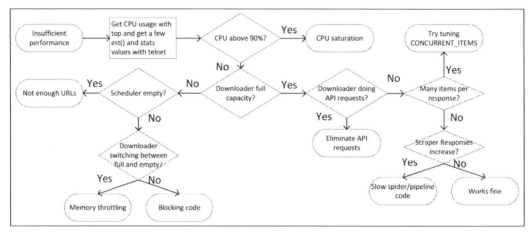

Figure 13. Troubleshooting Scrapy's performance problems

Figure 13 summarizes the procedure of diagnosing and repairing Scrapy's performance problems.

Summary

In this chapter, we tried to give you some interesting cases that highlight the fine performance implications of Scrapy's architecture. Details might change in future versions of Scrapy, but the intuition provided by this chapter should remain valid for a long time and might also help you with any high-concurrency asynchronous systems that are based on Twisted, Netty Node.js, or similar frameworks.

When it comes to the question of performance in Scrapy, there are three valid answers: I don't know and I don't care, I don't know but I will find out, or I do know. As we demonstrated many times in this chapter, the naive answer, "we need more servers/memory/bandwidth" is most likely irrelevant to Scrapy's performance. One really needs to understand where the bottleneck is and elevate it.

In our last chapter, *Chapter 11*, *Distributed Crawling with Scrapyd and Real-Time Analytics*, we will focus on elevating the performance further, beyond a single server's capacity by distributing our crawls across multiple servers.

11
Distributed Crawling with Scrapyd and Real-Time Analytics

We have come a long way. We familiarized ourselves with two fundamental web technologies, HTML and XPath, and then we started using Scrapy to crawl complex websites. Later, we gained a much deeper appreciation of the various features that Scrapy provides us with through its settings, and then we moved to an even deeper understanding of both Scrapy and Python when we explored its internal architecture and the asynchronous features of its Twisted engine. In the previous chapter, we studied Scrapy's performance and learned how to address complex and often counter-intuitive performance problems.

In this last chapter, I would like to give you some directions on how to further use this amazing technology to scale beyond a single server. We will soon discover that crawling is often an "embarrassingly parallel" problem; thus, we can easily scale horizontally and exploit the resources of multiple servers. In order to do this, we are going to use a Scrapy middleware as we usually do, but we will also use Scrapyd—an application that is specially designed to manage Scrapy spider's runs on remote servers. This will allow us to have on our own servers functionality that is compatible with the one that we presented in *Chapter 6*, *Deploying to Scrapinghub*.

We are finally going to perform real-time analytics on the extracted data with a simple system that is based on Apache Spark. Apache Spark is a very popular framework for large-scale data processing. We will use its Spark Streaming API to present results that get increasingly more accurate as we collect more data. For me, this final application showcases the power and maturity of Python as a language because, with just this, we can program the full stack from data extraction to analytics writing code that is expressive, compact, and efficient.

How does the title of a property affect the price?

The sample problem that we will try to solve is trying to find out how titles correlate with the prices of properties. We would expect terms such as "jacuzzi" or "pool" to be correlated with higher prices, while others such as "discount" with a lower price. Combining this information with location, for example, may be used to provide us with real-time alerts on properties that are bargains given their location and description.

What we want to calculate is the shift of the price for a given term:

$$Shift_{term} = \left(\overline{Price_{properties-with-term}} - \overline{Price_{properties-without-term}} \right) / \overline{Price}$$

For example, if the average rent is $1,000, and we observe that properties with jacuzzi have an average price of $1,300, while properties without it have an average price of $995, the shift for jacuzzi is $Shift_{jacuzzi} = (1300 - 995) / 1000 = 30.5\%$. If there's a property with jacuzzi and has just a 5% higher than average price, I would like to know about it!

Please note that this metric isn't trivial because term effects get aggregated. For example, titles with both jacuzzi and discount will likely show a combined effect of these keywords. The more data that we collect and analyze, then the more accurate our estimates. We will get back to this problem and how we implement a streaming solution in a minute.

Scrapyd

Right now, we will introduce scrapyd. Scrapyd is an application that allows us to deploy spiders on a server and schedule crawling jobs using them. Let's get a feeling of how easy it is to use this. We have it preinstalled in our dev machine, so we can check this immediately by going back to the code from *Chapter 3*, *Basic Crawling*. The exact same process that we used back then works here with just a single change.

Let's first have a look on scrapyd's web interface that we can find at `http://localhost:6800/`.

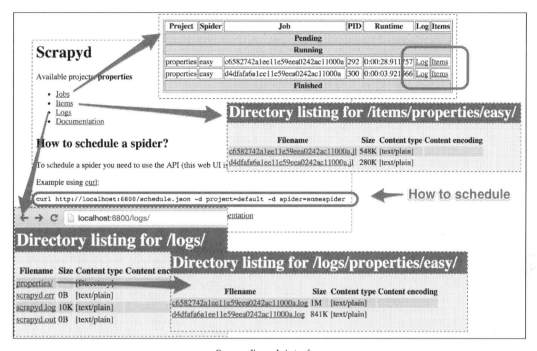

Scrapyd's web interface

You can see that it has different sections for **Jobs**, **Items**, **Logs** and **Documentation**. It also gives us some instructions on how to schedule jobs using its API.

In order to do so, we must first deploy the spider to the scrapyd server. The first step is to modify the `scrapy.cfg` configuration file as follows:

```
$ pwd
/root/book/ch03/properties
$ cat scrapy.cfg
...
[settings]
default = properties.settings

[deploy]
url = http://localhost:6800/
project = properties
```

Essentially, all that we need to do is to uncomment the **url** line. The default settings are suitable for us. Now, in order to deploy the spider, we use the `scrapyd-deploy` tool that is provided by `scrapyd-client`. `scrapyd-client` that used to be part of Scrapy, but is now a separate module that can be installed with `pip install scrapyd-client` (already installed in our dev):

```
$ scrapyd-deploy
Packing version 1450044699
Deploying to project "properties" in http://localhost:6800/addversion.
json
Server response (200):
{"status": "ok", "project": "properties", "version": "1450044699",
"spiders": 3, "node_name": "dev"}
```

As the deployment was successful, we will be also able to see the project mentioned in the **Available projects** section in the main page of the scrapyd web interface. We can now follow the instructions on the same page to submit a job:

```
$ curl http://localhost:6800/schedule.json -d project=properties -d
spider=easy
{"status": "ok", "jobid": " d4df...", "node_name": "dev"}
```

If we turn back to the **Jobs** section of the web interface, we will be able to see the job running. We can use the `jobid schedule.json` that returns us to cancel the job using `cancel.json` a bit later:

```
$ curl http://localhost:6800/cancel.json -d project=properties -d
job=d4df...
{"status": "ok", "prevstate": "running", "node_name": "dev"}
```

Please do cancel because otherwise you will be wasting computing resources for a while.

Great! If we visit the **Logs** section, we will be able to see the logs and on the **Items** section the Items that we just crawled. These get cleared periodically to free up space, so they might not be available after a few crawls.

If there's a good reason, such as a conflict, we can change the port using `http_port`, which is one of many settings that scrapyd has. It's worth being aware of them by having a look in scrapyd's documentation at `http://scrapyd.readthedocs.org/`. One important setting that we do change in our deployment for this chapter is `max_proc`. If you leave it with the default value of 0, scrapyd will allow as many as four times the number of CPUs that Scrapy jobs run in parallel. As we will be running many scrapyd servers, most likely in a VM, we set this number to four, allowing up to four jobs to run in parallel. This has to do with this chapter's needs and in a real deployment the default value will most likely be fine.

Overview of our distributed system

Designing this system was a great experience for me. I started adding features and complexity to the point where I had to demand that readers have high-end hardware to run the examples. What then became an urgent necessity was simplicity—both in order to keep the hardware requirements realistic and to ensure that this chapter remains focused on Scrapy.

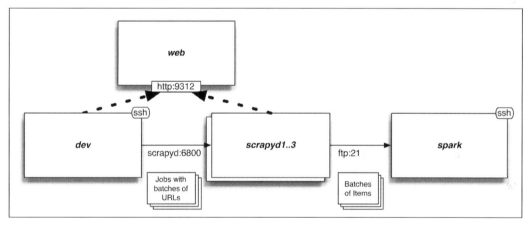

Overview of the system

At the end, the system that we are going to use in this chapter will contain our dev machine and a few more servers. We will use our dev machine to perform the horizontal crawling of the index and extract batches of URLs. We will then distribute these URL batches to scrapyd nodes in a round-robin fashion and crawl them. At the end, the `.jl` files with our `Items` will be transferred to a server running Apache Spark via FTP. What? FTP? Yes, I have chosen FTP and the local filesystem over HDFS or Apache Kafka because of its very low memory requirements and the fact that it's supported out-of-the-box as a `FEED_URI` backend by Scrapy. Please keep in mind that, with just a trivial change in the configuration of scrapyd and Spark, we can use Amazon S3 to store these files and enjoy redundancy, scalability, and so on. There would be nothing interesting and on-topic to learn using any more fancy technologies, though.

 One danger with FTP is that Spark may see incomplete files while their upload is in-progress. In order to avoid this, we use Pure-FTPd and a callback script that moves uploaded files to `/root/items` as soon as the upload completes.

Every few seconds, Spark probes a directory (`/root/items`), reads any new files, forms a mini-batch, and performs analytics. We use Apache Spark because it supports Python as one of its programming languages, and it also supports streaming. Up to now, we may have been using examples of relatively short-lived crawls, but many of the real-world crawls don't ever finish. Crawls run indefinitely 24/7 and provide streams of data that get analyzed, and their results just get more accurate with more data. That's exactly the case that we are going to showcase using Apache Spark.

 There's nothing special about Apache Spark and Scrapy. You are free to use Map-Reduce, Apache Storm, or any other framework that fits your needs.

In this chapter, we don't insert `Items` to databases like ElasticSearch or MySQL. The techniques that we presented in *Chapter 9, Pipeline Recipes*, would work in exactly the same way here, but their performance would be bad. Very few database systems are happy when you hit them with thousands of write operations per second and that's what our pipelines would do. If we want to insert in to databases, we have to follow a process that is similar to the one that we use for Spark, namely batch import the generated `Item` files. You can modify our Spark example process to batch import to any database.

One last thing to keep in mind is that this system is not particularly resilient. We assume that nodes are healthy and that any failures don't have a severe business impact. Spark has resilient configurations that provide high availability. Scrapy doesn't provide anything built-in apart from scrapyd's persistent queues, which means that failed jobs will restart as soon as the node is back. This may or may not be suitable for your needs. If resilience is important for you, you will have to build a monitoring and distributed queuing solution (for example, based on Kafka or RabbitMQ) that will restart failed crawls.

Changes to our spider and middleware

In order to build this system, we need to slightly modify our Scrapy spider and develop spider middleware. More specifically we will have to perform the following:

- Fine tune crawling the index to perform at maximum speed
- Write a middleware that batches and sends URLs to scrapyd servers
- Use the same middleware to allow batch URLs to be used at start-up

We will try to implement these changes as unobtrusively as possible. Ideally, the whole operation should be clean, easy to understand, and transparent to the underlying spider code. This is an infrastructure-level requirement and hacking (potentially hundreds) of spiders to enable it is a bad idea.

Sharded-index crawling

Our first step is to optimize index crawling to make it as fast as possible. Before we start, let's set some expectations. Let's assume that our spider will be crawling with a concurrency of 16, and we measure the latency of the source web server and it is about 0.25 sec. This gives us a maximum throughput of $16 / 0.25 = 64$ pages/second. The index has 50,000 detail pages / 30 details per index page = 1667 index pages. We expect the index download to take a bit more than $1667 / 64 = 26$ sec.

Let's start with the spider named `easy` from *Chapter 3, Basic Crawling*. We will comment out the `Rule` that performs the vertical crawling first (the one with `callback='parse_item'`) because we just want to crawl the index for now.

You can get all the source code of this book from GitHub. To download this code, go to:

`git clone https://github.com/scalingexcellence/scrapybook`

The full code from this chapter will be in the `ch11` directory.

If we time a `scrapy crawl` for just 10 pages before any optimizations, we get the following:

```
$ ls
properties  scrapy.cfg
$ pwd
/root/book/ch11/properties
$ time scrapy crawl easy -s CLOSESPIDER_PAGECOUNT=10
...
DEBUG: Crawled (200) <GET ...index_00000.html> (referer: None)
DEBUG: Crawled (200) <GET ...index_00001.html> (referer: ...index_00000.
html)
...
real    0m4.099s
```

If it takes 4 seconds for 10 pages, we have no hope of completing 1,700 pages in 26. By inspecting the logs, we will realize that each page comes from the previous page's next link, which means that we process at most one page at any given moment. Effectively our concurrency is 1. We want to parallelize and get the desired amount of concurrency (16 concurrent requests). We will shard the index and allow a few extra shards in order to be confident our crawler doesn't starve for URLs. We will split the index into 20 segments. Practically, any number above 16 will do and will increase the speed, but as we get beyond 20 we see diminishing returns. We will calculate the initial index IDs for each shard with the following expression:

```
>>> map(lambda x: 1667 * x / 20, range(20))
[0, 83, 166, 250, 333, 416, 500, ...  1166, 1250, 1333, 1416, 1500, 1583]
```

Consequently, we set our `start_urls` to the following:

```
start_urls = ['http://web:9312/properties/index_%05d.html' % id
              for id in map(lambda x: 1667 * x / 20, range(20))]
```

This would likely be something very different for your index, so it's not worth us making it any prettier at this point. If we also set our concurrency settings (CONCURRENT_REQUESTS, CONCURRENT_REQUESTS_PER_DOMAIN) to 16 and we run a crawl, we now get the following:

```
$ time scrapy crawl easy -s CONCURRENT_REQUESTS=16 -s CONCURRENT_
REQUESTS_PER_DOMAIN=16
...
real   0m32.344s
```

This is close enough to what we wanted. We download 1667 pages / 32 sec = 52 index pages per second, which means that we will generate *52 * 30 = 1560* detail page URLs per second. We can now uncomment the vertical crawling `Rule` and save the file as a new spider distr. We won't need to make any further changes to the spider's code, which shows how powerful and nonintrusive the middleware that we are about to develop is. If we were about to run `scrapy crawl` with our dev server only, assuming that we can process detail pages about as fast as index pages, it would take us no less than *50000 / 52 = 16* minutes to complete the crawl.

There are two key takeaways from this section. After studying *Chapter 10, Understanding Scrapy's Performance,* we are doing actual engineering. We can calculate exactly the performance that we can expect from our system and make sure that we don't stop unless we get it (within reason). The second important thing to remember is that as index crawling feeds details; crawling the total throughput will be the minimum of their throughputs. If we generate URLs much faster than scrapyds can consume them, URLs will be piling up in their queues. On the other hand, if we generate URLs too slowly, scrapyds will have excess unutilized capacity.

Batching crawl URLs

We are now ready to develop infrastructure that processes detailed URLs that are aimed at vertical crawling, batches them, and dispatches them to scrapyds instead of crawling them locally.

If we check Scrapy's architecture in *Chapter 8, Programming Scrapy*, we can easily conclude that this is the job for a spider middleware as it implements `process_spider_output()`, which processes `Request`s before they reach the downloader and has the power to abort them. We limit our implementation to support spiders that are based on `CrawlSpider`, and we also support only simple GET requests. If we need more complexity, for example, POST or authenticated Requests, we will have to develop more complex functionality that propagates arguments, headers, and potentially relogins at every batch run.

In order to get started, we will have a quick look on Scrapy's GitHub. We will review the SPIDER_MIDDLEWARES_BASE setting to see what reference implementations Scrapy provides us with in order to reuse as much as we can. Scrapy 1.0 has the following spider middleware: HttpErrorMiddleware, OffsiteMiddleware, RefererMiddleware, UrlLengthMiddleware, and DepthMiddleware. After a quick look at their implementations, we see that OffsiteMiddleware (just 60 lines) does something quite similar to what we want to do. It restricts the URLs to certain domains according to the allowed_domains spider attribute. Could we use a similar pattern? Instead of dropping URLs as OffsiteMiddleware does, we will batch them and send them to scrapyds. It turns out that we can. Here's part of the implementation:

```
def __init__(self, crawler):
    settings = crawler.settings
    self._target = settings.getint('DISTRIBUTED_TARGET_RULE', -1)
    self._seen = set()
    self._urls = []
    self._batch_size = settings.getint('DISTRIBUTED_BATCH_SIZE', 1000)
    ...


def process_spider_output(self, response, result, spider):
    for x in result:
        if not isinstance(x, Request):
            yield x
        else:
            rule = x.meta.get('rule')

            if rule == self._target:
                self._add_to_batch(spider, x)
            else:
                yield x


def _add_to_batch(self, spider, request):
    url = request.url
    if not url in self._seen:
        self._seen.add(url)
        self._urls.append(url)
        if len(self._urls) >= self._batch_size:
            self._flush_urls(spider)
```

`process_spider_output()` processes both `Item` and `Request`. We want to work only with `Request`; thus, we `yield` everything else. If we have a look at the source code of `CrawlSpider`, we notice that the way it maps `Request`/`Response` to `Rule` is by an integer field named `'rule'` on their `meta` dict. We check this number and if it points to the `Rule` that we target (the `DISTRIBUTED_TARGET_RULE` setting), we call `_add_to_batch()` to add its URL to the current batch. We then effectively drop this `Request`. We `yield` all other `Requests`, such as the ones from the next page links, without change. The `_add_to_batch()` method implements a de-duplication mechanism. Unfortunately, the sharding process that we described in the previous section means that we may extract a few URLs twice. We use `_seen` set to detect and drop duplicates. We then add those URLs to the `_urls` list, and if its size exceeds `_batch_size` (the `DISTRIBUTED_BATCH_SIZE` setting), it triggers a call to `_flush_urls()`. This method provides the following key functionality:

```
def __init__(self, crawler):
    ...
    self._targets = settings.get("DISTRIBUTED_TARGET_HOSTS")
    self._batch = 1
    self._project = settings.get('BOT_NAME')
    self._feed_uri = settings.get('DISTRIBUTED_TARGET_FEED_URL', None)
    self._scrapyd_submits_to_wait = []

def _flush_urls(self, spider):
    if not self._urls:
        return

    target = self._targets[(self._batch-1) % len(self._targets)]

    data = [
        ("project", self._project),
        ("spider", spider.name),
        ("setting", "FEED_URI=%s" % self._feed_uri),
        ("batch", str(self._batch)),
    ]

    json_urls = json.dumps(self._urls)
    data.append(("setting", "DISTRIBUTED_START_URLS=%s" % json_urls))

    d = treq.post("http://%s/schedule.json" % target,
                  data=data, timeout=5, persistent=False)

    self._scrapyd_submits_to_wait.append(d)

    self._urls = []
    self._batch += 1
```

First of all, it uses a batch counter (_batch) to decide which scrapyd server to send the batch to. We keep the available servers in _targets (the DISTRIBUTED_TARGET_ HOSTS setting). We then form a POST request to scrapyd's schedule.json. This is a bit more advanced than the one we performed with curl before because it passes several carefully selected arguments. Effectively, based on these arguments, scrapyd will schedule a run that is similar to this one:

```
scrapy crawl distr \
-s DISTRIBUTED_START_URLS='[".../property_000000.html", ... ]' \
-s FEED_URI='ftp://anonymous@spark/%(batch)s_%(name)s_%(time)s.jl' \
-a batch=1
```

Beyond project and spider names, we pass a FEED_URI setting to the spider. We get its value from our own DISTRIBUTED_TARGET_FEED_URL setting.

Since Scrapy supports FTP, we can have scrapyds upload crawled Item files through an anonymous FTP to our Spark server. The format contains the name of the spider (%(name)s) and the time (%(time)s). If we were using just these, we may have ended up with collisions if two files were created at the same time. In order to avoid accidental overwrites, we also add a %(batch)s parameter. Scrapy doesn't know anything about batches by default, so we have to find a way to set this value. One interesting property of scrapyd's schedule.json API is that every argument that isn't a setting or one of the few known arguments is passed to spiders as an argument. Spider arguments, by default, become spider attributes and, interestingly, unknown FEED_URI arguments are looked up on spider's attributes. As a result, by passing a batch argument to schedule. json, we can use it in FEED_URI and avoid collisions.

The last step is to compile a DISTRIBUTED_START_URLS setting with all the detail URLs of this batch encoded as JSON. There's no particular reason to use this format other than familiarity and simplicity. Any textual format will do.

> Passing lots of data to Scrapy via the command line is, at the very least, not elegant. At some point you want to store arguments in a data store (for example, Redis) and just pass Scrapy an ID. Doing so would require small changes in _flush_urls() and process_start_requests().

We perform the POST request with `treq.post()`. Scrapyd doesn't handle persistent connections very well; thus, we disable them with `persistent=False`. We also set a 5 second timeout—just to be on the safe side. Interestingly, we store the deferred for this request to a `_scrapyd_submits_to_wait` list that we will talk about it in a second. To close this function, we reset the `_urls` list and increase the current `_batch`.

Surprisingly, we will find lots of functionality on the close operation handler as follows:

```
def __init__(self, crawler):
    ...
    crawler.signals.connect(self._closed, signal=signals.spider_
closed)

@defer.inlineCallbacks
def _closed(self, spider, reason, signal, sender):
    # Submit any remaining URLs
    self._flush_urls(spider)

    yield defer.DeferredList(self._scrapyd_submits_to_wait)
```

`_closed()` is called either because we pressed *Ctrl* + *C* or because the crawl completed. In both cases, we don't want to lose any URLs that belong to the last batch, which haven't yet been sent. That's why the first thing we do in `_closed()` is to call `_flush_urls(spider)` to flush the last batch. The second problem is that being nonblocking, any of the `treq.post()` might or might not have completed by the time we stop crawling. In order to avoid losing any batches, we use the `_scrapyd_submits_to_wait` list that was mentioned earlier, which contains all of the `treq.post()` deferreds. We use `defer.DeferredList()` to wait until all of them complete. Since `_closed()` uses `@defer.inlineCallbacks`, we just `yield` it and resume when all requests complete.

Summarizing, jobs with batches of URLs in the `DISTRIBUTED_START_URLS` setting are sent to scrapyds, which run the same spider. Obviously, we need somehow to use this setting to initialize `start_urls`.

Getting start URLs from settings

You can feel how well tailored to our needs spider middleware is when you notice that it provides a `process_start_requests()` method, which can be used to process the `start_requests` that spiders provide us. We detect whether the `DISTRIBUTED_START_URLS` setting is set, and if so, we JSON to decode it and use its URLs to `yield` relevant `Request`. For these requests, we set the `_response_downloaded()` method of `CrawlSpider` as callback, and we set the `meta['rule']` parameter in order to have their `Response` processed by the appropriate `Rule`. Frankly, we look at Scrapy's source code, find the way that `CrawlSpider` creates their `Request` and do exactly the same. In this case it is:

```python
def __init__(self, crawler):
    ...
    self._start_urls = settings.get('DISTRIBUTED_START_URLS', None)
    self.is_worker = self._start_urls is not None

def process_start_requests(self, start_requests, spider):
    if not self.is_worker:
        for x in start_requests:
            yield x
    else:
        for url in json.loads(self._start_urls):
            yield Request(url, spider._response_downloaded,
                          meta={'rule': self._target})
```

Our middleware is ready. We enable it and set its settings in our `settings.py`:

```python
SPIDER_MIDDLEWARES = {
    'properties.middlewares.Distributed': 100,
}
DISTRIBUTED_TARGET_RULE = 1
DISTRIBUTED_BATCH_SIZE = 2000
DISTRIBUTED_TARGET_FEED_URL = ("ftp://anonymous@spark/"
                               "%(batch)s_%(name)s_%(time)s.jl")
DISTRIBUTED_TARGET_HOSTS = [
    "scrapyd1:6800",
    "scrapyd2:6800",
    "scrapyd3:6800",
]
```

Someone may reasonably argue that DISTRIBUTED_TARGET_RULE shouldn't be a setting as it may differ from one spider to another. You can consider it as a default value that you can override on your spiders using a custom_settings attribute, for example:

```
custom_settings = {
    'DISTRIBUTED_TARGET_RULE': 3
}
```

We don't need this in our case though. We can perform a test run that will crawl a single page that is provided as a setting:

```
$ scrapy crawl distr -s \
DISTRIBUTED_START_URLS='["http://web:9312/properties/property_000000.html"]'
```

After this succeeds, we can try a more ambitious one, which crawls a page and FTPs it to our Spark server:

```
scrapy crawl distr -s \
DISTRIBUTED_START_URLS='["http://web:9312/properties/property_000000.html"]' \
-s FEED_URI='ftp://anonymous@spark/%(batch)s_%(name)s_%(time)s.jl' -a batch=12
```

If you ssh the Spark server (more on this in a bit), you should be able to see a file, such as 12_distr_date_time.jl, in the /root/items directory.

This is a sample implementation of middleware that allows you to implement distributed crawling using scrapyd. You can use it as a starting point to implement one that fits your specific needs. The things you may want to adapt are as follows:

- The type of spiders that you support. An alternative solution that doesn't limit itself to CrawlSpider, may, for example, require your spiders to mark distributed requests with an appropriate meta and employ callback naming conventions.

- The way that you pass URLs to scrapyds. You may want to use domain-specific knowledge to reduce the amount of information that is passed. For example, in our case, we could pass just properties' IDs.

- You can use a more elegant solution with a distributed queue to make the crawler able to recover from failures and allow scrapyds to commit further URLs to batches.

- You can populate the list of target servers dynamically to support on-demand scaling.

Deploy your project to scrapyd servers

In order to be able to deploy the spiders to our three scrapyd servers, we have to add them to our `scrapy.cfg` file. Each `[deploy:target-name]` section on this file defines a new deployment target:

```
$ pwd
/root/book/ch11/properties
$ cat scrapy.cfg
...
[deploy:scrapyd1]
url = http://scrapyd1:6800/
[deploy:scrapyd2]
url = http://scrapyd2:6800/
[deploy:scrapyd3]
url = http://scrapyd3:6800/
```

You can query the available targets with `scrapyd-deploy -l`:

```
$ scrapyd-deploy -l
scrapyd1                http://scrapyd1:6800/
scrapyd2                http://scrapyd2:6800/
scrapyd3                http://scrapyd3:6800/
```

It's easy to deploy to any of them with `scrapyd-deploy <target name>`:

```
$ scrapyd-deploy scrapyd1
Packing version 1449991257
Deploying to project "properties" in http://scrapyd1:6800/addversion.json
Server response (200):
{"status": "ok", "project": "properties", "version": "1449991257",
"spiders": 2, "node_name": "scrapyd1"}
```

This process leaves us with a few extra directories and files (`build`, `project.egg-info`, `setup.py`) that we can safely delete. Essentially what `scrapyd-deploy` does is to pack your projects and upload them to the target scrapyd using `addversion.json`.

After this, if we query each of those servers using `scrapyd-deploy -L`, we can confirm that the project has been successfully deployed, as follows:

```
$ scrapyd-deploy -L scrapyd1
properties
```

I also use `touch` to create three empty files, `scrapyd1-3`, in the project's directory. This way `scrapyd*` expands to the names of the files, which are also the names of the target servers. You can then deploy to all servers with a bash loop: `for i in scrapyd*; do scrapyd-deploy $i; done`.

Creating our custom monitoring command

If you want to monitor the progress of your crawl across many scrapyd servers, you have to do it manually. This is a nice opportunity for us to exercise everything we've seen up to now to create a primitive Scrapy command, `scrapy monitor`, which monitors a set of scrapyd servers. We will name the file: `monitor.py`, and we add `COMMANDS_MODULE = 'properties.monitor'` to our `settings.py`. With a quick look at scrapyd's documentation, the `listjobs.json` API gives us information on jobs. If we want to find the base URL for a given target, we may correctly guess that it must be somewhere in the code of `scrapyd-deploy` so that we can find it in a single file. If we take a look at `https://github.com/scrapy/scrapyd-client/blob/master/scrapyd-client/scrapyd-deploy`, we will quickly notice a `_get_targets()` function (its implementation doesn't add a lot of value, so I omit it) that gives us target names and their base URLs. Awesome! We are ready to implement the first part of this command as follows:

```
class Command(ScrapyCommand):
    requires_project = True

    def run(self, args, opts):
        self._to_monitor = {}
        for name, target in self._get_targets().iteritems():
            if name in args:
                project = self.settings.get('BOT_NAME')
                url = target['url'] + "listjobs.json?project=" + project
                self._to_monitor[name] = url

        l = task.LoopingCall(self._monitor)
        l.start(5)  # call every 5 seconds

        reactor.run()
```

Given what we've seen up to now, this is fairly easy. It populates a `dict _to_ monitor` with the names and the API endpoints that we want monitor. We then use `task.LoopingCall()` to schedule recurring calls to our `_monitor()` method. `_monitor()` uses `treq` and `deferred`, and we use `@defer.inlineCallbacks` to simplify its implementation. Here it is (omitting some error handling and cosmetics):

```
@defer.inlineCallbacks
def _monitor(self):
    all_deferreds = []
    for name, url in self._to_monitor.iteritems():
        d = treq.get(url, timeout=5, persistent=False)
        d.addBoth(lambda resp, name: (name, resp), name)
        all_deferreds.append(d)

    all_resp = yield defer.DeferredList(all_deferreds)

    for (success, (name, resp)) in all_resp:
        json_resp = yield resp.json()
        print "%-20s running: %d, finished: %d, pending: %d" % \
            (name,  len(json_resp['running']),
            len(json_resp['finished']), len(json_resp['pending']))
```

These few lines contain almost every Twisted technique that we know. We use `treq` to call scrapyd's API and `defer.DeferredList` to process all the responses at once. Once we have all the results in `all_resp`, we iterate and retrieve their JSON objects. `treq` Response' `json()` method returns `deferred` instead of actual values that we `yield` to resume with actual values at some point in the future. As a final step, we print the results. The JSON response contains lists with information on pending, running, and finished jobs, and we print their length.

Calculating the shift with Apache Spark streaming

Our Scrapy system is fully functional at this point. Let's take a quick look at Apache Spark's functionality.

The formula $Shift_{term}$ that we presented at the beginning of this chapter is nice and simple, but it can't be implemented efficiently. We can easily calculate $\overline{Price}$ with two counters and $\overline{Price_{with}}$ with $2 \cdot n_{terms}$ counters, and each new price would have to update just four of them. Calculating $\overline{Price_{without}}$ though is very problematic because for every new price $2 \cdot (n_{terms} - 1)$ counters would have to be updated. For example, we will have to add a jacuzzi price to every $Price_{without}$ counter but the jacuzzi one. This makes the algorithm infeasible for a large number of terms.

To work around this problem, all we have to notice is that if we add the price of properties with a term and the price of properties without that same term, we get the price of all the properties (obviously!) $\sum Price = \sum Price|_{with} + \sum Price|_{without}$. The average price of properties without a term can, thus, be calculated using inexpensive operations as follows:

$$\overline{Price_{without}} = \frac{\sum Price|_{without}}{n_{without}} = \frac{\sum Price - \sum Price|_{with}}{n - n_{with}}$$

Using this form, the shift formula becomes the following:

$$Shift_{term} = \left(\frac{\sum Price|_{with}}{n_{with}} - \frac{\sum Price - \sum Price|_{with}}{n - n_{with}} \right) \Big/ \frac{\sum Price}{n}$$

Let's see how we implement this. Please keep in mind that this isn't Scrapy code, so it is very reasonable for it to feel unfamiliar, but you will still most likely be able to read and understand it with little effort. You can find the application in `boostwords.py`. Please note that it also contains lots of complex test code that you can safely ignore. Its core functionality is as follows:

```
# Monitor the files and give us a DStream of term-price pairs
raw_data = raw_data = ssc.textFileStream(args[1])
word_prices = preprocess(raw_data)

# Update the counters using Spark's updateStateByKey
running_word_prices = word_prices.updateStateByKey(update_state_
function)

# Calculate shifts out of the counters
shifts = running_word_prices.transform(to_shifts)

# Print the results
shifts.foreachRDD(print_shifts)
```

Spark uses something called DStream to represent streams of data. The textFileStream() method monitors a directory in our filesystem, and when it detects new files it streams data out of them. Our preprocess() function converts them to streams of term/price pairs. We aggregate these pairs on running counters with Spark's updateStateByKey() method using our update_state_function() function. We finally calculate shifts by running to_shifts() and print the best using our print_shifts() function. Most of our functions are trivial and they just shape data in an efficient-for-Spark way. The most interesting exception is our to_shifts() function:

```
def to_shifts(word_prices):
    (sum0, cnt0) = word_prices.values().reduce(add_tuples)
    avg0 = sum0 / cnt0

    def calculate_shift((isum, icnt)):
        avg_with = isum / icnt
        avg_without = (sum0 - isum) / (cnt0 - icnt)
        return (avg_with - avg_without) / avg0

    return word_prices.mapValues(calculate_shift)
```

It's really impressive that it follows the formulas so closely. Despite its simplicity, Spark's mapValues() makes calculate_shift run efficiently across our (potentially many) Spark servers with minimum network overhead.

Running a distributed crawl

I, typically, use four terminals to have a complete view of the progress of our crawl. I want to make this section self-contained, so I also provide the vagrant ssh commands that you need to open terminals to the relevant servers.

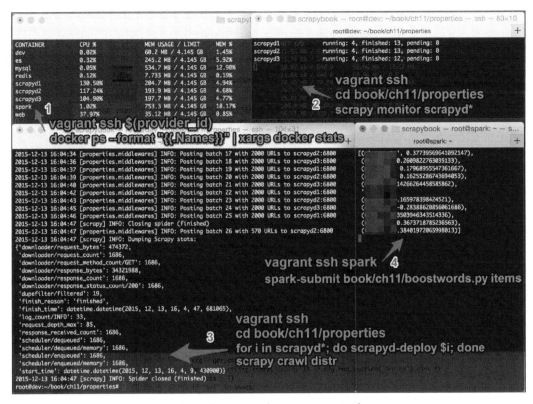

Using four terminals to oversee a crawl

With one terminal, **1**, I like to monitor the CPU and memory usage across the servers. This helps with identifying and repairing potential problems. To set it up, I run the following:

```
$ alias provider_id="vagrant global-status --prune | grep 'docker-
provider' | awk '{print \$1}'"
$ vagrant ssh $(provider_id)
$ docker ps --format "{{.Names}}" | xargs docker stats
```

The first two somewhat complex lines allow us to ssh the docker provider VM. If we aren't using a VM but we run on a docker-powered Linux machine, we need just the last line.

The second terminal is also diagnostic **2**, and I use it to run `scrapy monitor` as follows:

```
$ vagrant ssh
$ cd book/ch11/properties
$ scrapy monitor scrapyd*
```

Please keep in mind that using `scrapyd*` and the empty files with the server names, `scrapy monitor scrapyd*` expands to `scrapy monitor scrapyd1 scrapyd2 scrapyd3`.

The third one, **3**, is a terminal to our dev machine from which we kick-off the crawl. Apart from this, it's mostly idle. To start a new crawl, we perform the following:

```
$ vagrant ssh
$ cd book/ch11/properties
$ for i in scrapyd*; do scrapyd-deploy $i; done
$ scrapy crawl distr
```

The last two lines are the essential ones. First, we use a `for` loop and `scrapyd-deploy` to deploy the spider to our servers. Then, we start a crawl with `scrapy crawl distr`. We can always run smaller crawls using, for example, `scrapy crawl distr -s CLOSESPIDER_PAGECOUNT=100` to crawl about 100 index pages, which corresponds to about 3,000 detail pages.

Our last terminal, **4**, connects with the Spark server, and we use it to run the streaming analytics job:

```
$ vagrant ssh spark
$ pwd
/root
$ ls
book items
$ spark-submit book/ch11/boostwords.py items
```

Only the last line is essential, and it runs `boostwords.py`, giving it our local `items` directory to monitor. Sometimes, I also use `watch ls -1 items` to keep an eye on the item files as they arrive.

Which exactly are the keywords that most affect prices? I leave this as a surprise for those who managed to follow this far.

System performance

In terms of performance, our results greatly vary depending on our hardware, and the number of CPUs and memory that we give to our VM. In a real deployment, we get horizontal scalability allowing us to crawl as fast as our servers allow.

The theoretical maximum that one could get with the given settings is 3 servers · 4 processes/server · 16 requests in parallel · 4 pages/second (as defined by the page download latencies) = 768 pages/second.

In practice, using a Macbook Pro with 4 GB of RAM and 8 cores allocated to a VirtualBox VM, I got 50000 URLs in 2:40, which means about 315 pages/second. On an Amazon EC2 m4.large instance with 2 vCPUs and 8 GB RAM, it took 6:12 giving 134 pages/second due to limited CPU capacity. On an Amazon EC2 m4.4xlarge instance with 16 vCPUs and 64 GB RAM, the crawl completed in 1:44 giving 480 pages/second. On the same machine, I doubled the number of scrapyd instances to 6 (by slightly editing `Vagrantfile`, `scrapy.cfg` and `settings.py`) and the crawl completed in 1:15 with a speed of 667 pages/second. In this latter case, our web server seemed to be the bottleneck (this would mean an outage in real life).

The distance between the performance that we get and the theoretical maximum is more than justified. There are many little latencies that our back-of-the-envelope calculations don't take into account. Despite the fact that we claim a 250 ms page load latency, we've already seen in previous chapters that it's larger because, at the very least, we have additional Twisted and OS latencies. Then there are latencies, such as the transfer time of our URLs from dev to scrapyds, our crawled `Items` to Spark through FTP, and the time (2.5 seconds on average—refer to scrapyd's `poll_interval` setting) that it takes scrapyd to discover and schedule jobs. There's also a start time for both the dev and scrapyd crawls that we don't account for. I wouldn't try to improve any of these latencies unless I was certain they would increase throughput. My next step would be to increase the size of the crawl to, for example, 500k pages, load balance a few web server instances, and discover the next interesting challenges in our scaling endeavor.

The key take-away

The most important takeaway of this chapter is that if you are about to perform distributed crawling, always use suitably sized batches.

Depending on how fast your source websites respond, you may have hundreds, thousands, or tens of thousands of URLs. You would like them to be large enough—in the few-minutes level—so that any startup costs are amortized sufficiently. On the other hand, you wouldn't like them to be too large as this would turn a machine failure to a major risk. In a fault-tolerant distributed system, you would retry failed batches; and you wouldn't want this to be hours worth of work.

Summary

I hope you have enjoyed this book on Scrapy as much as I did writing it. You now have a very broad view of Scrapy's capabilities, and you are able to use it for simple and complex crawling scenarios. You have also gained an appreciation of the complexities of developing using such a high-performance system and making the most out of it. By using crawling you can leverage immediate network access to large real-world datasets on your applications. We have seen the ways to use Scrapy datasets to build mobile apps and perform interesting analytics. I hope that you use Scrapy's power to develop great, innovative applications and make our world a better place. Good luck!

Installing and troubleshooting prerequisite software

Installing prerequisites

This book uses a rich system of virtual servers to demonstrate the uses of Scrapy in a realistic multiserver deployment. We use industry standard tools—Vagrant and Docker—to set this system up. This is a book with strong dependencies on website content and layout, and if we were using websites outside our control, our examples would break in a few months time. Vagrant and Docker allow us to provide an isolated environment where examples run seamlessly now and in the future. As a side benefit, we don't hit any remote servers; thus, we can't cause any inconvenience to any webmaster. Even if we break something and examples stop working, by using two commands, `vagrant destroy` and `vagrant up --no-parallel`, we can tear down, rebuild the system, and continue.

Just before we start, I would like to clarify that this infrastructure is tailored to the needs of a book reader. Especially with regard to Docker, the general consensus is that every Docker container should run a single-process microservice. We don't do that. Many of our Docker containers are a bit heavy and allow us to connect to them and perform various operations via `vagrant ssh`. Our dev machine in particular looks nothing like a microservice. It's our user friendly *gateway* to this isolated system, and we treat it as a fully-featured Linux machine. Unless we bent the rules in this way, we would have to use a larger repertoire of Vagrant and Docker commands, delve deeper into troubleshooting them, and this book would quickly turn into a Vagrant/Docker book. I hope Docker aficionados will pardon us, and every reader appreciates the ease and benefits that Vagrant and Docker bring.

The containers for this book aren't by any means suitable for production.

It's impossible to test every software/hardware configuration out there. If something doesn't work, please, if possible, fix it and send us a Pull Request on GitHub. If you don't know how to fix it, search for a relevant issue on GitHub or open one if it doesn't exist.

The system

This is a reference section. Feel free to skip it at first read and return to it when you want to better understand the way that this book's system is structured. We repeat parts of this information in relevant chapters.

We use Vagrant to set up the following system:

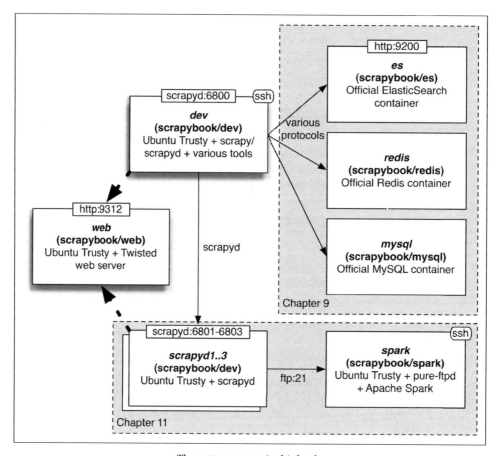

The system we use in this book

In the diagram, each box represents a server and the hostname is the first part of its title (dev, Web, es, and so on.). The second part of the title is the Docker image that it uses (`scrapybook/dev`, `scrapybook/web`, `scrapybook/es`, and so on.). Then there's a short description of the software that runs on the server. Lines represent links between servers, and their protocols are written next to them. Part of the isolation that Docker provides is the fact that connections beyond the ones that are explicitly declared aren't allowed. This means that if, for example, you want to run something that listens in the `1234` port on the spark server, nobody will be able to connect to it unless you expose this port by adding relevant declarations to the Vagrant file. Please keep this in mind in case you want to install custom software on any of those servers.

In most chapters, we use just two machines: `dev` and `web`. `vagrant ssh` connects us to the dev machine. From here, we can easily access every other machine using its hostname (`mysql`, `web`, and so on). For example, we can confirm that we can access the web machine by performing `ping web`. We use and explain various commands in each chapter. In *Chapter 9, Pipeline Recipes*, we demonstrate how to push data to various databases. In *Chapter 11, Distributed Crawling with Scrapyd and Real-Time Analytics*, we use three scrapyd Docker containers (which are in fact identical to our dev machine to reduce download size) with the `scrapyd1-3` hostnames. We also use a server with the `spark` hostname, which runs Apache Spark and an FTP service. We can connect to it with `vagrant ssh spark` and run Spark jobs.

We can find the description of this system in the `Vagrantfile` in the top-level directory on GitHub. As soon as we type `vagrant up --no-parallel`, the system will start building. This takes a few minutes, especially the first time, as we will see in more detail later in the FAQ. One can find this book's code mounted in the `~/book` directory. Any time someone modifies something in it on the host machine, changes propagate automatically. This allows us to hack files with our text editor or IDE and quickly check our changes on dev.

Finally, some listening ports are forwarded to our host computer and expose the relevant services. For example, you can use a simple web browser to access them. If you already use any of these ports on your computer, there will be a conflict and the system won't build successfully. We will show you how to fix these cases later in the FAQ. These are the forwarded ports:

Machine and service	From dev	From your (host) computer
Web — web Server	`http://web:9312`	`http://localhost:9312`
dev — scrapyd	`http://dev:6800`	`http://localhost:6800`
scrapyd1 — scrapyd	`http://scrapyd1:6800`	`http://localhost:6801`
scrapyd2 — scrapyd	`http://scrapyd2:6800`	`http://localhost:6802`

Machine and service	From dev	From your (host) computer
scrapyd3—scrapyd	`http://scrapyd3:6800`	`http://localhost:6803`
es—Elasticsearch API	`http://es:9200`	`http://localhost:9200`
spark—FTP	`ftp://spark:21 & 30000-9`	`ftp://localhost:21 & 30000-9`
Redis—Redis API	`redis://redis:6379`	`redis://localhost:6379`
MySQL—MySQL database	`mysql://mysql:3306`	`mysql://localhost:3306`

The `ssh` is also exposed on some machines and Vagrant takes care of redirecting and forwarding ports for us to avoid conflicts. All we have to do is run `vagrant ssh <hostname>` to the machine that we want.

Installation in a nutshell

The necessary software that we need to install is as follows:

- Vagrant
- git
- VirtualBox (on Windows and Mac) or Docker (on Linux)

On Windows, we also need to enable the `git ssh` client. You can visit their websites and follow the steps that they describe for your platform. In the following sections, we are going to try to provide step-by-step instructions, which are valid right now. They will certainly become obsolete in the future, so always keep an eye on the official documentation.

Installing on Linux

We start with instructions about how to install the system on Linux because it's the easiest. I will demonstrate with Ubuntu 14.04.3 LTS (Trusty Tahr), but the process should be very similar for any distribution, and well, the more unusual the distribution, the more—I guess—you know how to fill in the gaps. In order to install Vagrant, go to Vagrant's website, `https://www.vagrantup.com/`, and browse to its download page. Right-click on the **Debian package, 64-bit version**. Copy the link address:

We will use the terminal to install Vagrant because it's the most universal way, despite the fact that we could achieve the same with a few clicks on Ubuntu. To open the terminal, we click the Ubuntu icon in the top-left corner of the screen to open the **Dash. Alternatively**, we could press the **Windows** button. Then we type `terminal` and click on the **Terminal** icon to open it.

We type `wget` and paste the link from Vagrant's page. A `.deb` file should download after a few seconds. Type `sudo dpkg -i <name of the .deb file you just downloaded>` to install the file. That's it, Vagrant just installed successfully.

To install `git` just type the following two lines on the terminal:

```
$ sudo apt-get update
$ sudo apt-get install git
```

Now, let's install Docker. We follow the instructions from `https://docs.docker.com/engine/installation/ubuntulinux/`. On the terminal we type the following:

```
$ sudo apt-key adv --keyserver hkp://p80.pool.sks-keyservers.net:80
--recv-keys 58118E89F3A912897C070ADBF76221572C52609D
$ echo "deb https://apt.dockerproject.org/repo ubuntu-trusty main" | sudo
tee /etc/apt/sources.list.d/docker.list
$ sudo apt-get update
$ sudo apt-get install docker-engine
$ sudo usermod -aG docker $(whoami)
```

We log out and log in again to apply the group changes, and now, we should be able to use `docker ps` without a problem. We should now be able to download this book's code and enjoy the book:

```
$ git clone https://github.com/scalingexcellence/scrapybook.git
$ cd scrapybook
$ vagrant up --no-parallel
```

Installing on Windows or Mac

The process for the Windows and Mac environments is similar, so we will present them together while highlighting their differences.

Install Vagrant

To install Vagrant, we go to Vagrant's website, `https://www.vagrantup.com/`, and browse to its download page. We choose our operating system and go through the installation wizard:

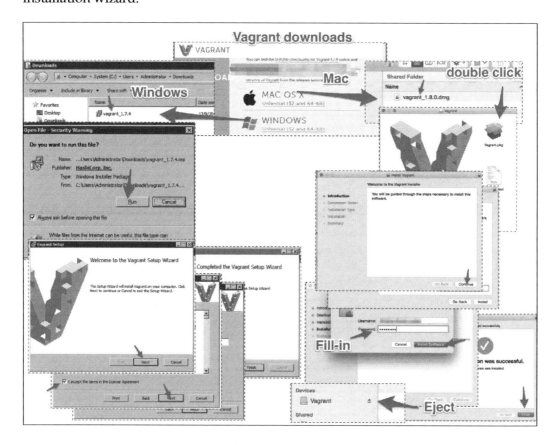

A few clicks later, we should have Vagrant installed. In order to access it, we will have to open the command line or the terminal.

How to access the terminal

On Windows, we press *Ctrl+Esc* or the *Win* key to open the applications menu and search for cmd. On Mac, we press *Cmd+Space* and search for terminal.

In both cases, we get a console window, and when we type vagrant, a few instructions will be printed. That's all we need for now.

Install VirtualBox and Git

In order to simplify this step, we will install the Docker Toolbox that contains both Git and VirtualBox. If we Google search for *docker toolbox install*, we end up at `https://www.docker.com/docker-toolbox` where we can download the appropriate version for our operating system. The installation is as easy as Vagrant's:

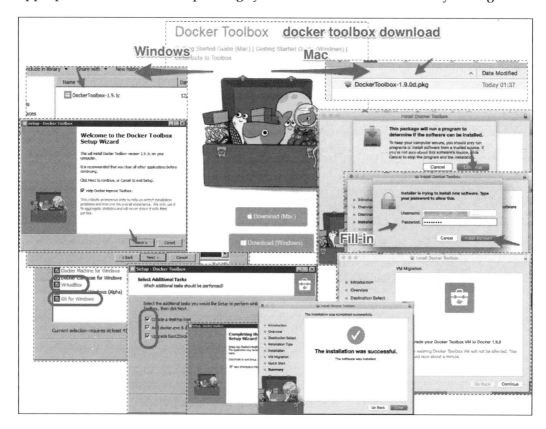

Ensure that VirtualBox supports 64-bit images

After the installation of Docker Toolbox, we should be able to find the VirtualBox icon in our Windows desktop or Mac's Launchpad (press *F4* to open it). It's important to check early whether our VirtualBox supports 64-bit images.

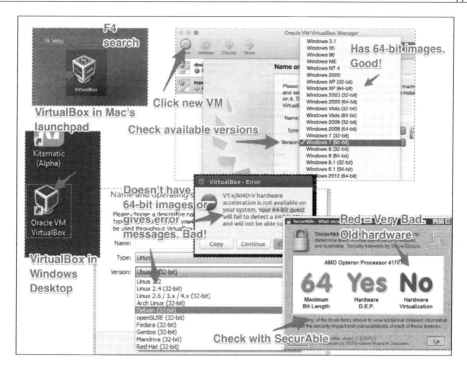

We open VirtualBox and click the **New** button to create a new virtual machine. We check the version drop-down menu, check the options, and then click **Cancel**. We don't really need to create a virtual machine right now.

 If the drop-down menu included 64-bit images, we can skip to the next section.

If the drop-down menu didn't include any 64-bit images or when we try to run a 64-bit VM it gives error messages such as **VT-x/AMD-V hardware acceleration is not available on your system**, we may be in a bit of trouble.

This means that VirtualBox can't detect VT-x or AMD-V extensions on our PC. If our hardware is old then it's reasonable and expected. If it's new, then these extensions may be disabled by the BIOS. If we are on Windows (most likely), an easy way to check is with a tool called SecurAble that we can download from https://www.grc.com/securable.htm. If the **Hardware Virtualization** is red and says **No**, it means that our CPU doesn't support the necessary virtualization extensions. In this case, we won't be able to run Vagrant/Docker, but we will still be able to install Scrapy and follow the examples using the online website (scrapybook.s3.amazonaws.com) as a source. Start using the spider from *Chapter 4*, *From Scrapy to a Mobile App*, which should work out of the box and build from there.

If the **Hardware Virtualization** is green, we will most likely be able to enable the extension from our BIOS. Google search for your PC model and how to change the BIOS settings that are related to VT-x or AMD-v. There's usually a key that we can press while rebooting that gives us access to BIOS. From here, we have to go to a security-related menu and enable the option of **Virtualization Technology (VTx)** or something similar. After rebooting, we will be able to run 64-bit virtual machines from our computer.

Enable ssh client for Windows

If we're on a Mac, we won't need this step, and we can skip to the next section. If we're on Windows, it doesn't provide us with a default ssh client. Fortunately, GIT (which we've just installed) has an ssh client that we will activate by adding it on Windows Path.

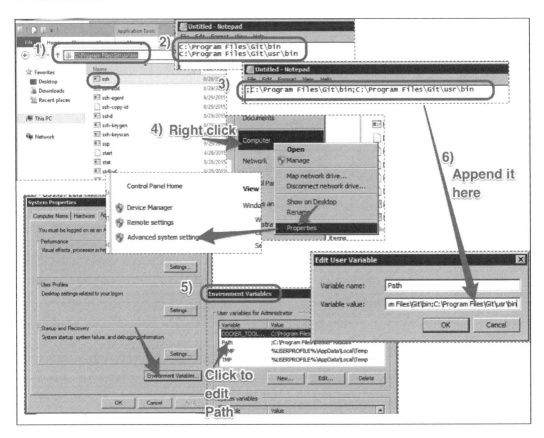

The `ssh` binary, by default, lives in `C:\Program Files\Git\usr\bin` (refer to 1). We will add both `C:\Program Files\Git\usr\bin` and `C:\Program Files\Git\bin` to the path. In order to do so, we put them in a Notepad, and we concatenate them adding `;` just before each one of them (refer to 3). The end result is as follows:

```
;C:\Program Files\Git\bin;C:\Program Files\Git\usr\bin
```

We now press *Ctrl+Esc* or the *Win* key to open the start menu and then find the **Computer** option. We right-click it (refer to 4) and select **Properties**. On the next window, we choose **Advanced System Settings**. We then click **Environment Variables**. This is the form where we edit our **Path**. Click on **Path** to edit it. On the **Edit User Variable** dialog, we paste at the end the two new concatenated paths that we have in Notepad. We should be careful not to accidentally overwrite whatever value our path previously had; we just append. Then we click **OK** a few times to exit all these dialogs, and our prerequisites are all installed.

Download this book's code and set up the system

Now that we have a fully functional Vagrant system, we open a new console/terminal/command line (we've seen how to do this earlier), type the following commands, and enjoy the book:

```
$ git clone https://github.com/scalingexcellence/scrapybook.git
$ cd scrapybook
$ vagrant up --no-parallel
```

System setup and operations FAQ

Next are the solutions to some of the problems you may run into while working with Scrapy for the first time:

What do I download and how much time does it take?

As soon as we run `vagrant up --no-parallel`, we don't have that much visibility of what's going on. The wall time is closely related to our download speed and the quality of our internet connection. Here's what one would expect to happen with an internet connection able to download about 5 MB per second (38 Mbps):

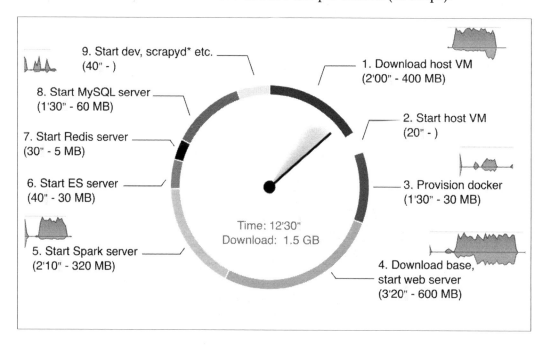

The first three steps aren't necessary if we're on Linux and have Docker already installed saving us 4' and 450 MBs of download.

Please note that all the preceding steps are relevant only to the first time when `vagrant up --no-parallel` downloads everything. Subsequent runs will typically take less than 10".

What should I do if Vagrant freezes?

Vagrant may freeze due to various reasons, and all we have to do is press *Ctrl+C* twice to exit. Then retry `vagrant up --no-parallel` and it should resume. We may have to do this a few times depending on the speed and quality of our internet connection. If we open the **Windows Task Manager** or the **Activity Monitor** on Mac, we can have a more clear view of what Vagrant is doing.

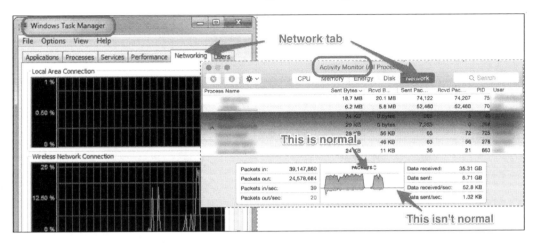

Short freezes of up to 60 seconds during or after download are expected because software gets installed. Longer periods of inactivity, though highly likely, mean that something went wrong.

If we interrupt and resume, `vagrant up --no-parallel` may fail with an error that is similar to this:

```
Vagrant cannot forward the specified ports on this VM... The forwarded
port to 21 is already in use on the host machine.
```

This is also a temporary problem. If we rerun `vagrant up --no-parallel`, it should resume successfully.

Let's assume the following failure takes place:

```
... Command: "docker" "ps" "-a" "-q" "--no-trunc"
Stderr: bash: line 2: docker: command not found
```

If this happens, shut down and resume the VM as shown in the next answer.

How do I shut down/resume the VM quickly?

If we use a VM, the fastest way to shut it down, for example, to save battery on a laptop, is to open VirtualBox, select the VM, and then press *Ctrl+V* or *Cmd+V*, or use the right-click menu and click **Save State**:

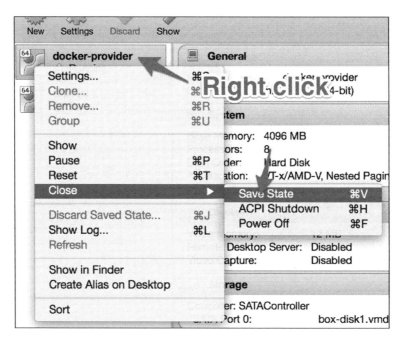

We can restore the VM by running `vagrant up --no-parallel`. dev, and Spark servers' `~/book` directories should work fine.

How do I fully reset the VM?

If we want to change the number of cores, RAM, or port mappings in the VM, we have to perform a full reset. To do this, we follow the steps of the previous answer but now chose **Power Off** or press *Ctrl+F* or *Cmd+F*. We can also achieve the same thing programmatically by running `vagrant global-status --prune`. We find the ID (for example, 95d1234) of the host virtual machine that is named "docker-provider". We then halt it with `vagrant halt`, for example, `vagrant halt 957d887`.

We can then restart the system with `vagrant up --no-parallel`. Unfortunately, dev and spark machines will most likely empty their `~/book` directories. To fix this problem, run `vagrant destroy -f dev spark` and then rerun `vagrant up --no-parallel`. This should fix these problems.

How do I resize the virtual machine?

We may want to change the size of the VM from, for example, using 2 GB of RAM to 1 GB or using 8 cores instead of 4. We can do this by editing the `vb.memory` and `vb.cpus` settings of `Vagrantfile.dockerhost`. Then, we follow the process of the previous answer to perform a full reset of the Virtual Machine.

How do I resolve any port conflicts?

Sometimes, we may have services running on a host that is occupying one of the ports that this system requires. First of all please keep in mind that if we open the two `Vagrantfile`, remove every `forwarded_port` statement, and reset as described in a bit, we will still be able to run the examples of this book. We just won't be able to easily inspect the services on these ports on our host machine (typically via a web browser).

That said, we can fix this more properly by remapping the conflicting ports. Let's use a conflict on port 9312 of the web server as an example. The process is slightly different depending on whether we run on Linux natively or using a VM.

On Linux using Docker natively

The problem will demonstrate itself with an error along these lines:

```
Stderr: Error: Cannot start container a22f...: failed to create
endpoint web on network bridge: Error starting userland proxy: listen
tcp 0.0.0.0:9312: bind: address already in use
```

Open the Dockerfile and edit the `host` value of the `forwarded_port` statement for the web server. We will then destroy the web server using `vagrant destroy web` and then restart it with `vagrant up web`, or if the problem happened during your initial load, resume loading with `vagrant up --no-parallel`.

On Windows or Mac using a VM

Here, we will get a different error message:

```
Vagrant cannot forward the specified ports on this VM, since they
would collide... The forwarded port to 9312 is already in use
on the host machine...
```

In order to fix this, we open `Vagrantfile.dockerhost` and remove the existing line with the port number. Then add a custom port forwarding statement below, for example, `config.vm.network "forwarded_port", guest: 9312, host: 9316`. This will forward to 9316 instead. We follow the process of the answer to the question *How do I full reset the VM?* to reset the Virtual Machine and everything should work fine.

How do I make it work behind a corporate proxy?

There are simple proxies and *TLS interception proxies*. Simple proxies require us to forward our requests to a proxy server before they reach the open internet. They may or may not require authentication, but in any case, the information that we need to use it is just a URL that we can obtain from our IT department. It's something along the lines of `http://user:pass@proxy.com:8080/`. If we are using Linux without a VM, most likely we've already set up everything correctly and no further adjustments are necessary. If we're using a VM though, we will need to make the proxy URL available to Vagrant, Docker provider VM, Ubuntu's aptitude, and the Docker service itself. All these operations get handled in the `Vagrantfile.` `dockerhost`, and all we need to do is uncomment the line that defines `proxy_url` and set its value appropriately.

Let's suppose that we get the following SSL-related problems:

```
SSL certificate problem: unable to get local issuer certificate
...
If you'd like to turn off curl's verification of the certificate, use
  the -k (or --insecure) option.
```

From either Vagrant or while provisioning Docker, we most likely have to deal with TLS interception proxies. These proxies aim to monitor both secure and insecure traffic by acting as a "man in the middle". They perform https requests verifying certificates as necessary on our behalf, and we perform https connections to them verifying their certificates. Our IT department most likely provides us a certificate, typically in the form of a `.crt` file. We place a copy of this file in our book's main directory (where `Vagrantfile` is). Further to setting `proxy_url` as in the previous case, we now have to further uncomment the line that defines the `crt_filename` variable and set its value to the name of our certificate file.

How do I connect with the Docker provider VM?

If we are on Linux and we aren't using a VM, then our machine is the Docker provider and we don't have to do anything. If we are using a VM, we can find the ID of our Docker provider by running `vagrant global-status --prune` and then find the machine named `docker-provider`. We can automate this on Linux and Mac with the following alias:

```
$ alias provider_id="vagrant global-status --prune | grep 'docker-
provider' | awk '{print \$1}'"
```

We can use `vagrant ssh <provider id>` or, in case we have the alias, `vagrant ssh $(provider_id)` to connect to the Docker provider. This is an Ubuntu Trusty 64-bit Virtual Machine.

How much CPU/memory does each server use?

If we use Docker natively or connect to the provider as described in the previous answer, we can see the resources that each individual Docker container consumes using `docker stats` as follows:

```
$ docker ps --format "{{.Names}}" | xargs docker stats
```

Here is an example of the output while running the code in *Chapter 11, Distributed Crawling with Scrapyd and Real-Time Analytics,* at the point where scrapyd's downloading intensively from the web server:

CONTAINER	CPU %	MEM USAGE / LIMIT	MEM %
dev	0.11%	63.61 MB / 2.099 GB	3.03%
es	0.46%	295.1 MB / 2.099 GB	14.06%
mysql	0.09%	54.3 MB / 2.099 GB	2.59%
redis	0.06%	12.28 MB / 2.099 GB	0.59%
scrapyd1	128.36%	208.4 MB / 2.099 GB	9.93%
scrapyd2	118.59%	198.7 MB / 2.099 GB	9.47%
scrapyd3	114.12%	205.4 MB / 2.099 GB	9.79%
spark	1.17%	374.2 MB / 2.099 GB	17.83%
web	45.79%	79.84 MB / 2.099 GB	3.80%

How can I see the size of Docker container images?

If we use Docker natively or connect to the provider as we have seen in the previous answer, we can find the size of Docker images as follows:

```
$ docker images
```

This book's containers are based on a single image with relatively little extra software installed on each variation. Consequently, the GBs one may see as virtual sizes aren't really used in terms of disk space. If we want to see how images are built hierarchically and individual sizes, we can set up an alias for the somewhat long `dockviz` command and then use it as follows:

```
$ alias dockviz="docker run --rm -v /var/run/docker.sock:/var/run/docker.sock nate/dockviz"
$ dockviz images -t
```

How can I reset the system if Vagrant doesn't respond?

We can perform a full reset of the system even if it ended up in a very confused state where even Vagrant can't reset it anymore. We can do this without resetting the host VM, which admittedly takes some time to complete. All we have to do is connect to the docker provider machine and force-stop all the containers, remove their images, and restart Docker. We can do this as follows:

```
$ docker stop $(docker ps -a -q)
$ docker rm $(docker ps -a -q)
$ sudo service docker restart
```

We could also use the following command:

```
$ docker rmi $(docker images -a | grep "<none>" | awk "{print $3}")
```

We use this to remove any Docker layers that we've downloaded, which means a few minutes of download time on our next `vagrant up --no-parallel`.

There's a problem I can't work around, what can I do?

We can always use VirtualBox and an image of Ubuntu 14.04.3 (Trusty Tahr) from osboxes.org (`http://www.osboxes.org/ubuntu/`) and follow the process for Linux installation. The code will then run entirely inside the VM. The only thing that we will miss is port forwarding and synced folders, which means that we either have to set them up manually or perform our development inside the VM.

Index

A

Amazon web services **115**
Apache Spark Streaming
  used, for calculating shift **218-220**
attribute **14**
automated data scraping
  communities, discovering **7**
  communities, integrating **7**
  forms, replacing **6**
  importance **4**
  quality applications, developing **5**
  quality minimum viable products,
     developing **5, 6**
  realistic schedules, providing **5**
  robust applications, developing **5**

B

benchmark system **183-185**
bottleneck
  identifying **178**

C

Chrome
  used, for obtaining XPath expressions **20**
collection
  creating **64-66**
component
  utilization getting, telnet used **180-182**
corporate proxy **240**
crawl URLs
  batching **209-213**
CRUD (Create, Read, Update, Delete) **148**
custom monitoring command
  creating **217, 218**

D

database
  creating **64-66**
  interfacing, with standard
     Python clients **159**
  populating, with Scrapy **66-69**
denial-of-service (DoS) attack **8**
distributed crawl
  running **220-222**
distributed system
  overview **205-207**
Docker
  URL **229**
Docker container images
  size, viewing **241**
Docker provider VM **240**
docker toolbox
  URL **232**
Document Object Model (DOM) **11**
Domain Name System (DNS) **12**
DOM tree representation **11, 12**

E

Elasticsearch
  about **148-151**
  geoindexing, enabling **158**

G

Git
  installing **232**

system
  peformance 223
  setting up 226-236

T

tag 13
telnet
  used, for getting components
       utilization 180-182
terminal
  accessing 231
tree representation 14
treq
  using 148
Twisted-specific clients
  used, for interfacing services 163

U

UR2IM process
  about 31
  item 34-39
  request and response 33, 34
  URL 32
URLs
  extracting 55-58
  two-direction crawling, with
    CrawlSpider 61, 62
  two-direction crawling, with spider 58-60

V

Vagrant
  about 29, 30
  installing on 230
  not responding 242
  URL 228
vagrant up
  freeze 237
VirtualBox
  64-bit images support 232-234
  installing 232

Virtualization Technology (VTx) 234
VM
  resetting 238
  resizing 239
  resuming 238
  shutting down 238

W

web scraping
  considerations 8
Windows
  installing on 230

X

XPath
  about 11, 12
  HTML element, selecting 16, 17
XPath expressions
  changes, anticipating 22, 23
  examples 21, 22
  obtaining, Chrome used 20
  using 17-20
XPath functions
  URL 19

Thank you for buying
Learning Scrapy

About Packt Publishing

Packt, pronounced 'packed', published its first book, *Mastering phpMyAdmin for Effective MySQL Management*, in April 2004, and subsequently continued to specialize in publishing highly focused books on specific technologies and solutions.

Our books and publications share the experiences of your fellow IT professionals in adapting and customizing today's systems, applications, and frameworks. Our solution-based books give you the knowledge and power to customize the software and technologies you're using to get the job done. Packt books are more specific and less general than the IT books you have seen in the past. Our unique business model allows us to bring you more focused information, giving you more of what you need to know, and less of what you don't.

Packt is a modern yet unique publishing company that focuses on producing quality, cutting-edge books for communities of developers, administrators, and newbies alike. For more information, please visit our website at www.packtpub.com.

About Packt Open Source

In 2010, Packt launched two new brands, Packt Open Source and Packt Enterprise, in order to continue its focus on specialization. This book is part of the Packt Open Source brand, home to books published on software built around open source licenses, and offering information to anybody from advanced developers to budding web designers. The Open Source brand also runs Packt's Open Source Royalty Scheme, by which Packt gives a royalty to each open source project about whose software a book is sold.

Writing for Packt

We welcome all inquiries from people who are interested in authoring. Book proposals should be sent to author@packtpub.com. If your book idea is still at an early stage and you would like to discuss it first before writing a formal book proposal, then please contact us; one of our commissioning editors will get in touch with you.

We're not just looking for published authors; if you have strong technical skills but no writing experience, our experienced editors can help you develop a writing career, or simply get some additional reward for your expertise.

Instant PHP Web Scraping

ISBN: 978-1-78216-476-0   Paperback: 60 pages

Get up and running with the basic techniques of web scraping using PHP

1. Learn something new in an Instant! A short, fast, focused guide delivering immediate results.

2. Build a re-usable scraping class to expand on for future projects.

3. Scrape, parse, and save data from any website with ease.

4. Build a solid foundation for future web scraping topics.

Instant Web Scraping with Java

ISBN: 978-1-84969-688-3   Paperback: 72 pages

Build simple scrapers or vast armies of Java-based bots to untangle and capture the Web

1. Learn something new in an Instant! A short, fast, focused guide delivering immediate results.

2. Get your Java environment up and running.

3. Gather clean, formatted web data into your own database.

4. Learn how to work around crawler-resistant websites and legally subvert security measures.

Please check **www.PacktPub.com** for information on our titles

Learning Data Mining with R

ISBN: 978-1-78398-210-3   Paperback: 314 pages

Develop key skills and techniques with R to create and customize data mining algorithms

1. Develop a sound strategy for solving predictive modeling problems using the most popular data mining algorithms.

2. Gain understanding of the major methods of predictive modeling.

3. Packed with practical advice and tips to help you get to grips with data mining.

Mastering Object-oriented Python

ISBN: 978-1-78328-097-1   Paperback: 634 pages

Grasp the intricacies of object-oriented programming in Python in order to efficiently build powerful real-world applications

1. Create applications with flexible logging, powerful configuration and command-line options, automated unit tests, and good documentation.

2. Use the Python special methods to integrate seamlessly with built-in features and the standard library.

3. Design classes to support object persistence in JSON, YAML, Pickle, CSV, XML, Shelve, and SQL.

Please check **www.PacktPub.com** for information on our titles

46270790R00152

Made in the USA
San Bernardino, CA
02 March 2017